Explaining and Predicting Elections: Issue Effects and Party Strategies in Twenty-Three Democracies

Explaining and Predicting Elections: Issue Effects and Party Strategies in Twenty-Three Democracies

IAN BUDGE and DENNIS J. FARLIE
University of Essex

London
GEORGE ALLEN & UNWIN
Boston   Sydney

George Allen & Unwin (Publishers) Ltd,
40 Museum Street, London WC1A 1LU, UK

George Allen & Unwin (Publishers) Ltd,
Park Lane, Hemel Hempstead, Herts HP2 4TE, UK

Allen & Unwin, Inc.
9 Winchester Terrace, Winchester, Mass. 01890, USA

George Allen & Unwin Australia Pty Ltd,
8 Napier Street, North Sydney, NSW 2060, Australia

First published in 1983

British Library Cataloguing in Publication Data

Budge, Ian
    Explaining and predicting elections.
1. Elections–History   2. Democracy–History
I. Title   II. Farlie, Dennis J.
324.6   JF1001
ISBN 0-04-324008-9

Library of Congress Cataloging in Publication Data

Budge, Ian.
    Explaining and predicting elections.
Companion vol. to: Voting and party competition.
c1977.
Includes index.
1. Political parties. 2. Elections. 3. Election forecasting. 4. Voting.
I. Farlie, Dennis.
II. Title.
JF2011.B79 1983   324.2   83-2732
ISBN 0-04-324008-9

Set in 10 on 12 point Times by Fotographics (Bedford) Ltd
and printed in Great Britain
by Mackays of Chatham

Contents

Preface

This is the second of two volumes on elections, reporting on research papers in which the order of authors' names has been alternated to indicate the full and equal nature of the collaboration. The first, *Voting and Party Competition*, which dealt with explanations of individual voting, was published by John Wiley in 1977. Both books have been supported by grants from the Political Science Committee of the British Social Science Research Council (HR5269/1). For the data-processing necessary to assess the present theory, we owe a great deal to Roger Barlow and to Peter Foster, our research assistant from 1977 to 1979. For general advice and comment on specific predictions we must thank Jim Alt, Ivor Crewe, Bill Irvine, Chris Goodrich, Derek Hearl, Larry Le Duc, John Meisel, Ken Newton, Stein Rokkan, Bo Särlvik, Berndt Solvang, Eric Tanenbaum, Ulf Torgersen, Derek Urwin, Henry Valen and Douglas Webber.

Seminars at the Universities of Bergen, East Anglia, Essex, Michigan State, Oslo and Windsor gave an opportunity to discuss many aspects of the theory and predictions of specific elections, as did a panel of the American Political Science Association in 1978 convened by Donald E. Stokes. Where we have followed the good advice so freely given, this book has obviously benefited. Where we have followed our own judgement we have undoubtedly committed some errors, but at least that makes them our own!

Introduction

Suppose we could say why one election differs from another, and thus account for party gains and losses. Why should we want to? What use does an explanation have? Is it even attainable?

We spend the rest of this book discussing and evaluating explanations, so the question of attainability must be decided at the end. The others can be answered here.

Obviously for some specialists there would be great advantages in a viable explanation of elections. They are key events which political scientists have been investigating intensively over the last forty years. A general theory would tie together many of the detailed discoveries that have been made, as well as providing a framework for further research.

Moving from the academic to the practical, politicians could use a systematic explanation to decide where to direct their efforts during an election campaign. This would not be a bad or manipulative consequence if it led to more vigorous campaigning and a clearer presentation of ideas. Better identification of the policies producing electoral gains should also enhance their chance of implementation and hence the chance of electors' wishes being carried through into government decisions. Voters themselves should gain some greater awareness of the factors entering into the election process, which could improve the quality of their party choice.

This is probably the most important contribution an explanation of elections could make, for the quality of voting choice is vital both to the functioning of democracy and to its justification. Elections are for most citizens the only occasion, even in a democracy, when they can directly act to influence government decisions, or where their preferences, expressed as issues in the party programmes, can be immediately taken up. Indeed, the regular occurrence of fair elections is commonly used to distinguish democracies from other, less free, political systems.

Systematic description and explanation are thus essential to any justification of democracy. For unless we know what goes on in elections we cannot argue convincingly for them as an institution which increases government responsiveness, nor for the overall political process which relies on them.

To play its full part a descriptive explanation must also be comparative – that is, it should if possible cover elections in all democracies rather than limiting itself to one or two. Only if we explain elections as involving similar processes everywhere can we argue that democracy is generally preferable to other political systems. Otherwise we stumble into the position that elections work for a few developed Western countries but not for the vast majority of the world population. Our explanation is in fact generalised to cover all democracies, and actually applied to the twenty-three which have existed independently since the war.

Certainly an explanation which emphasised the irrationality of electors, or their blind adherence to habit and tradition, would strike at the foundations of democratic beliefs, a faith in reasoned argument and its influence over the common man. Election theories usually stress the influence of party loyalty or group attachments on voting – quite naturally, given the massive underlying stability of individual choices. An unfortunate consequence has nevertheless followed, since this emphasis opens the way to inferences which undermine standard justifications of democracy. (For example, arguing that since most electors habitually vote for the same party, elections give little indication of popular preferences on questions of current importance.)

Such inferences are misleading, since all accepted theories recognise that results change in response to circumstances and with new issues and candidates. By giving both their initial emphasis and the major share of their attention to the role of social and political predispositions, existing formulations have not properly reflected this. Nor have they proved of practical use to politicians and voters who in the course of a single election campaign cannot hope to alter established loyalties, but who might look for some guidance on the emphasis to be put on issues.

Since issues often crucially decide results, the tendency to view their effects as unpredictable and residual has also resulted in partial rather than complete explanations of election trends. Even those analysts stressing the importance of 'policy voting' have been driven into a-theoretical demonstrations that it actually occurred in specific (usually American) elections; or into highly abstract 'rational choice' formalisations which deny the existence of standing loyalties (Budge and Farlie, 1977, ch. 5; Riker and Ordeshook, 1973). But this is as unrealistic in its way as ignoring the effects of issues, so again we end up with incomplete explanations.

Our attempt at a more rounded account starts from issues, because the concern that we take from classical democratic theory is whether elections do express popular wishes and needs, and whether these have any bearing on the result. We therefore focus on changing political conditions and voters' responses to them, and hence on issues and candidates. By estimating their impact we can also determine what role is played by tradition and loyalty so that we end by incorporating both predispositions and issue responses into our explanation.

This attention to issues should guard against any misinterpretation which undervalues the part played by electors' policy-related choices. Attributing a general rationale to such choices, which makes them predictable in certain circumstances, does not reduce democratic citizens to unthinking automatons. It demonstrates rather that there are sound general reasons for the choices electors make; that these are considered rather than random; and hence that they can be ascertained and discussed in general terms.

We take up some of these points in our conclusions, having said enough

to indicate the need for a viable, issue-based explanation of election outcomes. The question of whether we can produce this is naturally crucial
and prior to any further discussion of its bearings on democratic theory or
of its applications. Chapters 2 and 3 accordingly develop general
hypotheses and procedures, through which we can understand electors'
handling of issues and the relationship between their reactions and election
results. First, however, we consider previous attempts to estimate the
influence of issues in democratic elections. As this review is necessarily
detailed and technical, readers desirous of plunging immediately into the
heart of the discussion may prefer to start with Chapter 2 and refer back to
Chapter 1 as and when points become relevant. Some knowledge of the
present state of research is, however, useful for appreciating why our
investigation took the shape it did, and for validating some of our later
results. So it is a necessary starting point for the discussion.

Chapter 1

Previous Work

Earlier attempts to estimate the voting changes produced by issues have emerged from two bodies of research, both directed primarily to US elections but differentiated by methods and data. First, there are the studies, within the 'new political economy', which relate voting to economic conditions. Methodologically these base themselves on various types of multivariate regression equation and use aggregate data on actual voting, voting intentions, candidate popularity and economic expectations, together with economic time-series on seasonal unemployment, annual inflation and changes in real income.

The second set of studies are based on surveys and focus on individual voting rather than the overall election result. Since the overall result is produced by the aggregation of individual choices, a successful characterisation of the latter provides a basis for explaining the final outcome, so the two are closely related. The ways in which the survey evidence has been approached vary widely, from simple tabulations of issue preferences against vote, comparisons of actual vote with some kind of non-issue-based notional vote, to applications of econometric techniques and complex forms of non-recursive modelling. Substantively, the survey-based studies take in British, German and Canadian evidence as well as American.

In the first section of this chapter we outline the general development of econometric studies of voting and go on to derive estimates of issue effects which may be compared with estimates obtained on other bases. As will be seen, the substantial discontinuities between studies render them hard to relate to each other, let alone to other research. Thus, econometric estimates can be made comparable only on certain assumptions which we try to spell out as clearly as possible.

In Section 1.2 we go through the same stages with survey-based studies of the effects of issues. These are even more disparate than the econometric, so general estimates are harder to obtain even on extended assumptions. Individual studies of non-economic issues do, however, produce some figures, and certain approaches provide useful pointers for the development of our framework. These are considered in Sections 1.3 and 1.4. In Section 1.5 we review the overall convergence between various estimates, considering in particular whether discrepancies stem from real differences between elections, which rule out a comparative approach, or from divergences of method in the academic analyses, which need to be rectified but do not constitute an objection to comparative analysis in principle.

1.1   Econometric Estimates of Issue Effects

The methods here are primarily those of regression analysis.

The pioneering analysis of this type was Kramer's attempt to explain changes in US congressional results from 1896 to 1964 by prior changes in key economic variables (Kramer, 1971). Specifically, the parties' shares of the two-party vote over the two-yearly elections to the House of Representatives were related to real and monetary income, prices and unemployment rates, 'lagged' for an optimal period (i.e. their values were recorded as they were a year before the actual election, on the assumption that their influence needed time to work its way through to the vote). These variables were entered into multivariate regression equations. When applied to the Republican percentage of two-party vote, the conclusions were that change in real income a year before the congressional election had the expected positive effect, producing a 0·45 per cent increase or decrease in votes for each 1 per cent change in real income. Unexpectedly, unemployment had a positive coefficient in the regression equation, indicating that increased unemployment produced more votes for the incumbent party. However, the sampling error attached to that estimate was large relative to the size of the estimate itself, indicating that the finding could possibly be discounted, or attributed to an inverse relationship with inflation. Later estimates (Goodman and Kramer, 1975) indicated that only price movements had a significant effect on votes and that unemployment had the expected negative relationship with support for the governing party.

Stigler (1973) reacted to Kramer's initial findings not only by welcoming the lack of effect from fluctuations in unemployment but also by trying to demonstrate that no economic variable influenced vote. This contrasted with Kramer's finding that economic variables in total accounted for slightly under to slightly over half of the increase in the two-party vote. The contrast between Kramer's and Stigler's results is explained by the fact that in the first case the economic variables were 'lagged' by one year and in the second by two years. The surprising sensitivity of economic variables to the change in measure tends to support the idea that their influence needs to be carefully specified.

This introduced a first complication and discontinuity into the debate about economic effects on vote. Bloom and Price (1975), however, demonstrated that if effects over the two time-periods are allowed for separately, the immediately preceding year is undoubtedly important but effects from the year before that are insignificant and serve only to dilute the significance of the one-year variables if they are all considered together. This was confirmed by Hibbs (1978), who showed that 88 per cent of the vote effects of economic variables are attributable to changes in the immediately preceding year, leaving only 12 per cent to be covered by earlier changes. In general, therefore, it seems that developments in the year leading up to the election are the ones to concentrate on (certainly where economic and financial well-being are concerned).

What are the exact effects of economic factors within this time-period, however? Stigler argues that a rational voter will regard both parties as equally competent or incompetent in running the economy, and will choose between them on the criterion of which will redistribute resources more favourably to himself. The question of general effects was tackled again by Arcelus and Meltzer (1975), who replicated Kramer's analysis using slightly different measures for change in incomes, prices and unemployment (see Table 1.1, pp. 8–9, for a specification of the exact differences involved). The individual effects of these were for the most part insignificant, price inflation having the only sizeable coefficient. When all the economic variables were included, however, along with others representing (i) the 'coat-tails' effect of the successful presidential candidate in pulling up the congressional vote of his party every four years, and (ii) changes in voting alignments in 1920 and 1932, about 70 per cent of the variance of the congressional vote could be accounted for. This is a reasonably high level but the result owes more to the influence of the purely political variables than to the economic issues as such.

Bloom and Price (1975) also sought to specify the influence exerted by economic issues more precisely, by distinguishing between the effects on voting of rising and falling income. This again introduces another complication and change of direction to the debate on economic effects, since they are arguing that previous analyses were mistaken in implicitly treating effects as symmetrical (a rise increases votes to the same extent as a fall diminishes them). Bloom and Price, on the contrary, argue that the effects are asymmetric – electors' gratitude for an increase in prosperity may not match their desire to punish the incumbents for a decline. They demonstrate this by relating changes in real per capita income – as the independent, explanatory variable – to deviations from the vote expected on the basis of Party Identification (a measure of long-term loyalty to a party) as the dependent variable. On the basis of these measures, a remarkable difference emerged between the effects of rising and falling income. The Republican Party under its Presidents loses 0·59 per cent of the vote for each 1 per cent drop in real income. The Democrats under their Presidents lose more heavily – 0·79 per cent of the vote for each 1 per cent drop. When real income rises, on the other hand, neither party gains more than a negligible proportion of the vote.

A further interesting implication from their findings, if we assume that only falling income affects vote, is that it has exerted minor effects in the postwar period compared with the interwar years. Falls in income were slight and infrequent after the Second World War, but quite massive in the Depression. This suggests that economic variables as a whole had little importance postwar, but produced changes of up to 10 per cent of vote before the war. Bloom and Price do not, however, examine the possibility that some of this massive effect might be due to underlying realignments or presidential effects of the sort allowed for by Arcelus and Meltzer: indeed, they do not examine the effects of falls in real income in conjunction with those of any other variable, political or economic, so it is perhaps premature to generalise from their findings.

However, Tufte (1975), concentrating mainly on the postwar period (congressional elections in the middle of presidential terms from 1938 to 1972 inclusive), finds significant effects being exerted by income on vote. He relates presidential popularity and absolute changes in real income to vote for the incumbent party (measured as deviations in the current mid-term election from their average voting percentage over the last eight). The relationship between vote and changes in real income was higher than that for vote and presidential popularity. For each 1 per cent change in income, vote would change about 0·6 per cent. For each 1 per cent change in popularity, vote would change about 0·13 per cent. However, income and popularity are themselves related, constituting perhaps the strongest relationship in the model. There is a commonsense ordering of the predicting variables, since income changes may influence presidential popularity but the reverse influence is implausible.

Tufte implicitly assumes symmetry between rises and falls in real income, in terms of effects on vote. In view of the strong possibility of asymmetry, it is worthwhile noting that the years in which real income has fallen in the United States since the First World War are 1920, 1930, 1932, 1938, 1946, 1954 and 1958. The years underlined are those of mid-term congressional elections, and there are obviously a disproportionate number of these. In fact from the start of Tufte's series of mid-term elections in 1938, the *only* years in which real income had fallen up to the early 1970s were those of mid-term elections. It is conceivable, therefore, that Tufte's findings on the effects of income change really rest on the loss of votes associated with falls in income for these years. Real income also fell in 1974 – the year in which Tufte, alone among the econometric analysts of voting, made a prediction of future voting – specifying congressional voting percentages in advance, on the basis of his model. If the seemingly well-attested reasoning about the asymmetry of gains and losses in income holds up, any correspondence with results could be largely due to the fall in income in that particular year. (Two weeks in advance of the election his prediction was for a 39·2 per cent Republican vote compared with an actual 41·1 per cent.)

In a later report (1978) Tufte related income and presidential popularity to congressional voting in the same years as presidential elections, confirming the links he had discerned for off-year elections, but with slightly different values. In the on-year elections a 1 per cent change in real disposable income per capita seems to produce a 1·1 per cent change in national vote – an impact of almost double the strength of that observed for off-years. For presidential elections, a 1 per cent improvement in real disposable income benefits the incumbent presidential candidate by 1.3 per cent of the national vote. However, in the context of this intensely personal confrontation between the two presidential candidates, popularity has more of an impact than in congressional elections. Measured in terms of the balance of 'likes' over 'dislikes' in response to general survey questions, a net gain of one 'like' on average over the whole electorate produces a voting gain of 7·6 percentage points.

The research cited above by no means exhausts the burgeoning literature covering economic influences on voting. It does, however, include all the estimates that have been made, to our knowledge, of the exact relationships between economic factors and vote. It is significant that these are all American and practically all directed to congressional rather than presidential voting – a point to which we shall return later. This narrowness of focus immediately raises the question of how generalisable these findings are outside the United States, since our interests are primarily in comparative estimates.

In a study which raises this point with regard to Scandinavia, Madsen (1980) concludes that in two countries, Norway and Denmark, voting does not seem to depend on economic conditions even at the weak level detected by Kramer. Only in Sweden did net change in unemployment and increases in real income appear to have a significant relationship with voting. Unfortunately this result is not reported in a form which enables us to derive precise estimates of effect which could then be compared with the American.

Much research in this area has also been carried through in Britain, starting from the work of Goodhart and Bhansali (1970) and ably reviewed and advanced in a recent book by Alt (1980). This raises new questions on how far declining party fortunes are related to economic circumstances at all, and how far they constitute a secular decline in support. Unfortunately this extensive and sophisticated body of work produces nothing directly comparable with the American figures cited above, and no estimates of issue effect we can use. Economic factors are not related to actual voting but to the voting intentions revealed by quarterly opinion polls.

Naturally a relationship exists between voting intentions and voting, but its precise nature is obscure, and it has even been suggested that such intentions have, over the postwar period, increasingly taken on the nature of emotional and non-competitive popularity ratings rather than serious projections of voting behaviour (Miller and Mackie, 1973). A recent cross-national review (Paldam, 1981) stresses that giving a split-second answer to an unexpected question in an interview is not the same as choosing a party over several weeks or months in an election campaign.

The British studies certainly demonstrate a connection between economic conditions and voting intentions and suggest that it may be asymmetric in the sense that income losses are punished more heavily than gains are rewarded (Alt, 1980, ch. 5): for Australia, see also a similar finding by Kemp (1978). Alt's study indicates, moreover, that subjective expectations and measurements of inflation and income have a stronger influence over voting intentions than 'objective' indicators. But for measures of effect on actual vote we have to turn again to the relationships between the latter and congressional voting.

Differences between these various analyses produce considerable confusion. The basic strategy has been to concentrate on selected major problems (inflation, unemployment, prosperity) which appear as issues in most contemporary elections, and to relate them to votes over a fairly long series of elections, in some of which these factors may not have appeared as issues at all. This procedure entails an important assumption that attitudes to such issues have remained stable over periods ranging from thirty-five to seventy years, through two world wars and many social upheavals. The practice of assimilating results from econometric analyses in many countries (cf. Paldam's 1981 review), and of treating results from analyses of actual vote as equivalent to analyses of voting intentions, also involve very strong assumptions. Existing evidence seems in the latter case to indicate that vote and popularity are not equivalent in anything but a very broad and imprecise sense, this is the reason for not considering detailed findings on voting intentions here.

The econometric studies have equated factors like inflation and un-employment with commonly used economic indices. This has proved a less straightforward procedure than it may have seemed initially, owing to the several ways in common use of measuring such factors, each of which makes a difference (sometimes a considerable one) to the result.

Another unresolved question is the selection of variables in conjunction with which the effects of each factor should be estimated. Since each 'captures' some of the influence of the others when used on its own (as noted above with regard to Kramer's puzzling finding on unemployment), the decision on what combination of economic variables is to be employed in the regression equation is crucial in determining the magnitude of estimates. In practice, purely economic variables have been used in different combinations so there is non-comparability even here. There is also a wider problem in that economic factors are only one of the possible influences on elections, which must include political and perhaps social factors as well. Paldam (1981, p. 181) notes that economic factors on average are associated with only one-third of total voting changes. This has been tacitly acknowledged through the inclusion by Arcelus and Meltzer of an allowance for presidential incumbency and underlying realignments, and by Tufte of a measure of presidential popularity. The nature and comprehensiveness of the non-economic variables included will, however, also crucially affect the influence over voting attributed to each of the leading economic variables.

Discontinuities both in the actual variables combined in the final equation, and in their measurement, are illustrated in Table 1.1. This table covers the studies of congressional voting discussed at the beginning of this section. Columns refer (by the names of authors and dates) to the particular study from which estimates were taken, and within this to the different dependent variables used. (All except Tufte's in the last column relate to congressional voting, but sometimes to absolute vote, sometimes to Republican or Democratic percentage of the two-party vote, or to their percentage of the total vote including third parties.) Rows in the table are distinguished in terms of the particular variable employed and the method of operationalising this. Cells left blank in the table indicate that that variable (or particular operationalisation) was not used in the estimating equation. The numeric entries themselves are based on the regression co-efficients in the estimating equations reported by the original papers. All have been reduced to two decimal places. From the fact that few of the coefficients in different columns fall into the same rows, the non-cumulative nature of the research is obvious.

Discounting Stigler's two-year variables, and Arcelus and Meltzer's economic variables the effects of which were insignificant compared with the political, mainstream research points to changes in real income as the major economic influence over congressional voting. Kramer's original estimate was that a 10 per cent change in income produces a 4–5 per cent change in vote; Tufte's that it produces approximately 6 per cent change in vote for the incumbent party, for congressional off-year elections (though 11 per cent for on-year elections); and Bloom and Price's that such a (negative) change costs the Republicans about 6 per cent and the Democrats about 8 per cent when the presidency is occupied by their party. Changes in real income have varied considerably over the interwar and postwar periods, from 1–3 per cent (generally in the postwar period), through a middle 'band' of 5–7, to large changes, commonly around 10 per cent but including a catastrophic 15 per cent in the year of the Depression. These have favoured different parties at different times (usually affecting the party holding the presidency) so that both direction and magnitude of the voting changes they produce have been found to be erratic.

Obviously we cannot regard the estimates as more than rough approxi-mations. It is probably more useful though less exact to estimate the vote effects of small, moderate and large shifts in income. If we take small changes in real income as those up to 3 per cent, these produce something like a 1·5 per cent change in vote if we roughly average Tufte's off-year and Kramer's estimates. A large change of about 10 per cent (which has not, however, occurred postwar) produces about 5·5 per cent on this basis.

One must note also that economic effects have always been shown to account for less than half of the total changes in vote percentages (some-times none at all). This points to the necessity of allowing for political and social effects. Some attempt has been made to allow for political variables in studies of voting intentions and government popularity, by such devices as giving arbitrary scores decreasing by one unit each month, to represent

Table 1.1 *Effects of Political and Economic Variables in US Elections as Estimated by Econometric Techniques using Aggregate Data*

Author	Arcelus and Meltzer (1975)			Bloom and Price (1975)			Kramer (1971)		Stigler (1973)	Tufte (1975)	Tufte (1978)
Predicted Variable*	V1	V2	V3	V4	V4	V4	V4	V4	V4	V5	V6
Predicting Variable*											
Political:											
CM											7·64
PE	11·78	6·81	5·35								
PI										0·13	
PP							0·00	0·00	0·01		
RI				0·86	1·19	0·61					
RP	0·76	−2·12	2·68								
T20	16·39	7·05	4·51								
T32	11·39	8·67	1·58								
Economic:											
C1	0·11	−0·00	0·04								
C1×RI		−0·09	−0·07								
I1							+0·53	−0·64			
P1	−0·23	−0·52	−0·03				−0·16	+0·55			
P1×RI		+0·62	+0·38								
P2						0·21					
R1									−0·21		
R2									0·17	0·04	1·32
R3				0·12							
R4					−0·75						
U1	+0·01	−0·01	+0·01				+0·20	+0·17			
U1×RI		+0·02	−0·02								

* The explanation of these variable names is as follows:

Political

CM Advantage to incumbent party in average number of candidate like/dislike mentions.
PE Dummy variable, equals +1 for a presidential election, 0 otherwise.
PI Predicted Republican percentage of the vote based on registered party identification.
PP Presidential popularity measured by opinion polls.
RI Dummy variable, equals +1 for Republican President, 0 otherwise.
RP RI×PE.
T20 Dummy variable, equals +1 if election before 1920, 0 otherwise.
T32 Dummy variable, equals +1 if election in or after 1932, 0 otherwise.

Economic

C1 Relative change in real compensation over previous year.
I1 Relative change in actual income over previous year.
P1 Relative change in price index over previous year.
P2 Relative change in price index over previous two years.
R1 Relative change in real income over previous year.
R2 Relative change in real income over previous two years.
R3 $\frac{1}{2}(R1+|R1|)$, i.e. change if an increase.
R4 $\frac{1}{2}(|R1|-R1)$, i.e. change if a decrease.
U1 Relative change in unemployment rate over previous year.

Voting

V1 Percentage of electors voting (1896 to 1970).
V2 Percentage of electors voting Democrat (1896 to 1970).
V3 Percentage of electors voting Republican (1896 to 1970).
V4 Percentage of two-party vote voting for incumbent party (1896 to 1970).
V5 Difference between the percentage of the two-party vote voting for the incumbent party and a moving average of this percentage in congressional elections (1938 to 1970).
V6 Percentage of two-party vote voting for incumbent party in presidential elections (1940 to 1972).

initial 'honeymoon' support for a government, or entering deaths in the Vietnam War into equations (e.g. Paldam, 1981, p. 193). These devices work because, over a series of monthly or three-monthly observations, related to percentages expressing support in opinion polls, they show significant variation. When related to actual votes, however, with only one or two elections occurring in the lifetime of the issue, the range of values would be too limited to support useful estimates.

The main analysis of the actual vote effects of a political variable remains Tufte's estimate of the effects on off-year congressional vote of presidential popularity (the second variable in his estimating equation along with changes in real income). Using the straight percentage of respondents in Gallup's three-monthly polls who approve of the way the President is doing his job, Tufte reckons that a 1 per cent shift in popularity will produce a 0·13 per cent shift in vote. Between mid-term elections presidential popularity may vary from 42 to 56 per cent. The more relevant figure is, however, the extent by which popularity varies during the run-up to the election. An extreme case here is the drop in President Ford's rating in 1974 from 71 to 55 per cent – 16 per cent, which on the estimate produces approximately a 2·1 per cent vote loss for what must be taken as a large negative impact.

On the other hand, presidential candidates are likely to have a different and stronger effect in the election they are actually contesting, than in one where they campaign to a limited extent on behalf of their party, but where all sorts of other candidates appear and where particular local factors come into play. Indeed, Tufte himself in his later study notes the considerably greater effect of popularity in presidential elections themselves, though it is uncertain exactly how this translates into net votes. However, he does observe that on average real disposable income increases by 3·3 per cent in presidential years, so that the net vote gain to the incumbent is of the order of 4·3 per cent.

Exact comparisons are really impossible given the different bases on which figures were reached. What can be said is that net effects of economic issues in the United States seem to fall within a broad range of around 1·5–6·0 per cent. Contrasting electoral and temporal contexts, and discrepancies among econometric studies themselves, prevent us from concluding anything more than this.

1.2   Attitudinal Components of Policy Voting

The factors related to vote through multivariate regression equations need not, of course, be purely economic in character. In an influential study D. E. Stokes (1966) related electors' evaluations of the two US presidential candidates, of group interests, foreign and domestic policy, and general party competence, to their individual votes. The influence of these attitudes upon the overall percentage result (which is the focus of our investigation) can then be found by combining information from the regression equation with information on the distribution of evaluations among the electorate.

Specifically, each elector's favourable or unfavourable evaluation of a party can be measured on a scale running, for example, from −10 through zero to +10. Scores represent the net balance of favourable and unfavourable mentions of a party on each of the six attitudes mentioned above, in response to survey questions on what is liked and disliked about the party and its presidential candidate. They give a very good indication of the way the individual voted: as appears from the research by Kelley and Mirer (1974) discussed below. However, aggregating the individual scores for and against a party may result in zero, because positive and negative scores balance out. Here the attitude could not be said to exert any overall effect although important in individual decisions. To the extent that the scores deviate in the same direction from zero, the attitude makes a larger overall contribution to the final outcome. This can be summarised for the voters as a whole by the difference between the mean of the overall distribution of scores which may deviate in response to strongly positive or strongly negative attitudes and the zero score for each attitude. How influential a strongly pro or anti attitude is in relation to electors' other attitudes depends also on how strongly it influences the final voter choice – in other words, on the size of its coefficient in the general regression equation. Multiplying this by the difference between actual mean and zero score gives a measure of the effect of that particular attitude which can be readily expressed as a net vote percentage.

Using this framework, Stokes concluded that for the 1952 presidential election the Republican advantage from Eisenhower's candidacy was 3·5 per cent and for 1956 nearly 8 per cent. For the election of 1960 Nixon's gains were 2·5 per cent, but in 1964 Johnson's candidacy produced a 5 per cent advantage for the Democrats. This is evidence for presidential incumbents exerting a large and positive effect, confirming the general historical impression that an incumbent President generates considerable popular support when he stands for re-election. Ford's defeat in 1976 supports rather than refutes this. Given his distinctly unimpressive record, he did well to come nearly equal to Carter. The latter's defeat in 1980 constitutes a genuine counter example. Of the other types of issues investigated by Stokes, foreign policy generally favoured the Republicans at 3·5 per cent net in 1952, 2·5 per cent in 1956, 2·0 per cent in 1960 and zero in 1964. Presumably Vietnam and the crises of the 1970s pushed these effects up.

Using Stokes's methods, with a significant modification mentioned below, Klingemann and Taylor (1977) have obtained estimates of the impact both of candidates and of various specific issues on the percentage vote in West Germany. In elections from 1961 to 1976 inclusive the incumbent Chancellor produced net gains for his party of the order of 1·0 per cent, 0·5 per cent, 5·5 per cent, 2·6 per cent and 0·2 per cent. Since both the Christians (CDU) and the Socialists (SPD) were in office at different times over this period, these figures imply that candidate effects vary in both direction and magnitude, but are somewhat smaller on average than the American.

Klingemann and Taylor note explicitly, however, that their estimates for the impact of issues are conservative. They are based only on sympathisers with the *other* party, who are induced by the candidate or issue to vote on this occasion for its rival. Estimates are not based on the electorate as a whole. Since Stokes's estimates allow all electors to contribute to net gains or losses, they are almost bound to be higher.

Survey-based estimates of net effects are available from the same German study for both domestic and foreign issues. These show that both parties benefit from foreign-policy issues and from the issue of price stability. On 'law and order', however, only the CDU benefits, while on the issue of old-age security only the SPD gains. Foreign-policy issues generally have small effects, while price stability produces fluctuating net gains. When law and order and old-age security emerge as issues they have a more stable effect, of the order of 1·0 – 1·5 per cent. This seems low for such issues, but we have already explained the very conservative basis on which figures are calculated. Nevertheless, the impact of candidates and foreign policy does seem less in West Germany compared with the United States.

The inability to make straightforward, direct comparisons between figures is irritating but not confined to these particular reports. It is endemic in a field where there has been little cumulative research or awareness of the quantitative findings and assumptions in other investigators' work. This is nowhere more apparent than in the literature on 'policy voting' in the United States, whose whole concern is with the electoral impact of issues. To a large extent this has been directed towards demonstrating that issues have some effect, rather than providing precise estimates of what it is. Unfortunately, even such a broad objective has been bedevilled by conceptual and methodological difficulties, partly because of the lack of a clear idea about when an elector has voted on issues. Is it necessary for an elector to express an opinion on the issue, to perceive what policies are being furthered by the government, and grasping what differences exist between the parties? (Campbell *et al.*, 1960, p. 170; Margolis, 1977). Or is an elector without any opinion, who does not vote, also expressing his (non-)opinion? Suppose also that an elector has a preference on an issue, and votes in line with friends who have similar opinions, without having himself formulated clear ideas about party differences or government policy. Can he be said to be voting on issues just as much as an elector who has resolved these points? (Budge and Farlie, 1977, p. 286).

A further question is whether issue voting occurs only when a voter changes from his previous party? (Switchers are found to be generally more in agreement with the party they move towards than the one they move from.) Or may an elector still be choosing on issues when he remains in general agreement with the party of his traditional loyalty? For stand-patters the two influences are hard to disentangle. Recently non-recursive modelling has been applied to presidential voting in 1972 and 1976 in an attempt to resolve the question, that is, issue stands have not only been regarded as determining immediate votes but also as shaping party identification (or, more broadly, long-term party loyalties) and through this influencing later voting (Page and Jones, 1978). However, this makes it even harder to get a clear-cut estimate of the total effect of issues since in any one election part of the influence of party loyalty has also to be attributed to them, while part of the direct influence of issues has to be reattributed to other factors. An earlier paper on the 1964 presidential election by Jackson (1975, pp. 193–4), which originated this line of research, estimated that each additional issue on which people felt closer to a party increased their propensity to vote for that party by 0·21. However, without knowing the percentages who did feel closer to each party on the issues, we have no way of estimating their effects over the total electorate.

Clearer figures on immediate issue effects (which, however, ignore possible background links between issues, loyalties and other factors) are obtainable from 'Normal Vote' analyses. The basic procedure here is to compute the vote 'expected' for each group on the basis of its proportion of electors identifying with a particular party, and its likely turnout. The discrepancy between this expected percentage and the actual observed vote then provides some idea of the effects of the issue on the group under consideration. Many of these analyses concentrate on particular groups rather than on the total electorate and so do not provide any basis for comparison with our estimates. In what is in many ways the most thorough and systematic use of a 'Normal Vote' analysis of the impact of issues (the 1968 presidential election study by R. W. Boyd, 1972), electors are divided into groups with different views on issues. The expected vote for each opinion group is calculated and compared with an estimate of the observed vote, using the Survey Research Centre survey of that election. The purpose of the analysis is to show the deflection of these groups from the way they would have voted on the basis of party identification. Since the absolute number of voters in each opinion group is given, as well as the percentage discrepancy between expected and actual vote, it is also possible to calculate the net gain or loss to the Democrats over all groups, to provide a general idea of the impact of the issue. This generally comes out at a level of around 15 per cent net, which is substantially higher than most of those cited previously, but which can be explained almost entirely as effects being calculated on the assumption that issues are independent of each other, when in fact they are overlapping. Their independent effects must thus be substantially less than 15 per cent. Moreover, the estimates are based only on voters with opinions on the issues and exclude those with no opinion, whose inclusion would tend to lower the extent of change attributable to the issue. (We should emphasise that these estimates are calculated by us from figures reported by Boyd. He himself does not use them.)

Our basic conclusion must be that there is not enough information from the 'Normal Vote' analyses of issue effects to produce firm quantitative estimates of their magnitude.

1.3   Aggregating Electors' Likes and Dislikes: 'The Simple Act of Voting'

The approaches we have discussed generally base themselves on precoded agree/disagree responses to preselected issues, though sometimes respondents are asked to express their strength of feeling. Jackson's analysis used precoded questions giving respondents' perception of their location and of the location of parties or candidates. The combination of these provides a measure of the similarity of individual preferences to different parties' policies. The problem with preselected questions of both kinds is that the choice of relevant issues then depends wholly on the survey-designer's judgement. Omission of salient issues or inclusion of some which are not salient can seriously distort judgements about the real extent of issue voting.

One solution is to identify issues which concern electors themselves through answers to 'open' questions (such as 'What do you consider the most important problems facing yourself/the country?') – or through reactions to general inquiries about likes and dislikes of parties and candidates. Such questions have advantages in allowing electors to identify issues salient for themselves. Their disadvantage is that measures based on them are not strictly comparable with ones based on preselected issues. Moreover, by deriving estimates from some kind of count of electors' positive and negative reactions to parties, one loses sight of individual issues and the effects they may exert on the outcome, since purely idiosyncratic and personal responses weigh equally with reactions to general questions of policy.

The outstanding study based on 'non-directive' questioning is 'The simple act of voting' analysed by Kelley and Mirer (1974). This hypothesises a 'voter's decision rule' which directs choice of that (presidential) candidate towards whom the individual has the greatest net number of favourable attitudes. Where no candidate has such an advantage, the voter votes consistently with his party affiliation, if he has one. Where neither of these criteria applies, the choice is indeterminate. Favourable and unfavourable attitudes are ascertained from electors' responses to standard questions on what was liked and disliked about each of the candidates and major parties in turn. On the basis of such responses the decision rule correctly characterised over 80 per cent of voters' choices (not electors' choices, because it did not purport to cover non-voting).

This is obviously very successful in a postdictive and potentially predictive sense, and constitutes a plausible account of how the individual elector makes up his mind on the basis of the political stimuli impinging on him. It is extremely suggestive, in that it underlines the need for electors to simplify drastically in order to cope with problems of information overload and calculation costs which would otherwise paralyse their political judgement. In this sense it exerts a considerable influence over our own approach below.

To some extent, however, the admirable simplicity of the formulation is also a weakness, since it deprives the rule of general explanatory relevance. When we inquire why the Democrats won in 1964, or the Republicans in 1952, we want to know more than that the majority of electors decided to vote for them on the basis of considerations that they considered individually relevant at the time. With such a question we really wish to discover what distinguished the two elections and produced the different outcomes. The rule does not provide estimates of the impact of individual issues, which sink without trace in the mass of individual responses. Its application to these nevertheless produces an illuminating finding of a different and unexpected sort, which bears on our later discussion of campaign strategies. The error rate in characterising votes from attitudes decreased, naturally, with the net number of attitudes favouring a candidate, but rose sharply with increases in the total number of attitudes from which the net scores were computed. In other words, the balance of positive over negative responses might result from the expression of a small number of attitudes, all positive. Or it might result from a large number of positive responses outweighing a still substantial number of negative responses. In the latter case voting choices are less predictable than in the former.

This could be seen as reflecting greater uncertainty in the voters' own minds, produced by the perception of more and more party issue stands which oppose one's own preferences. Where only a few issues impinge, electors are more likely to see one party in wholly positive terms. This point is important for our analysis of campaign strategies. If party leaders think electors become more uncertain as they place more issues before them, they will have a powerful incentive to limit their appeals to the three or four they think will have most effect (see Table 7.1, Assumption 9, p. 150 below). However relevant to our later argument, the finding bears only peripherally on the question of issue effects. Indeed, none of the American policy voting literature yields very clear findings about the impact of individual issues.

To supplement it we turn in the next section to British and Canadian studies, using different methodologies again, which give more precise figures of the type we are seeking.

1.4   Survey-Based Estimates of Issue Effect: British and Canadian Evidence

A study by W. L. Miller (1978) of the effects of the immigration issue in the British general election of 1970 brings an alternative approach to estimation. Basing himself on the national election survey of that year, he used a five-option question on immigration: Britain should (1) assist in sending immigrants home; (2) stop further immigration but allow immigrants already here to stay; (3) allow in immediate families of immigrants already here and a few skilled workers only; (4) allow in new workers and their families; or (5) allow free entry. Options thus ranged from a fairly hostile position to a highly sympathetic one. Respondents were asked to locate themselves, and both parties, on these positions. Taking aggregate perceptions as being the actual position of the party for the election gives a measure for each respondent of his closeness to the party, which can be used in conjunction with answers to a further question on which party he personally thought was closer to him.

Respondents can thus be divided successively into those who voted Labour, Conservative and 'Other' in 1966 (the preceding election); each of the resulting groups into those actually close to Labour or Conservative or equidistant; and those in turn into electors who *perceived* themselves as closer to Labour, to Conservatives, or as equidistant. This division enables Miller to calculate swings for the various groups. His percentage figures relate to the total electorate rather than just to voters.

The total swing from Labour to Conservative in the 1970 election, calculated on this basis, was 4·6 per cent. Distrusting the stability of Party Identification in Britain, Miller does not compare actual swing with the figure which might have been expected on the basis of the proportions of Conservative and Labour identifiers in each group. Instead, he estimates what might have happened had there been no immigration effect by averaging the swings among electors unaffected by the issue. These he takes operationally as being the groups who perceived themselves as equidistant from the parties on immigration. Applied to the whole electorate this gives an overall swing of 3·1 per cent to the Conservatives. Subtracting this estimated baseline figure from the actual swing in the election gives an estimate of 1·5 per cent as the effects of the immigration issue in increasing support for the Conservatives.

This figure is, however, based on the total electorate rather than the total number of voters. Without knowing the actual numbers of voters and non-voters which entered into the calculation, we cannot convert the estimate to a form which is directly comparable to the ones made earlier, in terms of net percentage gains of votes. Certainly, however, electors moving into the Conservative Party and thus constituting the Conservative gain must have voted. Knowing that the overall turnout at 72 per cent was roughly three-quarters of the electorate, we can adjust the figure of 1·5 per cent upwards by a third to get a voter-based estimate of the Conservative swing. This now appears as about 2 per cent.

However, this figure represents the average of Conservative gain and Labour loss. In the likely event that the Conservatives attracted other than former Labour voters, their contribution to average swing would have been somewhat higher than Labour's, so the estimate of their gain would fall between 2·0 and 2·5 per cent.

This figure gains support from the conclusions of an independent study of immigration applying quite different methods. In order to isolate voting effects attributable to the issue as such, Studlar (1978) related opinions on immigration, along with other significant background influences, to vote (measured as 0 for Labour and 1 for Conservatives). The resulting multiple regression was applied separately for those who perceived Labour as harder on immigrants, those who saw no difference between the parties and those who perceived the Conservatives as harder. By multiplying the regression coefficient associated with immigration opinions by the numbers in each group, and adding these algebraically, Studlar was able to estimate the gain to Conservatives in 1970 as 3·3 per cent net. Recalculations of his data (allowing for an observed shift towards Labour among the group seeing 'no difference' between the parties, which Studlar does not include) brings the estimate of Conservative gains on the issue to under 3 per cent. Given the very approximate nature of all the calculations, this is close enough to Miller's results to give some confidence that we have a reasonable measure here of the voting effects of a major election issue in Britain.

Parallel estimates for the effects of a specific campaign issue are given in 'The majority government issue and electoral behaviour in Canada' (Le Duc, 1975: slightly revised in Le Duc, 1977). This study isolated Liberal and Progressive Conservative voters who had switched, or entered the electorate for the first time, between the elections of 1972 and 1974, and who reported that they were influenced 'a great deal' in their decision by the majority government issue (thus we are as sure as we can be with survey responses that we are dealing with electors who changed purely under the impact of that issue). Analysis was restricted to these voters, on the reasoning that concern about majority government could only have the effect of inducing electors to vote for one of the two parties which had any hope of a majority. The various flows of votes between parties produced a figure of 1·3 per cent net gain to the Liberals from the electorate as a whole. To calculate a net percentage gain in terms of voters, we have to make allowances for turnout in the 1974 election. Seventy-one per cent voted in 1974 and since the changers under consideration are all voters we have to add roughly a third to this percentage to get an estimate comparable with those made earlier. This produces 1·7 per cent net gain in voters for what Le Duc regards as an issue of medium impact.

Such an estimate fits well with those for the more central issue, in 1970, of immigration in Britain, for which the ascribed effects are clearly greater. It also falls within the range identified for most of the West German issues, from 1 to 3 per cent net gain in voters. The broad agreement between these quite diverse analyses seems to contrast with the effects of US issues, which on the basis of both the econometric estimates and of Stokes's work seem to be within a higher and broader range from 1·5 to 6·0 per cent of voters, with one or two even higher examples. Given the institutional and cultural differences between the United States and other countries, it would not be surprising if issue effects were larger there: a greater dominance of short-term cues over American electors' voting choices has already been identified on the basis of comparative survey data (Budge and Farlie, 1977, pp. 332–48).

1.5   Prospects for Comparative Investigation

Given the range of very disparate studies which we have to draw upon, our ability to make even rough generalisations is encouraging. The different estimates do converge and they point to conclusions which make sense. Given the limited extent of change between one election and another, we could not expect a single issue to produce very extensive switches of support. This is particularly so when we consider only the net shifts which show up in overall results rather than all of the movements, often counter-balancing, which may well take place between different groups in the electorate. Net effects must be counted in single, low percentages rather than double figures. The higher estimates for US issues also gain plausibility from general impressions, reinforced by survey evidence and election outcomes themselves, of greater volatility among US electors.

The feasibility of a comparative investigation does not, of course, depend upon the figures for different elections being the same, although there is an unexpected bonus if they are. Rather it depends on being able to relate figures to each other on the assumption that they measure the same underlying processes. That is, that issues such as immigration and inflation do not entail such totally different reactions in different countries at different times that the resulting shifts cannot be compared.

There are, of course, many descriptive studies of single elections which do not explicitly bring in other cases. However, these do not rule out the possibility of doing so. They simply refrain from explicit comparisons. Such studies depend upon implicit comparison in raising such obvious points as turnout being unusually low or an issue engaging exceptional attention (how could we tell except in contrast with previous elections or other countries?).

Surveys of particular elections depend even more heavily on the assumption that questions used elsewhere convey the same meaning to respondents as those in current use. Cross-national and time-series analyses are committed on this point, as we noted in regard to econometric studies which assume that inflation or unemployment evoke similar reactions, for as long as seventy years, and in different national contexts.

Though the necessity of assuming a limited comparability may be admitted, it is always easy to point to the many circumstances differentiating elections as proof that a general approach is inappropriate and that each should be treated on its own terms within its own time and place. This would rule out general estimates of the kind we have tried to construct, and certainly inhibit general explanations which used them.

There is no easy answer to such an objection. Elections do differ in their specific circumstances and no general explanation may be forthcoming. On the other hand, the same point can be made about practically any area of scientific investigation. Were it always accepted we should have no physical, economic, or indeed political theory – which talks about democracy as a general concept, not one bounded by a specific place or time. The role of elections in democracy creates at least a presumption that they should be studied generally and comparatively. If, in the event, a general explanation cannot be constructed, then we can fall back on specific description. But an attempt at generalisation should first be made.

Of course, our selection of twenty-three democracies for investigation has already reduced some of the undoubted variation in electoral systems. There are, for example, no political systems in our analysis that admit only one or no parties. We have also (see Table 3.1, p. 61 below) made countries more comparable by concentrating analysis on only two opposing parties or blocs, thus ignoring other complexities of multi-party systems.

The econometric studies and all survey analyses are committed to comparative generalisations, since they freely transfer techniques and assumptions between historical periods and countries. Too often, however, the transfers have been piecemeal and unconsidered, resulting in a diversity of results and conclusions which do not relate clearly to each other. This is more the result of analytic decisions than of real differences between countries or elections. For, in spite of analytic confusion, certain underlying similarities are glimpsed. These encourage comparative analysis, but the prevailing state of disorganisation suggests this will prove most valuable where it is integrated and systematic, applying a common approach to many countries rather than varying methods within a few.

One positive result stemming from the use of different methods is that, where they agree, findings are relatively well attested. For if common estimates emerge they are more likely to reflect reality than if they derived from the systematic biases of a single approach. The same point applies to our later results. If a new technique produces similar figures, both its own validity and that of the previous investigation will be strengthened. The important point is not whether one technique is 'better' than another in some absolute sense which does not exist (since all have biases and errors), but whether all lead to concurring estimates which we can then use with some confidence.

Chapter 2

Saliency Theory

Every approach to the study of elections has its own weaknesses and strengths. As we cannot hope to evolve a totally unbiased, error-free method, it seems sensible to adopt one which will remedy some of the weaknesses of previous investigations and offer a basis for alternative estimation and interpretation. It is in the agreement of the different approaches on these, rather than in an attempt to develop one method to the exclusion of others, that the prospects for constructive explanation lie.

Two weaknesses of earlier investigations stand out. One is the absence of cumulative research, since the variety of methods, variables and measures renders comparison difficult. The other is the limited cross-national basis of comparison: broadly comparable estimates of voting gains from issues can be obtained only for US elections, which are probably atypical; for West German elections; and for single issues in one British and one Canadian election.

The non-cumulative nature of research derives partly from the absence of any systematic theory of how issues affect electors, other than the general assumption that electors vote for parties which serve their aspirations and vote against those which do not. This assumption is insufficiently specified to tie investigations down to any particular line of approach, or any agreed set of influences. It also ignores the considerable potential of competing parties and alternatives to influence electors' reactions. In isolation, electors might vote against a government which decreased income. But what if they believe that any government would decrease it to the same extent (as Stigler, 1973, suggests)? And how precisely do they trade off decreased income, for example, against decreased immigration, which might be on offer as well?

An alternative to proliferating *ad hoc* studies to deal with these points is to develop a consistent theory to cover them systematically, and then to check it against the data which seem most relevant and available. This is the approach followed below. The estimates produced within this framework can then be compared with those discussed in Chapter 1, to see how far they support each other.

A comprehensive theory cannot readily be developed for a single country. It has to cope with the processes operating in a variety of democracies. Consequently it requires checking against a variety of national experiences, to ensure that it offers at least a reasonably adequate account of them. For that reason we try to cover all the countries that have operated with regular and competitive elections over most of the period from 1950 to 1981. Through this approach we hope to offset the restricted national basis on which studies of issue effects have been undertaken up until now. Inevitably more breadth implies less depth. With a wider selection of countries we cannot hope to deal with their internal processes in as much detail as a single-country study could. We are not seeking to replace such studies, however, but to complement them, and for this a large-scale comparative investigation seems most useful.

If one develops a complete theory about the way election processes work, this will in the present state of research rest on some initially unsupported postulates. However much one bases oneself on previous work this is, as we have seen, so fragmentary that gaps have to be filled with plausible assumptions. This does not imply that these need remain unchecked, however. Once the argument has been stated, we can see if relevant evidence departs significantly from theoretical expectations. Rigorous and extended tests are, in fact, applied in Chapters 3–5. The procedure of first stating hypotheses and then checking them reverses previous work, which has tried to provide findings first and interpretations afterwards. There is room for both types of approach but it should be noted that neither is free from theoretical assumptions. In order to make the estimates described in Chapter 1 very strong assumptions had to be made. The fact that we state ours first does not imply that our approach is more subjective, but rather that it is more explicit.

Since a theoretical and comparative method has most to contribute at the present time, the rest of this chapter develops one. In Section 2.1 we discuss the theory of party competition and electoral reactions which fits best with existing evidence. Section 2.2 describes the broad issue types in terms of which judgements about parties are made, while Sections 2.3 and 2.4 show how the varying importance of these in the campaign triggers aggregate voting shifts on the part of the electorate.

2.1   Party Competition and Electoral Reactions

Any explanation of how electors make voting choices rests on beliefs, explicit or implicit, about party behaviour. This is because parties provide the main political guidance for most electors, by simplifying and focusing the complex world of politics in terms of their own policies and stands. It is on the basis of the alternatives parties offer that most electors make their only direct political decisions.

Most data-based studies concentrate their analysis on individual voting, assuming by the way that parties seek office and so make themselves as attractive as possible in order to gain votes. Where such assumptions are taken further, they have generally been developed into mathematical models too formal and abstract to relate closely to empirical studies (e.g.

Budge and Farlie, 1977, pp. 156–81; Budge *et al.*, 1981). Here, our view of the way electors decide to vote stems directly from the way parties approach them, thus recognising the strong interaction between party and electoral decisions.

How do parties approach voters? A common view is that they stage a 'great debate' in which government spokesmen defend their programmes on the important questions of the day, while the opposition criticises them and argues that its own preferred policies are better (Bryce, 1921, p. 124).

The actual evidence offers only limited endorsement for this view. Far from discussing details of their opponents' plans, parties tend in their public pronouncements to ignore them so far as possible, and to deflect popular attention to other policies which have not been mentioned by their rivals. The latter in turn promote their own favourite issues, usually quite different ones, so that reading different party statements made in the course of the same campaign fosters the illusion that several quite separate elections are taking place!

Supporting evidence for this revised interpretation comes from analyses of campaign documents, particularly the authoritative policy statements made by designated representatives, on behalf of the whole party. In Britain this takes the form of a short- to medium-length document composed under the direction of the party leader and termed the election manifesto (Kavanagh, 1981). In the United States a similar document is issued by the platform committee of the party convention under the name of the party platform. Elsewhere the statement of the party position may take a variety of forms, from radio and television speeches, newspaper advertisements and statements, declarations of principle by various party organs, special pamphlets, etc. (For the variety of practices see Budge and Robertson (eds), forthcoming.)

The most extensive studies of such documents are of British manifestos and American party platforms (Robertson, 1976; Budge and Farlie, 1977, pp. 421–33). When their sentences were systematically examined, a major finding was the very limited extent to which the rival parties mentioned each other at all, let alone mentioned the others' policies. In some no reference at all is made to the other party; in none do references occur in more than a quarter of all sentences; and the overall average is 7 per cent. Less than half of these references, even at the most generous estimate, can be taken to concern policies. Broadly, this avoidance of direct reference is found to characterise a variety of campaign material from the postwar period collected from over twenty countries (Budge and Robertson (eds), forthcoming).

Parties therefore do not compete by arguing directly with each other, but by trying to render their own areas of concern most prominent. Practically, this means that the only way to analyse the way they vary their appeals is to discover general 'issue types' or 'issue areas' within policy statements. These can then be located and counted within each document and their incidence compared between parties and elections. The effect on voters is to induce them to think in terms of similar broad 'issue types', so those discovered in manifestos and their equivalents offer a first lead to the categories used by electors themselves to evaluate issues (see Table 2.1, p. 28 below).

In line with the documentary findings cited above, Saliency Theory sees party competition in terms of varying emphases on policy areas. In their public pronouncements, parties do not scrupulously consider each topic of public interest in turn, contrasting their own detailed policies with those of their opponents. If they did, electors might well react differently. Instead, they devote most attention to the types of issue which favour themselves, discuss these with less reference to details than to general reviews of their past achievements and promises for the future, and give correspondingly less attention to issues which favour their opponents (see Table 6.1, p. 132 below). Party competition is only secondarily a direct confrontation of opposing policies. Most frequently it produces selective emphases on the strong points of one's own case. Rather than promoting an educational dialogue, parties talk past each other.

Why should selective emphases prove helpful to a party? Underlying them are certain beliefs about electoral behaviour which party leaders endorse, at least implicitly. They seem to think that certain policy areas attract a net inflow of votes to the party when they become salient. Conversely, other areas favour rivals: mentioning them at all (even to refute mistaken policies) runs the risk of rendering an unfavourable issue salient and helping to push voters into another party.

To see why this should be, one has only to envisage a party identified with support for expanded welfare services, for example. So long as it mentions this generally favoured position it can be sure of arousing only positive feelings. Suppose, however, it goes on to emphasise taxation policy. Generally, increased welfare policies have to be paid for by higher taxes – an unpopular suggestion. If the party emphasises both areas equally rather than emphasising welfare and ignoring taxation, it will at most fail to gain and very probably lose votes. By linking the two areas it has to deal with the disadvantages as well as advantages of its policies; by stressing only welfare it purveys only positive inducements. The same logic applies to the party associated with low taxation. To gain votes it has to emphasise taxation policy and ignore consequential cuts elsewhere. An incident from the 1979 general election in Britain underlines this. Sir Keith Joseph, a leading Conservative spokesman, undertook to show how his party's policy of lower taxes would be financed through cuts in social and other expenditures. After two speeches he totally abandoned the topic, presumably as a result of appalled reactions from his colleagues. The danger lay in directing attention from the group which was to be benefited (taxpayers) to the group, to which most taxpayers also belong, which would be hurt – welfare users. The politician's art lies in persuading electors to vote in terms of their membership of the benefited group rather than of the disadvantaged one.

As the parties themselves talk of welfare without regard to taxes, and take credit for prosperity, regardless of its consequences, or of whether it really follows from their policies, electors can hardly be expected to take a more sophisticated view. They, too, are likely to see issues as divided into a number of broad policy areas quite divorced from each other, so that a policy can be advocated within one area without repercussions for the others. This is encouraged by the fact that even specialists are unclear about the nature of possible interconnections – for example, lowered taxes need not involve welfare cuts if tax receipts increase through inflation or general prosperity, or if the government increases the budget deficit, or if it has simply underestimated future revenues.

The selective emphases of the parties have other consequences for electors' decisions. They imply that particular parties normally benefit from the importance of a *particular* issue area. Hence they will do all they can to stress this in the hope that they will not lose by doing so and may gain substantially if they make it prominent. Party strategists assume, in other words, that electors make a clear connection between a certain party and good government performance on a particular issue. The working assumptions of experienced politicians on this point are to be respected, quite apart from the fact that they constitute a self-fulfilling prophecy. If the political bodies with most impact on electors choose to structure their appeals in this way, it is of course likely that electors will react along the same lines.

In any case, when they are unsure of what causes what in the tangled chain of political developments, people faced with practical choices are forced to rely on the general association between certain events and a particular party's tenure of office. It may be simplistic for US electors to prefer Republicans to Democrats on foreign policy, on the ground that Democrats have always been in office when the country went to war, but who is to say the belief is totally unfounded? Simply because the issue works to their advantage, Republican Presidents may in fact devote more care to international developments than Democrats, while the latter are especially careful (for similar reasons) in handling the economy. Similarly, welfare is less likely to be increased under a right-wing than under a left-wing government (Castles, 1982, ch. 2). In addition to this, parties have commitments to their activists and to change these would produce radical upheavals to little electoral advantage. Who would even believe a Christian Democratic pledge to reduce the powers of the Church? Certain electoral commitments simply make no sense for parties, and therefore they can be relied upon not to make them. The result is that parties are widely perceived as 'owning' certain issue types, such as support of traditional morality and religion, or law and order, or the expansion of welfare. This vastly simplifies voting for electors. When an issue type is of prime importance voters can (with some important exceptions) automatically choose the appropriate party.

Electors' decisions are thus largely shaped by the public behaviour of parties. While this reaches them through the media, parties themselves select the emphases which are likely to get through. Of course electors will seldom be able to decide how to vote on the basis of only one issue in an election. Often three, four or five separate policy areas may be important for them. In reaching a decision about the balance of issue advantages, electors are again likely to simplify and to react in the most direct way possible. An indication of how they actually simplify comes from a study by Kelley and Mirer of US presidential elections (1974, pp. 572–91). Their index of individual voting choices sums positive and negative references to the parties and assumes, very successful, that electors vote for the side with the highest positive score. In other words, simple self-contained emphases are added up and balanced out: there was no apparent attempt by the elector to evaluate these or to discount some in favour of others, as would be the case if they were not taken at face value and weighted equally. In the context of Saliency Theory, it therefore seems likely that electors will weight important issues equally (i.e. give each a score of one), attribute these scores to each of the parties on the basis of which 'owns' each issue, and vote for the party with the highest score over all the issues important to them.

From the fragmentary evidence available, we should expect electors to take their lead from party statements of policy positions, and thus to preserve the same drastic separation between different areas of politics, the same focus on broad goals within each area rather than detailed policies, and the same fixed connections between most goals and choice of a particular party. In Sections 2.2 and 2.3 we shall see how individual decision processes build up into aggregate votes of the whole electorate when particular issue areas come to prominence in the course of an election campaign.

2.2   Types of Issues

The major questions raised by this account are (a) what policy areas electors see issues as falling into; (b) how many electors feel affected when one of these areas comes to the forefront; and (c) which parties 'own' which areas and so may expect to gain votes when they become prominent. The first is tackled in this section and the others in Sections 2.3 and 2.4.

A preliminary point is why parties and electors should locate issues within broad areas of policy rather than tackling each specific issue as it comes up. A moment's reflection, however, suggests that simplification cannot stop at selective emphasis. To make decisions at all on the basis of issues which were not related to anything that had gone before, one would have to go into the antecedents of each as it emerged, laboriously tracing its development and likely consequences. It is easier to group the new issue with others into a broad policy area, where each party has a general record for which it can be held responsible. Thus a party's future behaviour on a new problem can be gauged from how it has performed on related issues in the past.

Parties themselves help electors to simplify in this way. Their pamphlets and documents group topics under headings such as 'foreign affairs', 'welfare' and 'agriculture'. Media discussion follows suit. So to a certain extent electors have relevant policy areas defined for them. Since some of the headings used by parties shift from election to election, however, they cannot themselves altogether form the stable groupings of issues which electors need to make consistent decisions.

Analyses of election surveys from many countries suggest that electors group certain issues together on the basis of their relationship to enduring social cleavages. It is natural and familiar to see certain issues as touching on religious and moral practices; others affecting race relations or regional or rural interests; others as involving class division or the relation of government to society (Lipset and Rokkan, 1967, pp. 1–39; Budge and Farlie, 1977, pp. 352–5). Relating issues to cleavages in this way also has the advantage that parties possess relatively clear group images which make them likely to react to associated issues in a predictable way. A labour or socialist party mobilising lower-paid workers may cut welfare payments but will at least cut them less than other parties under foreseeable circumstances. The same might be said for an agrarian party in regard to farm incomes, or to conservative parties' propensity to lower taxes.

The side a party takes on societal conflicts thus provides a ready guide to policy on the issues these generate, and a general inducement for electors to group issues round such cleavages. On the other hand, by their nature some issues cannot be related to cleavages. A firm foreign policy could be pursued by any kind of party. Ideology is no sure guide to competent handling of government business.

Comparative survey investigations demonstrate the existence of a range of issues, some of great importance outside continuing social cleavages (Budge and Farlie, 1977, pp. 352–5). Fortunately such issues cluster spontaneously within their own broad areas, such as foreign affairs, constitutional relationships and defence. Often these groupings are related to the relatively invariant categories used in party documents.

Specific issues thus tend to fall into the fourteen broad types or policy areas summarised in Table 2.1. As electors' categorisations of issues are strongly influenced by party pronouncements, the third column of the table lists the groupings of topics which emerge from analyses of actual party documents (Robertson, 1976, pp. 72–6; Budge and Farlie, 1977, pp. 421–3; Budge and Robertson, forthcoming, chs 1 and 2). These relate quite closely to electors' issue types, but coming from a relatively more sophisticated political discussion are more finely differentiated. The fact that the manifesto topics all fit within broad issue types makes it easier to relate them to each other and thus ultimately to make some judgements on the effect party emphases have in bringing election issues to prominence (see Chapter 6 below).

Turning now to a more detailed consideration of the issue groupings in Table 2.1, the first six types cover the specific issues which crop up in many elections but fall outside continuing social cleavages. For example, a threatened breakdown of civil order is of major concern but can be substantially unrelated (as in France in 1958) to class or religion or to region. The same can be said for constitutional rights and guarantees, for foreign relationships and defence. 'Defence' covers a fairly compact and obvious group of issues. 'Foreign relationships' involve several distinct clusters – lumping decolonisation along with fishing limits, membership of NATO, or entry to the European Economic Community. All such issues, on the other hand, involve general considerations of national independence and prestige. They also involve dealings with much the same set of countries. Membership of the EEC has been tied up with consolidation of the Western Alliance and relations with the Eastern bloc, which in turn is linked to détente. Consequently, this group of questions hangs closely together in politicians' and electors' usages.

Table 2.1   *Broad Groupings into which Electors Classify Issues*

Broad Grouping	Specific Campaign Issues within Each Broad Grouping	General Topics in Party Document Analysis found in Each Broad Grouping
1 Civil order.	Law and order; measures against crime; death penalty; rioting, strikes and demonstrations; anti-system parties and problems caused by their strength.	Law and order. Defence of way of life.
2 Constitutional.	Questions involving established institutions (e.g. monarchy, presidency, parliament and relations between them); democracy; civil rights.	Constitutionalism. Democracy.
3 Foreign relationships.	Membership of NATO and other foreign alliances; détente; attitude to communist powers; entry to EEC; national prestige abroad;	Foreign special relationships; colonies; decolonisation. Peace; internationalism; isolationism.

Table 2.1 (*continued*)

Broad Grouping	Specific Campaign Issues within Each Broad Grouping	General Topics in Party Document Analysis found in Each Broad Grouping
	colonies and decolonisation; overseas aid; attitudes to war and peace (Vietnam).	
4 Defence.	Military spending increases, reduction, importance *vis-à-vis* other policy areas; nuclear arms.	Defence. Military.
5 Candidate reactions.	Likes and dislikes about candidates; leading candidates' performance.	
6 Government record and prospects.	Current financial situation and prospects, expectations; economic prosperity, depression. Incidence of inflation and unemployment; government corruption, inefficiency; satisfaction with government in general and in any specified area in ways not stipulated in other categories. Is tax money spent wisely? Desire for majority government, strong government.	Government efficiency. Government corruption. Economic stability.
7 Moral-religious.	Support of traditional/ Christian morals and church; abortion and birth control; temperance; anti-clericalism–danger from clergy/church; religious schools and education.	Support of morality. National effort.
8 Ethnic.	Immigration and foreign workers; attitudes to minority groups and their advancement; discrimination; school and housing integration; language questions.	Underprivileged minority groups; culture.
9 Regional.	National unity; devolution and regional autonomy; regional equalisation of resources.	Regionalism; national unity.

Table 2.1 (*continued*)

Broad Grouping	Specific Campaign Issues within Each Broad Grouping	General Topics in Party Document Analysis found in Each Broad Grouping
10 Urban–rural.	Farmers and rural interests; agricultural subsidies.	Agriculture.
11 Socioeconomic redistribution	Social service spending; importance of social welfare; housing as a problem; housing subsidies; rent control; food subsidies; health and medical services; social reform; pensions; aid to other services such as education; action in regard to unemployment; full employment, employment guarantee.	Social justice; social services; labour and other underprivileged demographic groups.
12 Government control and planning.	Nationalisation; state control of the economy; general government power and control; management and regulation of environment.	Controlled economy, economic planning, conservation.
13 Government regulation in favour of the individual.	Action against monopolies; big business power, trade union power; protectionism and free trade.	Regulation protectionism and free trade.
14 Initiative and freedom.	Closed shop and action in relation to it; incentives; level of taxation; support for free enterprise economics.	Freedom, enterprise, incentives, productivity, technology, economic orthodoxy.

'Candidate reactions' cover assessments of the personalities and individual capabilities of national leaders. Since leaders change frequently, often for situational and personal reasons, reactions here can be rapidly modified between elections, which lends this type of issue considerable importance where it occurs.

These points are true also for 'government record and prospects' which refers either to a party's achievements while in office, or its ability to provide a credible alternative government if in opposition. Party documents often draw attention to the unity of their own leadership and divisions among their rivals, or to corruption or inefficiency in handling affairs. While these considerations refer to the style of implementation rather than to the content of policy, they form obvious separate grounds for assessing parties. Linked with reactions to the handling of affairs, are the economic conditions associated with the government's term of office. An association is commonly made between 'economic stability and 'government efficiency' in the party documents (see column 3 of Table 2.1). Apart from electors' natural tendency to use what is presented to them as a basis for judgement, there are good reasons why a government's style and economic achievements enter simultaneously into the broader assessment. Economic policy, in the modern state, is more closely under government control (because effected by and large through administrative action) than other areas, which normally require legislation. The general competence of government thus impinges closely on its handling of the economy. Poor management in one is likely to be paralleled by poor management in the other. Hence judgements about competence and ability to govern are based on a broad balance of stylistic and economic considerations, rather than on either viewed separately. Neither, moreover, forms the preserve of any one party (see Table 2.6, p. 50 below). Parties with quite different fixed positions on other issues may gain from administrative competence and association with prosperity. The oscillating nature of electors' reactions to parties on these broad areas of domestic policy forms another ground for distinguishing such issues jointly from others.

Categories 7–14 relate to the societal cleavages discussed earlier. As these form a common reference point they are of course paralleled (sometimes exactly) in the party documents. Religion stems directly from one of the common social cleavages. Analogues in manifestos are references to support of morality and traditional behaviour, which is often put in a Christian framework. The equation between morality, tradition and religion is also made in non-Christian countries – as is natural, since an attack on one often forms an attack on the other. Consequently, religious and moral considerations are lumped together by most electors.

While traditions are often associated with the maintenance of linguistic and group distinctiveness, ethnic differences are less likely to involve a clash of basic moral principles. At the practical level, the specific issues produced by religious cleavages differ in kind from those associated with ethnicity. Anti-clericalism in Catholic countries contrasts with questions involving immigration and foreign workers. Linguistic differences often cross-cut religious ones and vice versa. Similarly, among the manifestos and party programmes, questions of culture and of underprivileged minorities are usually presented independently of questions of morality.

The different nature of the specific issues involved also accounts for the separation of 'regional' from 'urban–rural' cleavages. The clash of material interests between farmers and town dwellers, which can occur potentially within any region, is quite distinct from (though it may in practice overlap with) clashes between centre and periphery. The same differentiation is made in party documents.

The remaining issue types all relate to facets of class divisions. They are distinguished, however, because different class issues have different and indeed contrasting effects on party support. The point about welfare expenditures and taxation has already been made (p. 24 above). Having no practical reason to tie the two together, and indeed being encouraged by media headlines and party stands to view them separately, electors react to these issues in terms of their immediate interests. These indicate both an increase in welfare and a reduction in taxation. But the first is a characteristic programme of socialist parties and the second a habitual stand of the right, so reactions to the two types of class issue will tend to push electors towards opposing partisanships. The same is true for welfare expenditures and centralised planning or attitudes to trade unions and monopolies. However interconnected these policies may seem to planners, they do not strike electors as being so. Indeed, we have much evidence for differences in perceptions, given the widespread opposition which has existed to nationalisation compared with majority support for housing programmes or general health services (Butler and Stokes, 1971, pp. 222, 417; Blondel, 1964, p. 78).

The broadest difference lies between the welfare programmes which are at the heart of traditional social democratic programmes and measures for extending government control. Although the range of issues included under category 11 is wide, they have an obvious common rationale in promoting an immediate redistribution of benefits to the poorer and more numerous classes in the population. Housing and social service proposals are closely associated in party manifestos and appeals, often combined with food subsidies. Education is stressed, in line with the general emphasis on public services. Particularly where unemployment is widespread, its reduction is seen as an essential foundation for other social reforms, while greater expenditure in these areas, under the influence of Keynesian economics, has been advocated as a contribution to greater employment. Since the specific issue proposals in this area are so closely associated, equally congenial to socialists and reformers, and all justified by a redistributive rationale directed to obvious areas of need, mention of one acts as a codeword for the others.

Measures for extending government control, on the other hand, constitute various aspects of a class-based appeal which provoke quite different reactions. A consideration mentioned above is that parties think it ill-advised (if not suicidal) to stress the negative as well as the positive aspects of their programme. Greater welfare will not be publicly associated with less freedom. Nor will a left-wing party, advocating rational planning and allocation of resources, spell out the consequences of this in terms of rationing, and restrictions on business initiative and freedom of action. Conversely, advocates of uninhibited free enterprise will stress freedom but not the pollution or social disparities which accompany the relentless pursuit of individual advantages. Following party leads, electors too react to the immediate aspects of planning, or free enterprise, rather than linking the two together. This is the reason for separating government control from freedom, even though they represent two faces of the same coin. In practice, from the manifesto and issue material we have examined there is no difficulty in differentiating them. Where government management and planning are stressed they go into category 12; where freedom and enterprise are slogans they belong to category 14. These themes are seldom presented in a balanced way which might cause difficulty in distinguishing them.

The argument over government control is not wholly between central-ised planning and individual freedom. There is also a grey area where government intervention can increase individual freedom. The most obvious example is action against monopolies. Such regulatory action is also undertaken by populist or right-wing governments against trade unions, so that it may encompass groupings on both sides of the class struggle. Or it may favour both sides, as with protectionism directed against foreign imports. Government action here has quite a different character from the extension of central planning and management, often being invoked in the name of free enterprise. This is reflected in the issue type we have labelled government regulation, and separated from direct govern-ment control. Similar distinctions are reflected in the topics from party documents, listed in the third column.

As the campaign prominence of one or other of these issue types may affect the voting results quite considerably, it is interesting to see how far their importance has varied since the last world war in the twenty-three democracies included in our investigation. We determine which issues have been important on the basis of observers' reports. The sources for these are cited in Appendix B, which also lists all the specific issues cropping up in these countries for postwar elections – information which, so far as we know, is not available elsewhere. Specific issues are grouped into the broader issue types used below on the basis of Table 2.1 supple-mented by the detailed coding instructions in Appendix C. In this way we can summarise the major differences between countries in terms of the types issues fall into, and investigate tendencies over time towards the replacement of one leading type by another.

One point of difference lies in the number of issue types which become salient: does an election focus narrowly around one type, or does it range over a variety of differentiated topics? Note that this is not quite the same thing as the number of specific issues entering into the election. A wide number of questions relating to housing, education, pensions, minimum wages and health would all be recorded as a single emphasis on socio-economic redistribution, while an election that covered crime, state of the economy and foreign immigration would appear as throwing up three types of issue (civil order, government record and ethnic). The first set of issues inter-relate more closely than the second, a fact that emphasises that the number of *issue types* can differ from the number of actual issues. Generally, of course, the two go together, since the larger the number of specific issues, the more likely they are to fall into a broader range of types.

Table 2.2 looks directly at the number of issue types in the different countries with which we are concerned. These countries are listed down the left-hand side of the table; they have been selected on the basis of having had reasonably competitive elections since the war, or since independence shortly after the war. A more detailed account of the basis for selection appears in Appendix B.

Turning to the occurrence of issue types, the first point to note is the differing number of elections in each country (shown in brackets after the name of the country). This varies quite considerably. Australia, for example, has nearly double the number of elections (thirteen) of France or Germany (seven apiece) and more than double those studied for Luxembourg or Sri Lanka (six and five). The reason for this variation is partly institutional – Australia has more frequent elections than other countries. It is also affected by our choice of starting dates.

The resulting variation in numbers means that comparisons between countries should be based on the second column, showing the average number of issue types per election in each country rather than the total number given in the first column of Table 2.2. This reveals that the United Kingdom, Israel, Australia, the United States, India, France, Sri Lanka, Germany, Finland and Canada (in that order) have the highest number of issue types per election. On the whole, larger countries (where problems are presumably more complicated) with a competitive two-party system (which may serve to project these into elections) throw up higher numbers. The exceptions are Israel and Finland – where an unusually exposed international situation and a complicated internal one may contribute. The countries with exceptionally low numbers of issue types are Switzerland, where many elections seem not to involve national issues at all and real debate takes place at cantonal level, and Iceland, where postwar election politics have centred on the US base at Keflavik, fishing limits, and employment. Here the small size of the country, its internal homogeneity and isolation have all contributed to reduce the range of issues which might emerge.

Behind the totals in Table 2.2 lie the overall distributions over each of the individual issue types in each country. These are presented in Table 2.3, which provides an opportunity to examine national differences more closely. From this we can see that the most widespread type of issue which enters into the great majority of elections in all countries is government record. This is hardly surprising, since elections are designed to choose a government and the most immediate ground for choice is how well the contestants have performed in the past or seem likely to perform in the future. In most countries government record is as predominating a concern as it is overall. In Belgium, however, it enters into only six out of ten elections – buried very often by the disruptive linguistic divisions of recent years. Switzerland is the other country where government record is not prominent, but this is a reflection of the absence of national issues from many Swiss elections rather than a downgrading of government record in relation to other types of issue.

Table 2.2   *Number of Types of Issues Salient in Postwar Elections, for Twenty-Three Democracies*

	Total Number of Types	Average Number of Types for Each Election
Australia (13)	59	4·5
Austria (9)	29	3·2
Belgium (10)	34	3·4
Canada (13)	46	3·5
Denmark (13)	37	2·9
Finland (11)	39	3·6
France (7)	27	3·9
Iceland (12)	26	2·2
India (7)	28	·4·0
Ireland (10)	32	3·2
Israel (10)	46	4·6
Italy (8)	27	3·4
Japan (9)	29	3·2
Luxembourg (6)	18	3·0
Netherlands (11)	38	3·5
New Zealand (10)	28	2·8
Norway (8)	25	3·1
Sri Lanka (5)	19	3·8
Sweden (11)	30	2·7
Switzerland (8)	5	0·6
United Kingdom (10)	54	5·4
United States (9)	37	4·1
West Germany (7)	26	3·7
All countries (217)	739	3·4

The personal characteristics of candidates (usually for the chief executive office) enter into slightly more than half the elections. Again it is unsurprising that the qualities of potential leaders should form such a widespread basis of assessment. Being less widespread than government record, however, there is more room for variation between countries. The United Kingdom, West Germany, India and Sri Lanka have candidates entering as a major consideration into all elections, followed by Australia (eleven out of thirteen), Canada (ten out of thirteen), Ireland and Israel (nine out of ten) and the United States (six out of nine). On the whole it seems that countries with a broadly Anglo-Saxon parliamentary tradition

Table 2.3   Types of Issue Salient over All Postwar Elections, for Twenty-Three Democracies

Country	Civil Order	Constitutional	Foreign Relationships	Defence	Candidate Reactions	Government Record and Prospects	Moral-Religious	Ethnic	Regional	Urban-Rural	Socioeconomic Redistribution	Government Control and Planning	Government Regulation in Favour of Individual	Initiative and Freedom
Australia (13)	4	2	3	2	11	13	1	0	2	2	11	2	2	4
Austria (9)	2	1	1	1	5	7	1	0	0	1	5	2	0	3
Belgium (10)	1	6	1	2	3	6	1	6	3	0	3	0	0	2
Canada (13)	0	3	5	3	10	13	0	0	6	0	1	2	0	2
Denmark (13)	1	2	2	3	3	13	0	0	0	1	7	0	0	6
Finland (11)	3	1	8	0	3	11	0	0	1	4	5	2	3	0
France (7)	0	4	3	0	5	6	0	0	0	0	2	2	0	2
Iceland (12)	2	2	6	1	3	10	0	0	0	0	1	4	0	0
India (7)	1	1	3	0	7	7	0	1	0	0	4	1	1	0
Ireland (10)	2	1	3	3	9	9	1	0	3	0	3	0	0	3
Israel (10)	3	4	6	0	9	10	4	3	0	0	2	3	2	1
Italy (8)	2	1	4	3	3	6	0	0	1	2	5	0	0	0
Japan (9)	2	2	6	1	4	9	3	0	1	0	2	1	0	0
Luxembourg (6)	0	0	0	1	1	6	2	0	0	0	5	0	1	1
Netherlands (11)	2	0	3	0	2	11	0	1	0	2	2	5	3	4
New Zealand (10)	1	0	4	0	6	8	2	0	1	0	2	1	0	3
Norway (8)	0	2	6	0	1	8	0	1	0	0	1	3	1	2
Sri Lanka (5)	0	0	1	0	5	4	0	0	1	0	1	0	0	1
Sweden (11)	0	0	2	0	4	8	0	1	0	0	5	4	1	5
Switzerland (8)	1	1	0	0	1	3	1	2	0	0	0	0	1	0
United Kingdom (10)	1	0	6	3	10	10	0	1	1	0	7	7	0	3
United States (9)	2	1	7	1	6	9	0	0	0	0	5	0	4	3
West Germany (7)	3	1	5	1	7	6	0	0	0	0	2	1	1	0
Total (217)	33	35	85	25	118	193	16	16	20	12	81	40	20	45

Note: For totals of salient issues country by country, see Table 2.2.

and tendencies to a two-party system tend to focus attention on candidates (however, West Germany does not follow the Anglo-Saxon tradition and Israel has not until very recently had anything like two-party competition). Democracies with least stress on candidates are Denmark, Finland, Iceland, Italy, Japan, Norway, Switzerland and the Low Countries. These are on the whole the smaller North European countries, with the significant exceptions of Italy and Japan. Perhaps the factionalism of the dominant party in the last two countries prevents national leaders appearing as more than nominees of special interests. The institutionalisation of the parties, and traditions of collective leadership in the smaller North European democracies, may inhibit assessment through individual personalities.

Foreign relations appears as an important issue in rather less than half the elections. It is particularly important in the United States – naturally, in a country at the centre of a world system of alliances which has been engaged in two major conflicts within the last thirty years. The United Kingdom (six out of ten) and France (three out of seven) have been in a similar situation. Foreign relations are also important to smaller countries next to a powerful or threatening neighbour, such as Finland *vis-à-vis* the USSR (eight out of eleven elections), West Germany (five out of seven), Japan (six out of nine), India (three out of seven) and Norway (six out of eight). Iceland (six out of twelve) and Canada (five out of thirteen) have been particularly concerned over relations with the United States.

The last leading issue type again cropping up in nearly half the elections is socioeconomic redistribution, at the core of which stand welfare policies. In Australia these were debated in eleven out of thirteen elections, attaining almost similar prominence in the United Kingdom (seven out of ten). They were raised also in more than half the elections held in Italy, India and, rather surprisingly, the United States. Elsewhere they appeared in a significant number of elections, except in Canada (one out of thirteen), France (two out of seven), Sri Lanka (one out of five) and Switzerland (no election at all). Possession either of a socialist party or strong two-party competition appears to contribute to the raising of this issue, although the exceptions indicate that the relationship is not strong.

All remaining issue types appear in the range between fourteen and forty-five elections (i.e. between about 8 per cent and 20 per cent of the total). In all cases, low general representation stems from their uneven distribution within different countries. All are raised frequently in one or two countries, but do not appear at all elsewhere. Thus civil order has been a recurring concern in France and West Germany (three out of seven elections) and peculiarly – because of fears about communist subversion – in almost a third of Australian elections. Constitutional changes have been debated a great deal in Belgium (six out of ten elections), primarily because of the need to conciliate Flemish speakers by bestowing greater autonomy. Defence has been of particular concern in Canada, where it unleashes tensions between francophones and anglophones, and towards the United States; in Denmark and the United Kingdom debate has revolved around the overall level of defence expenditures within a precarious economy. Religion has entered into politics in Italy, Netherlands and Luxembourg through the Christian parties there and in Sri Lanka through the fears of the Buddhist priesthood about its position. Ethnic rivalry has dominated Belgian politics over the last ten years, and has emerged in Britain and Israel through problems of assimilation posed by recent immigration. Regional issues are related to ethnic tension in Belgium, while in Canada the position of French-speakers is symbolised by the power of Quebec. Farming problems are important to Finland, not only because of the relatively greater numbers of the rural population, but because of the pivotal position of the Agrarian Party. Nationalisation and associated powers of government control have been particularly controversial in the United Kingdom, but also in Sweden, Norway and the Netherlands, while its converse – an emphasis on individual freedom and initiative – was prominent in Denmark even before the dramatic emergence of Glistrop's anti-tax party in 1973. Government regulation has emerged in about a quarter of elections in Finland, the United Kingdom and the Netherlands, mainly in relation to strikes. Since these are an endemic problem in modern economies, we may expect this type of issue to become increasingly prominent in future. Even generally under-represented issue types thus emerge as important for the analysis of elections in at least one country.

Issue types vary not only across countries but over time – some recurring more frequently in later elections, some declining in saliency. Table 2.4 traces the incidence of issues in each election 'period' of the postwar years. Such periods have been selected simply to group contiguous elections, without any deeper theoretical justification. They seem short enough to capture significant changes.

Government record is such a ubiquitous type of issue that no particular trend can be traced; if anything it appears to have become an even more widely used basis of assessment in recent years than formerly. The same can be said more strongly of candidates – from a third of elections in the late 1940s to three-quarters since the mid-1970s. Foreign relations appear more sensitive, as one might expect, to the state of international affairs – relatively more prominent in the late 1940s with the Cold War, then in the late 1950s and early 1960s with détente, then from 1965 to 1974 with Vietnam and its aftermath. Socioeconomic redistribution appears in a quarter to a half of the elections in each time-period, attaining most prominence in the early 1950s during the first wave of postwar prosperity, and least prominence most recently.

Of the less generally recurring issues, civil order comes to much greater prominence in the politically disturbed periods after 1965, with student demonstrations and terrorism. Constitutional issues come to prominence

Table 2.4 Differences in the Types of Issue Salient over Twenty-Three Democracies, for Each Postwar Election Period

Election Period	Civil Order	Constitutional	Foreign Relationships	Defence	Candidate Reactions	Government Record and Prospects	Moral-Religious	Ethnic	Regional	Urban-Rural	Socioeconomic Redistribution	Government Control and Planning	Government Regulation in Favour of Individual	Initiative and Freedom	Total
1945–49 (14)	2	1	9	1	5	13	1	0	2	1	5	6	2	2	50
1950–54 (28)	4	3	7	2	11	21	1	0	0	2	14	5	2	7	79
1955–59 (31)	3	5	12	4	16	28	4	1	1	3	10	6	1	5	99
1960–64 (31)	2	6	12	5	11	27	2	3	1	2	12	1	1	5	90
1965–69 (34)	8	6	16	4	18	30	2	3	6	0	13	3	2	6	117
1970–74 (34)	5	6	19	4	23	33	2	4	6	4	15	6	4	5	136
1975–79 (36)	7	7	9	2	24	33	4	4	3	0	10	9	8	11	131
1980–81 (9)	2	1	1	3	10	8	0	1	1	0	2	4	0	4	37
Totals (217)	33	35	85	25	118	193	16	16	20	12	81	40	20	45	739

earlier, from 1955. Defence shows a rising trend to the early 1960s, and a slow decline thereafter. Religious-moral questions remain at a low level throughout, with a slight peak in the late 1950s. Reflecting the growth of separatist and autonomist movements in Europe, and the increasing numbers of foreign workers in all countries, ethnic issues show a distinct rise over the postwar period. Regionalism reached a sudden peak in 1965–74 but an indication of decline is seen in the thirty-three elections out of thirty-six in which it failed to appear in 1975-9. Urban–rural questions, on the other hand, show no distinct tendencies, though they reached their highest level in 1970–4.

The three non-redistributive class issues all show a tendency to grow in prominence over the postwar years. The extent of government control (involving such questions as nationalisation) was much debated during the postwar reconstruction, slipped almost out of sight in 1960–4, then returned to prominence in the 1970s with the breakdown of Keynesian approaches to economic management and the advent of neo-capitalist modes of thought. A broadly similar pattern, though different in detail, can be seen for the antonym of government control – individual initiative and freedom. Regulation, increasingly discussed in relation to industrial unrest and strikes, again rises sharply to prominence in the 1970s.

Most of these tendencies are understandable in terms of a postwar history which in most countries involved initial reconstruction, followed by a relaxed enjoyment of restored prosperity from about 1955 to 1965, succeeded in turn by the increasing problems of a complex economy and intergroup tensions connected with this (foreign affairs proceeding, meanwhile, from a consolidation of Cold War alliances, through détente, to a concern with American involvement in Vietnam, and further dissolution of previous alliances). That the appearance and disappearance of election issues can be related to general tendencies, outside the control of politicians in any one country, carries implications for our later analysis of campaign strategies. For if politicians have only a limited ability to emphasise or de-emphasise issues, which become independently salient in elections, one can attribute only a partial influence over victory or defeat to their actions. Rather than seeing their strategy as determining the outcome, we must ask instead whether they made the most of their appeal under given circumstances which they could not wholly (or perhaps even substantially) affect.

The inference, that salient election issues relate broadly to significant events in the outside world, and are not sham debating topics designed to divert attention from real problems, is consistent with the evidence and is a cheering conclusion for the democrat, if somewhat daunting for ambitious politicians. We shall follow up the implications of issues emerging from events rather than being artifically created when we discuss politicians' impact on election outcomes in Chapter 6. An essential intervening factor, however, is the perception by electors of a connection between parties and approved courses of action within the various issue areas, the question which we now consider.

2.3 Direction and Magnitude of Issue Effects

Our statement of Saliency Theory has already referred to politicians' and electors' perceptions of a fixed link between achievement of certain goals and choice of a particular party. One would not normally associate a left-wing party with upholding traditional religious and moral standards. This results in it playing such questions down, thus ceding 'ownership' of the issue to the right while emphasising those appeals which the right cannot make. In the case of electors to whom traditional values are very important, this results in habitual voting for some right-wing party.

For many electors, in fact, certain issue areas will be permanently important, regardless of what macro-issues dominate the campaign. The very poor will always be conscious of welfare, for example. Such electors as a result of their permanent preoccupations will vote for the same party all the time – often as part of a cohesive social group concerned with the same issue.

Because of their abiding fixation on one issue area they will provide stable core support for the parties. Such support can be estimated in part through the 'Basic Vote' (Sections 3.4 and 5.3 below) – that part of party percentage vote left when the gains or losses attributable to campaign issues are taken away. There are enough marginal electors, however, forming a changeable group sensitive to the issue areas salient in the current campaign, to produce the net shifts of votes anticipated by politicians if they succeed in bringing 'their' issues to prominence.

Therefore a crucial question is what effects the campaign salience of a particular issue type can be expected to have on a party's electoral fortunes? Here politicians' expectations are clearly that certain issues favour a party because the majority of electors likely to shift under its impact have in mind an 'obvious' policy which one or the other party appears best qualified to pursue. Evidence on which issues politicians expect to favour which party comes from manifesto emphases favoured by each party (Budge and Farlie, 1977, pp. 304–55, 421–55; Robertson, 1976, pp. 78–89; Budge and Robertson (eds), forthcoming). Evidence that politicians' expectations are actually reflected in electors' behaviour comes from a mass of diffuse historical and survey material, the best-focused discussion being Crewe and Sarlvik's (1980) assessment of 'Party strategies and issue attitudes', from the British election studies of the 1970s. But it also appears in much of the survey evidence cited in Chapter 1 and from comparative investigations over many countries (Budge and Farlie, 1977, pp. 257–409).

What this evidence indicates is that socialist parties, and their analogues elsewhere, through their association with change and reform, are widely viewed as lowering standards on morality and crime; 'soft' on other countries and on ethnic and regional minorities; prone to extend bureaucracy and controls, to raise taxes and to cut down on personal initiative. Some groups (ethnic minorities, for example) may see themselves as beneficiaries of these changes but the majority do not. As a result, socialist or reformist parties have little to gain from the prominence of these issues and may even lose. It is the bourgeois parties who are seen as upholding popular preferences here and it is they who will gain in aggregate when these issues become salient.

On 'foreign relations', 'candidates' and 'government record', everything depends on the current situation, who are the party leaders, and what the government has done. Such issues are not permanently owned by any party but may be annexed temporarily. Often, of course, the result of the election will depend on which party takes them over at the time. Hence most direct argument and confrontation will be focused in this area.

This leaves 'socioeconomic redistribution', the core of the traditional social democratic programme, where the majority of electors do stand to gain immediately from an extension of welfare and health care, better education or straight money transfers. While richer electors may react against discussion of this question, socialist and reformist parties should make large net gains from it.

One can discern in these reactions of electors to the parties a reasonably consistent underlying rationale. Most electors, when they consider politics at all, naturally think in terms of immediate, concrete, costs and benefits rather than long-term, abstract goals. They are also liable to attach greatest weights to personal and family effects. Thus they share a generalised distrust of proposals for change which cannot be clearly shown to produce these immediate personal and family benefits, but may instead cause inconvenience or disruption. Hence there is a tendency to react against proposals for change, and against the party of the majority of electors. Minorities who are helped by the changes will, of course, provide support, but because of the antipathy of the majority the net gains will be made by the party which broadly upholds the *status quo*.

The socialist commitment to change is thus a major political landmark in most party systems. Often, indeed, it is the only distinct landmark, since the goals of non-socialist parties are much more diverse and in many cases can best be clarified through their opposition to socialism. We therefore take the contrast between socialist parties and non-socialist parties (often termed 'bourgeois' parties, whatever the social origins of their voters) as our major point of reference in characterising parties associated with change and opposed to it.

Of course, public stances are not the same as actual government policy. In office, bourgeois parties have introduced far-reaching changes while some socialist administrations have done very little to alter the *status quo*.

Over time, however, it is hard to deny that the former will do less to change things than the latter. In any case, they are more likely to oppose change in public and to have a reputation for opposing it. It is, after all, upon this reputation (broadly related to reality) that electors base their judgements.

A further reason for starting from the position of the socialist party is that socialists tend to be less fragmented than bourgeois parties. Some democracies (United Kingdom, Australia, New Zealand, France, Sri Lanka) have only two major parties so it is easy to identify the main contenders for power in the national electoral struggle. In countries with many parties, however, there is often only one large party – usually socialist or labour but occasionally communist. As the emergence of left-leaning governments is bound up with this party's electoral fortunes, we focus our attention on it – ignoring smaller parties which may be crucial for some government coalitions but which in the long run cannot contribute substantially to the strength of the socialist alternative.

Having concentrated attention on the large socialist party, we then look for its main rival within each national system. Sometimes this is a single large conservative or liberal party, as in the countries already cited. Some-times it is a Christian democratic party which is large but does not monopolise the bourgeois vote – as in the Low Countries there is often a secular, free enterprise liberal party which is even more ideologically opposed to socialism. However, it is the Christians who contribute the major electoral opposition to the socialists, so it is upon their voting gains or losses that we focus. Elsewhere, as in most of Scandinavia, socialists may be faced by a bloc of small bourgeois parties whose only hope of office is to act together against the socialists. There we analyse their performance in combination, as a bourgeois bloc.

Underlying our choice of parties picked out for analysis is this clash of socialist and bourgeois ideologies and long-term prospects for the promotion of these by the participation of their main 'carriers' in govern-ment. The bourgeois contender is selected because it forms the main obstacle to the electoral rise of the large socialist party, rather than on its classic conservatism or liberalism. Agrarian, regional, or religious parties have all in the past criticised aspects of the prevailing *status quo* but, having carried their original points fifty or more years ago, they now defend the existing set-up. So there is no real difference in terms of electoral opposition to socialism among the bourgeois parties.

The socialist–bourgeois dichotomy does not cover competition in three countries where none of the major parties is socialist. However, the under-lying distinction between parties of change and others does extend to them, in the sense that each has a major party which is more 'reformist' than the other – the Democrats in the United States, the Liberals in Canada, and Fianna Fáil in Ireland. For each of these we have to make different judge-ments about electoral effects, and so we discuss them separately in Section 2.4. But these assessments are still informed by the analogy with socialist–

bourgeois differences. Generally, therefore, these form a basis for linking issue effects with the major parties in all twenty-three democracies, making truly comprehensive explanation possible.

Table 2.5   *Parties in Twenty-Three Democracies Included in our Analysis and Labelled as Socialist–Reformist or as Bourgeois–Conservative*

Country	Socialist or Reformist	Bourgeois or Conservative	Significant Party Omitted
Australia	Labour Party	Liberal–Country Party coalition	None
Austria	Social Democrats	People's Party	Freedom Party
Belgium	Socialist Party	Christian Social Party	Liberals; Nationalist Parties
Canada	Liberal Party	Progressive Conservative Party	New Democratic Party; Social Credit
Denmark	Social Democrats	Conservatives; Liberals; Radicals	Progress Party; Christian People's Party
Finland	Finnish People's Democratic Union; Social Democrats	Agrarian and Conservative; National Coalition Liberals (Progressive Party)	Swedish People's Party
France	Communist and Socialist	All major non-left parties	None
Iceland	People's Alliance	Independence Party	Progressive Party; Social Democrats
India	Congress Party	Not represented	Several parties which helped found Janata
Ireland	Fianna Fáil	Fine Gael	Labour Party
Israel	Labour and Allies, ultimately forming Alignment	Likud and its founder parties	Religious parties
Italy	Communist	Christian Democrats	Social Democrats; Socialist; Liberals; Monarchists–Social Movement (MSI); Republicans
Japan	Japan Socialist Party	Liberal Democrats	Komeito
Luxembourg	Socialist Party	Christian Social Party	Communists; Democratic Party
Netherlands	Labour Party (P v. d. A)	Christian Democrats and precursors	Liberals
New Zealand	Labour Party	National Party	Social Credit
Norway	Labour Party	Conservative; Liberal; Agrarian; Christian People's and Joint Non-Socialist	None

Table 2.5 (*continued*)

Country	Socialist or Reformist	Bourgeois or Conservative	Significant Party Omitted
Sri Lanka	SL Freedom Party	United National Party	Communist; Lanka Sama Samasta; Federal Party; Tamil Congress; SL Freedom Socialist Party
Sweden	Social Democrats	Conservatives; Agrarian People's Party; Liberals	None
Switzerland	Social Democrats	Conservatives; Radical Democrats; Farmers, Traders and Citizens or People's Party	None
United Kingdom	Labour Party	Conservative Party	Liberals; Nationalists
United States	Democrats	Republicans	None
West Germany	Social Democrats	Christian Democrats	Free Democrats

Table 2.5 specifies the major parties in each country listed as socialist and bourgeois (for the United States, Canada and Ireland the parties listed are generally reformist and innovatory in the left-hand column, and generally conservative and more opposed to change in the right-hand column). There is little that could be considered controversial about these placements, which are used in both academic and practical analyses of the countries concerned. Outside Scandinavia we have generally taken the single largest party in each *tendance* as representing 'bourgeois' and 'socialist' respectively (such as the Christian Democrats and Communists in Italy, and the Christian Party and Socialists in the Low Countries). Where a third party is thereby left out, we have noted the omission. In India the elements making up Janata were so diverse, and included so many elements of the Congress, that no continuing alternative to Congress can be traced. Our specific analytic decisions for each country will be presented in Chapter 3. The most difficult judgements are involved in France, where different combinations with different names have opposed the 'union of the left' (Socialist plus Communist) in almost all elections. We discuss these complexities in regard to our prediction of the French Assembly election in Chapter 4.

One final point about the typology of parties is its basis in the ideology and enduring outlook of leaders and activists, rather than in electoral cleavages. This is important because it avoids the danger of tautology which might otherwise arise in the relationship with election issues. If we defined party types in terms of their appeal to electors and then found that stressing these appeals increased support, little that was new would be added. Having distinguished parties in terms of the degree of leaders' endorsement of the Marxian diagnosis, we are free to ask whether a heavy public emphasis on that diagnosis produces more votes than playing it down (and we shall pursue this point systematically in Chapter 6). Obviously the leaders' ideology imposes considerable constraints on what a party can claim electorally and socialist parties will almost always emphasise redistribution and government control more than their opponents. But this is a matter of the leaders' choice, guided by strategic and ideological considerations, not of our definition.

The distinction between socialist and bourgeois parties now provides the basis, given electors' reactions to change, for deciding who will benefit from the presence of different types of issue in an election. Underlying the whole argument is the public commitment of socialist leaders to widespread social and political change, of the bourgeois leaders to upholding the *status quo* with only minor change, and electors' suspicion of change without immediate advantages. The only area where such benefits are clear is that of welfare and redistribution. We consequently expect socialist parties to benefit from the emergence of this issue. Centralised planning may be objectively linked to this but the tendency to view issues in discrete and unrelated terms indicates that it will be assessed on its own merits as a negative development which will generate gains for the bourgeois parties and losses for the socialists. Bourgeois parties, on the other hand, are likely to present plans for intervention in terms of maintaining the position of the small man against large, impersonal interests and (possibly unfairly) are likely to gain credence and support on such an appeal. But they will also gain from presenting themselves as defenders of individual initiative and free enterprise, and of established regional and majority rights and traditions against centralised planning and newfangled ideas. Their regional and rural appeals may be reinforced by association with a regional or agrarian party, as in Scandinavia. As upholders of the *status quo*, bourgeois parties are likely also to appear as more reliable supporters of the constitution and of security and law and order.

Overall, then, we expect only one type of issue to act consistently in socialist parties' favour. This does not imply that they are at a disadvantage compared with non-socialist rivals. As we have seen from Table 2.2, socioeconomic redistribution is by far the most likely of those issues with 'fixed' effects to come up in elections. Moreover, the three types of issue which may potentially favour any party occur even more regularly. Provided a socialist party can associate itself with a better record on, or even plausible promises of, greater prosperity, with popular candidates or a good foreign policy, it can win even though some of the other fixed issues are also salient.

Consequently we do not anticipate the socialist party being necessarily penalised by its dependence on socioeconomic redistribution. But its choice of issues, if we are correct in our characterisation, is more restricted than that of the bourgeois parties. This has advantages and disadvantages. It does, on the one hand, render its strategy clear-cut and obvious, if these constraints are recognised. On the other hand, it renders its response less flexible. Socialists, if our diagnosis is correct, are rarely able to explode an electoral mine under their opponents. They cannot bring in last-minute fears about communist threats; they are less likely to be able to substitute fresh appeals between elections. The position of the bourgeois parties, able to appeal on a wide range of issue types which are less likely than redistribution to find some resonance, means that they depend more than the socialists on clever improvisation and entrepreneurial leadership. Both need to take advantage of the immediate situation in order to 'capture' the erratic types of issue – government record and candidate appeals in particular – if they are going to win. Neither side is assured of victory on long-term appeals alone. The positions they can occupy differ, however, and this should have far-reaching consequences for their choice of campaign strategies.

Issues affect election results not only in terms of direction – which party is favoured by their prominence in the campaign, but also in terms of magnitude – the size of the voting changes they can be expected to induce over the whole electorate. Note that we are concerned here with net and not with gross changes. The distinction is important for all subsequent discussion. Obviously any policy emphasis by a party will please some electors and offend others, so we never encounter an unmixed movement of support in its favour. But the crucial point bearing on the election outcome is the extent to which favourable movements of support outweigh negative movements – the net gains (or losses) accruing to a party from the issues it has emphasised. Net movements associated with any one type of issue are likely to be small when measured in percentage terms – a 'large' movement may be no more than 2 or 3 per cent of all voters, where the corresponding gross total of counterbalancing switches might reach as much as 10 or 12 per cent. Where parties are competing closely for support, even a net change of 1 or 2 per cent may prove vital to the outcome.

One approach to the size of the voting changes is to assume that once any issue type becomes salient it has the same impact. The very fact that it confronted electors as a problem would ensure equal effects, on this line of argument. To emerge at all it must have a powerful sway over some people. The relevant distinction between issues would lie not in their impact after they emerged but in their different potential for emerging at all.

This is a plausible argument which has also technical advantages; for if all salient issue types carried equal effects, we could score one for their presence and zero for their absence, sum the scores for all issues favouring or disfavouring a particular (socialist or bourgeois) party in an election, and then relate these summed issue scores to the votes it received. Scoring one for the presence of a characteristic and zero for its absence is an intuitively justifiable practice, so this would be a quick and efficient way to get estimates of the likely effects of issues on aggregate votes.

Because of its simplicity and directness, we report in Appendix D an experiment with this method of scoring issues (along with a number of other approaches). We have doubts, however, about the hypothesis that all issues carry equal effects once they become salient; for this is to equate routine grumbles about bureaucracy, which may be entirely salient and genuinely felt, with lively apprehension of an incipient coup and the breakdown of civil order. For some electors, indeed, bureaucracy may be the sole problem involved in the election, but one would think that when civil order became salient it held a resonance for many more. To score both types of issue equally, once they had emerged, would blur this distinction. Our own expectation is that it would hold and therefore we do distinguish different magnitudes of effect for the different types of issue.

We do not, on the other hand, wish to go into impossibly refined speculation about the effects each type might carry. So basically we distinguish 'large' and 'small' effects, allowing one or two types to fall between as 'medium'. As with direction, there will be a majority of 'fixed' effects. Were it possible, it would be better to have fixed magnitudes as well as fixed directions for all issue types, since this would eliminate situational judgements based on the events of a particular election. But there is, of course, an inevitable variation in the impact of 'government record and prospects', depending on what the government has actually done, or has failed to do, which cannot be judged in a general fashion for all governments but must depend on the specific situation. The impact of candidates will also vary with the strength of their personality and the particular impression they make, except in contexts where candidate effects are particularly important (see the United States, Canada and Ireland below).

On the other hand, foreign relationships will in most countries involve technical matters somewhat remote from the average citizen, with few direct repercussions on everyday life. Hence although the party favoured by this type of issue may vary with the situation, its effects will generally be small. Defence is another highly technical area where without the presence of an impending attack few electors are heavily involved.

Other issues with small effects are questions involving government control and planning and regulation and initiative and freedom. This is because the growth of bureaucracy, the power of large organisations *vis-à-vis* the small man and the decline of private initiative are routine grumbles for most people. Experienced all the time, they are irksome rather than particularly threatening. The same can be said for urban–rural issues. While agricultural payments (the most common topic in this area) are particularly important to the minority who stand to gain, the resulting negotiations are highly technical and have a delayed, indirect connection with food prices in the shops. The precise linkages are indeed likely to be disputed by the economists hired by both sides, so they are imperceptible to most electors. Net movements produced even by salient issues of this type should generally prove small.

On the other hand, regional and ethnic disputes, when they come to the fore, arouse strong passions among considerable numbers of electors. Where such issues are important they involve friction among a heterogeneous population, as in Belgium. When this comes to the centre of political debate it will involve large numbers of electors. The same, with necessary modifications, can be said for religious and moral questions; these will generally engage large groups fairly intensely, as with proposals to extend or abolish the right to abortion.

A threatened breakdown in law and order, whether from soaring crime rates, popular unrest or prospective coups, is naturally an infrequent occurrence in the countries we are dealing with. When it arises, however, more citizens are likely to feel more affected personally than by any other type of issue – even where it exists as threat rather than actuality. Constitutional problems do not have the same urgency, particularly in stable democracies. Nevertheless they affect enough people's rights and freedoms to produce a fair resonance where they arise, so this is classed as the only type of issue with fixed medium effects.

All the fixed impacts discussed above belong to issue types working in favour of bourgeois parties. In view of electors' reactions, we should, however, expect the socialist-owned issue of socioeconomic redistribution to exert a large impact, since it carries immediate benefits for the majority of the population. A large-impact issue which regularly gains prominence is a considerable electoral asset, even though socialists lack other fixed appeals.

Table 2.6 summarises the effects of all types of issue. Levels of magnitude are given in the second column and direction in the third. We are here describing effects for bourgeois–socialist competition only, leaving the three countries with a different party structure for further discussion. Parties expected to gain from the emergence of a particular issue type are indicated by '+ bourgeois' or '+ socialist' as the case may be. Parties expected to lose by its emergence are indicated by '–bourgeois' or '–socialist'. We do not expect gains and losses to accrue simultaneously from the emergence of a particular issue type: either the bourgeois party gains or the socialists lose, or vice versa. Normally we should expect the favoured party to gain. But there may be circumstances (such as flagrant neglect by a government of necessary social reforms) which redound more to the discredit of one party than to the credit of the other(s). In such a case one side will lose rather than the other gain. This is spelt out in greater detail in Appendix C.

In Table 2.6 we have a complete summary of where discussion has taken us so far. We have a set of issue types which should trigger off mutually independent electoral reactions: we have indications of the type of party favoured by these reactions, and of the relative size of the net gains or losses associated with each type. To go further, into the precise degree to which each type of issue enhances a party's vote, we must proceed to an analysis of available data. In Chapter 3 we base initial estimates of issue effects on voting returns from the twenty-three countries; and use these to assess the Basic Vote parties can obtain, independently of issues (through habit and tradition, for example). Since this analysis follows the assignments of direction and magnitude summarised in Table 2.6, and these apply only to competition between bourgeois and socialist parties, we need first to consider issue effects for the United States, Canada and Ireland.

Table 2.6   *Expected Magnitude and Direction of Net Changes in Support Associated with Each Type of Election Issue, for Socialist–Bourgeois Party Competition*

Type of Issue	Magnitude of Changes Produced	Direction of Net Changes in Support
1 Civil order	Large	+Bourgeois −Socialist
2 Constitutional	Medium	+Bourgeois −Socialist
3 Foreign relationships	Small	Erratic
4 Defence	Small	+Bourgeois −Socialist
5 Candidate reactions	Erratic	Erratic
6 Government record and prospects	Erratic	Erratic
7 Moral-religious	Large	+Bourgeois −Socialist
8 Ethnic	Large	+Bourgeois −Socialist
9 Regional	Large	+Bourgeois −Socialist
10 Urban–rural	Small	+Bourgeois −Socialist
11 Socioeconomic redistribution	Large	−Bourgeois +Socialist
12 Government control and planning	Small	+Bourgeois −Socialist
13 Government regulation in favour of individual	Small	+Bourgeois −Socialist
14 Initiative and freedom	Small	+Bourgeois −Socialist

2.4   Exceptional Cases: the United States, Canada and Ireland

What makes these countries exceptional is the fact that the major parties do not include a socialist alternative (though in both Canada and Ireland this comes an important third). In addition, Canada and Ireland experience crises of national unity absent on the whole from the other democracies. In the United States presidential elections take the place of general parliamentary elections in the other countries (congressional elections are so locally oriented as to make presidential elections a much better comparison even though certain differences still remain; Budge and Farlie, 1977, pp. 331–43, figs 9.12–9.14). Because their party systems and elections show considerable differences, we discuss issue effects in each country separately. We start with the United States because in many ways its party system most resembles the socialist–bourgeois ones just discussed.

It has in fact been convincingly argued that the United States possesses a mass social democratic movement in the form of the trade union, liberal welfare state planning and New Politics wings of the Democratic Party (Lipset, 1976, pp. 19–55). This makes it reasonable to view the Democrats as a reformist party with a public reputation for being on the side of change, rather like the socialist party in the other systems. The Republicans can then be regarded as analogous to bourgeois parties. Generally speaking, this implies that the Republicans will be seen by electors opposed to change as the safe party on most types of issue, with corresponding gains when these come up. On socioeconomic redistribution, however, where immediate gains accrue from change, the Democrats will pick up votes (or Republicans occasionally lose them). Government record and candidate reactions will be erratic in direction, varying as in other countries with the candidates and the government.

Table 2.7 summarises these expectations. Since both the party system and the circumstances of the United States differ from those of the countries previously considered, the impact of some types of issue alters somewhat in both direction and magnitude.

Taking direction first, foreign relationships move from being an erratic to being a fixed type of issue, favouring the Republicans. It is curious and perhaps not wholly accidental that since 1916 wars have always been initiated under a Democratic administration and, in the case of Korea and Vietnam at least, terminated under a Republican one. This has produced a widespread belief among American electors, possibly not unfounded, that Republicans are better at handling foreign affairs (Key, 1963, pp. 172–4). On the other hand, the Democrats' general promotion of ethnic rights, and the identification of local machines with particular minorities, imply that most ethnic issues will favour them. Ethnics are now in the voting majority. Regional issues, on the other hand, mostly setting the South and sometimes the East Coast – major areas of traditional Democratic support – against the other regions (in combination more populous), should continue to favour the more conservative party. American farmers are volatile in their voting behaviour (Campbell *et al.*, 1960, pp. 425–39), and likely to switch between Republicans and Democrats in line with their particular interests. Urban–rural issues therefore change from being fixed in a conservative direction to being erratic. Finally, the Democrats' record as a trust-busting party in the United States, fighting monopolies and big business profiteering to maintain the rights of the small man, has been more convincing than that of the Republicans for the last fifty years – nor have they been unduly identified with the interests of big unionism. Hence issues under government regulation favour the Democrats rather than the Republicans.

Table 2.7　*Expected Magnitude and Direction of Net Changes in Support Associated with Each Type of Election Issue for US Democrats and Republicans*

Type of Issue	Magnitude of Changes Produced	Direction of Net Changes in Support
1　Civil order	Large	+Republican −Democrat
2　Constitutional	Large	+Republican −Democrat
3　Foreign relationships	Large	+Republican −Democrat
4　Defence	Medium	+Republican −Democrat
5　Candidate reactions	Large	Erratic
6　Government record and prospects	Erratic	Erratic
7　Moral-religious	Large	+Republican −Democrat
8　Ethnic	Large	−Republican +Democrat
9　Regional	Large	+Republican −Democrat
10　Urban–rural	Medium	Erratic
11　Socioeconomic redistribution	Large	−Republican +Democrat
12　Government control and planning	Small	+Republican −Democrat
13　Government regulation in favour of individual	Small	−Republican +Democrat
14　Initiative and freedom	Small	+Republican −Democrat

Viewing Table 2.7 as a whole, Democrats are seen in a more favourable strategic position than socialist parties. Not only can they utilise the appeals of the latter for social and distributive reforms, while presenting attractive candidates and seeking to put forward an attractive government record; they can also court farmers, build on their inherent ethnic appeal, and abandon controversial questions of government control for the electorally attractive platform of regulating selfish interests. Democrats should therefore have a wider range of strategies available to them than European and Asian socialist parties, increasing their problems of choice but also their vote-winning potential.

On the other hand, the Republican potential is perhaps also greater than that of most bourgeois parties. While they have slightly fewer issue types at their disposal, their 'capture' of foreign relationships gives them a frequently recurring and, in the US context, large-impact issue. Foreign relationships have a great impact on American voters because of the country's status as a world power, at the centre of a web of alliances and commitments. The possibility of involvement abroad is always present, and even small wars carry immediate consequences for electors which are absent in smaller countries. Defence is elevated for the same reason to medium impact in the United States.

Constitutional issues which in the United States as elsewhere favour the more conservative party are also classed as large-impact issues given the importance which the written constitution and its Supreme Court interpretations have in national politics. The relative importance of farming and of farmers as a key electoral group which is markedly volatile raises the impact of urban–rural issues to medium rank. Candidates are recorded as having an invariant large effect (when salient) because of the peculiar form taken by the presidential election, which focuses attention as much on the individual personalities and characteristics of the two nominees as on their party affiliations or policies. Such a concentration must produce correspondingly large electoral reactions. A sitting President standing for re-election cannot help but enter as an issue into the election, thus generally producing large gains for his party. This recognises the advantage which incumbent Presidents traditionally enjoy when standing again for office.

While differences are apparent, Democrat–Republican competition can evidently be discussed without strain within the broad framework used for socialist–bourgeois parties. We shall see in Chapter 3 whether this gives equally convincing estimates for the effects of issues; the theoretical analysis at least supports Lipset in discerning a prototype of socialist–bourgeois party competition in the United States.

Canada is a country with affinities both to her North American neighbour and to Europe, along with peculiarities of her own. These are all reflected in Table 2.8. The first change is in the basic typology itself, reflecting the existence in Canada not only of large regional disparities and differences, but also of strains on national cohesion. These derive not only from the pull of the United States on certain provinces, but also from the rivalries of French- and English-speaking Canadians. While some aspects of these are reflected in the allowances already made for religious, ethnic and regional differences, the new category for national unity allows for the secession of Quebec arising as an election issue. Needless to say, this invokes considerable resonance, and it favours the Liberals because they have rested much more than the Conservatives on an alliance of French and English, and thus have displayed a consistent interest in maintaining national unity which has allowed them to annex the issue.

Table 2.8   *Expected Magnitude and Direction of Net Changes in Support Associated with Each Type of Election Issue for Canadian Liberals and Conservatives*

Type of Issue	*Magnitude of Changes Produced*	*Direction of Net Changes in Support*
1 Civil order	Large	+Conservative −Liberal
2 Constitutional	Medium	+Conservative −Liberal
3 Foreign relationships	Erratic	Erratic
4 Defence	Large	−Conservative +Liberal
5 Candidate reactions	Large	Erratic
6 Government record and prospects	Erratic	Erratic
7 Moral-religious	Large	+Conservative −Liberal
8 Ethnic	Large	+Conservative −Liberal
9 Regional distribution of resources	Large	+Conservative −Liberal
9A National unity	Large	−Conservative +Liberal
10 Urban–rural	Large	Erratic
11 Socioeconomic redistribution	Large	−Conservative +Liberal
12 Government control and planning	Small	+Conservative −Liberal
13 Government regulation in favour of individual	Small	−Conservative +Liberal
14 Initiative and freedom	Small	+Conservative −Liberal

Foreign relations is described as erratic in magnitude as well as direction, because it often covers relations with the United States where nationalism may produce large effects, though other issues in this area arouse little interest. Defence is ascribed large effects because it tends to involve issues such as conscription (in the aftermath of the Second World War) which strain relationships between the two language communities, or the placement of radar and missile systems which again brings in relations with the United States. Mostly such issues favour Liberals rather than Conservatives because on these points they appear as defenders of the *status quo*. Candidates may attract voters to either party, but their impact is fixed as large. This judgement does not derive from institutional aspects of the election, which is parliamentary and not presidential, but from continuing cultural traditions which encourage the extraordinary longevity in office (or at least in politics) of a few notable figures, each strongly dominant.

For the same reasons as in the United States, but with even more force in Canada where farmers constitute a larger and economically more important group, urban–rural issues are noted as having large but erratic effects. And regulatory types of issue, as with the Democrats, favour the Liberals. Otherwise the size and direction of effects are the same as those noted for bourgeois and socialist parties.

Again, the Liberals' strategic position is not too dissimilar from that of socialists, but like the American Democrats it encompasses a wider range of appeals. Given the strong and popular leaders they have typically put forward, and combining social reforms with preservation of national unity, Liberals are practically unbeatable. In a naturally prosperous country with no serious international threats, the party longest in government gets automatic electoral bonuses. Perhaps this accounts for the dominance of the Liberal party in Canadian electoral politics, along with the weakness of its rivals, the Progressive Conservatives, who have lost some of the issues which elsewhere belong to bourgeois parties.

Although the Republic of Ireland is located geographically in Europe, the ethos of its party system diverges more from the general spirit of socialist–bourgeois party competition than does that of either North American country (see Table 2.9). This is primarily because the dominant party, Fianna Fáil, has engrossed such a wide variety of electoral appeals. Not only does it share the general reformist ability to rally support with socioeconomic redistribution, it has also constituted itself the guardian of republican legitimacy, of religious traditions and of the underprivileged regions of the west. It is the stalwart anti-partition party and so gains when questions of national unification come to the fore. In a nation of farmers, where urban–rural issues have a large impact, it is the champion of the country. It has also made itself an excellent reputation by using govern-ment power to support the small man. Coupled with its attractive candidates for the premiership (de Valera, Lemass, Lynch) in a country where personality has a large impact, these appeals have ensured its growth to almost double the size of its conservative rival, Fine Gael.

While Fine Gael appears for historical reasons as the best guarantor of order against gunmen and the machinations of the IRA, it can otherwise only count on some fixed support when vestigial Anglo-Irish interests are at stake or when criticising excessive bureaucracy or restrictions on economic freedom. Otherwise Fine Gael must rely on situational issues and on an alliance with the labour third party.

A party system with its roots in a domestic civil war of sixty years ago has obvious differences from others which have on the whole evolved around less contentious issues, more slowly, over a longer period of time. Again the overall typology provides a basis for specifying these differences. Whether they carry over into data-based estimates remains to be seen. At any rate, we now have overall schemes for twenty-three countries (supplemented by precise coding instructions in Appendix C), which enable us to process reports of issues for each postwar election. Once identified and assigned to types these can be given a direction and magnitude of effect and roughly aggregated to provide some general idea of the forces acting for and against particular parties in individual elections. How we proceed from this to gains and losses of actual votes is the concern of the next chapter.

Table 2.9   *Expected Magnitude and Direction of Net Changes in Support Associated with Each Type of Election Issue for Irish Fianna Fáil and Fine Gael*

Type of Issue	Magnitude of Changes Produced	Direction of Net Changes in Support
1 Civil order	Large	–Fianna Fáil +Fine Gael
2 Constitutional	Large	+Fianna Fáil –Fine Gael
3 Foreign relationships	Medium	Erratic
4 Defence	Small	Erratic
5 Candidate reactions	Large	Erratic
6 Government record and prospects	Erratic	Erratic
7 Moral-religious	Large	+Fianna Fáil –Fine Gael
8 Ethnic	Small	–Fianna Fáil +Fine Gael
9 Regional distribution of resources	Large	+Fianna Fáil –Fine Gael
9A National unity	Large	+Fianna Fáil –Fine Gael
10 Urban–rural	Large	+Fianna Fáil –Fine Gael
11 Socioeconomic redistribution	Large	+Fianna Fáil –Fine Gael
12 Government control and planning	Small	–Fianna Fáil +Fine Gael
13 Government regulation in favour of individual	Small	+Fianna Fáil –Fine Gael
14 Initiative and freedom	Small	–Fianna Fáil +Fine Gael

Chapter 3

Issues and Votes

If we wish to explain election outcomes in terms of the issues prominent in the campaign, we must have some idea of how these relate to the voting gains or losses of the parties. Ideally we should be able to state just what percentage of the party vote was attributable to the salience of an issue of a particular type. The joint effects of all issues salient in the election, added to or subtracted from the Basic Vote contributed principally by long-standing party supporters, should then sum up to the total percentage vote received by the party in the election.

Only if we can consistently account for party votes in this way can we be sure that we have a valid explanation of election outcomes. To do so, however, we must first have estimates of issue effects in terms of the per-centages of vote affected by their appearance in the election.

The research cited in Chapter 1 indicates that the impact of an individual issue on vote ranges between 1 and 3 per cent of the vote in most countries, and approximately double that in the United States. These studies, however, focused on individual issues over a limited time period. In this chapter we try to provide general estimates over all types of issues for all the countries examined through the entire postwar period, as the basis for a comparative analysis of the impact of issues on election out-comes. Quantifying issue effects also allows us to say what proportion of party vote is *not* due to campaign issues and hence mainly attributable to loyalist voting. Measures of the Basic Vote, contributed in part by loyalists, are considered in Section 3.4.

First, however, we have to obtain the general measures of issue effects. The division of issues into types (Table 2.1 above) and assignments of magnitude and direction (Tables 2.6–2.9) help here, along with the coding instructions in Appendix C. With their aid we can identify and classify issues arising in an election and at least approximately identify the level of voting effects associated with them and the way in which they favour one party rather than another. In Sections 3.1 and 3.2 we show how issues can be identified and scored within a specific election context. In Section 3.3 we go on to provide comparative estimates of issue effects which can then be deployed to measure the Basic Vote of each party as well (Section 3.4).

3.1 Scoring Issues from Documentary Sources

In Appendix B we provide a comprehensive list of salient issues, with the direction and magnitude of their effects, for postwar elections in twenty-three democracies. All such issues have been identified and scored from reports made by qualified observers. These belong to the historical tradition of electoral analysis, consisting of detailed descriptions of the issues, personalities and events of each campaign. These are seldom integrated closely with theoretical and statistical work; but they should be. Individual decisions cannot be explained without reference to ongoing events, while a correct appreciation of the significance of events depends on the effects they have on voting.

The use of this material should be of particular interest to historians, as similar descriptions exist for earlier elections, for which evidence is otherwise lacking. Our procedures can be applied to past as well as to foreign elections, thus broadening the scope of electoral investigations considerably.

As with other sources of political data (for example, surveys and government statistics), difficulties appear when election reports are analysed systematically. One possibility is that observers may differ over the issues they think important in a particular election. In fact, serious descriptions of the same campaign seldom contradict each other. Rather they are complementary in the sense of one account adding to the tally of issues reported in another. As different commentators have different, but equally valid, insights into what is going on, we accept issues mentioned by any competent source as salient (sources are described in Appendix B).

Another possibility is that accounts may be imprecise and ambiguous so that each reader takes from them a different impression of the issues involved. Again this is not a unique problem. Cost of living and inflation indices may well be based on different sets of products in different countries or at different times, so that seemingly 'objective' index numbers are actually non-comparable. Survey responses can be notoriously ambiguous.

To cope with the problem of coding documentary material into relevant categories, certain procedures are followed to ensure that ambiguity and subjective differences are kept to a minimum. Basically these involve (1) drawing up clear overall directions which indicate how a given reference should be treated and (2) checking decisions of coders independently applying the instructions to the same material, to see how far they agree.

Naturally we have applied the standard checks to our documents and achieved a high level of agreement between independent coding judgements (for details see Appendix C). Before going on to analyse derived numbers, however, it will clarify matters to see in detail how they are obtained. The example we use also demonstrates how precisely and explicitly issues can be identified from public commentaries. To these we apply the classification in Table 2.1 (p. 28 above) and the scoring system associated with Table 2.6 (p. 50 above) thus demonstrating in detail how to get from a general verbal discussion to numeric scores, which can then be related to votes.

The example consists of two leading editorials in *The Times* (London) devoted to a discussion of issues in the anticipated general election of early October 1978. The first, entitled 'The Conservative agenda' (*The Times*, 10 April 1978), reviews the issues on which the Conservatives had an advantage and which they might therefore be expected to stress. The second, entitled 'Twenty weeks to polling day' (*The Times*, 25 May 1978), does the same for Labour. It is particularly illuminating to take this source because it shows how we identified and scored issues for the election predictions in Chapter 4. For such predictions serious newspaper analyses were the only source of informed comment as they were the only discussions to identify issues in advance for a forthcoming election. We combined the *The Times* commentaries at the end of May 1978 to produce issue scores and a prediction of the outcome four months *before* the anticipated election. We try, incidentally, even when identifying issues for elections held in the past, to select them on the basis of reports made *before* the election in question. This ensures that scores are uninfluenced (as far as possible) by knowledge of the actual voting, so that they form genuinely independent measures. Expectations about the result formed on this basis can then be checked against actual outcomes, just as a future prediction can, to see if they are correct, that is they can be used *post*dictively, though not *pre*dictively (since we are coming to them after the event). True predictions of future elections are presented and discussed in Chapter 4: the characterisation of issues made on the basis of the *The Times* editorials would have constituted a similar prediction had the October election taken place as expected.

In order to give the flavour of the actual discussion, we quote extensively, noting issues when they appear by the general type and number assigned in Table 2.1 (shown in square brackets to indicate our interpolation):

It has become part of the conventional wisdom of British politics that elections are won and lost ... on the economic performance of the government of the day. But it is evident that the Conservatives intend to base their appeal on other issues as well. They know that on a number of social questions public opinion is moving in a tough-minded direction that is broadly in accordance with Conservative thinking, and they intend to take electoral advantage of that trend.

One of the questions is of course immigration [8 Ethnic] ... the Conservatives are making the most of a popular issue ... the Conservatives [are] associated in the public mind with toughness on immigration and this is not ... a question in which political interest will die away before election day.

Another of the issues is ... individualism in tune with much of the rather vague but widespread public resentment of bureacracy and excessive government [14 Initiative and freedom].

The third of these extra-economic issues on which the Conservatives are concentrating is law and order, [1 Civil order] which offers electoral benefits at least as great as either of the other two . . . their proposals do not amount to grand strategy that is radically different from existing policy. That may not matter, however, in electoral terms. The public will have gained a general impression that the Conservatives are the party that would be tougher on crime . . . on such issues as law and order and immigration it is the impression that often matters most politically. (From 'The Conservative agenda', *The Times*, 10 April 1978)

This editorial concentrated on issues favourable to the Conservatives. Over a month later the balance was maintained by considering issues from the Labour point of view, in a leading editorial entitled 'Twenty weeks to polling day' (*The Times*, 25 May 1978):

The election strategy of the Government has been settled for some time . . . Mr Callaghan aims to present himself as the champion of moderation, common sense and national unity, hoping to manoeuvre Mrs Thatcher into an increasingly aggressive counter-attack, which he believes will alienate the public. The Labour Party also hopes to catch the turn of the economic tide . . . after the recovery has reached the voters before inflation starts to accelerate again . . .

Mr Callaghan has so far succeeded in presenting himself to the country as a calm, capable and moderate Prime Minister . . . reassuring to the electorate. Again and again . . . he leaves the ordinary but interested elector thinking: "that is what I would have done myself".

Mrs Thatcher's position is therefore a difficult one. She has to maintain public interest . . . Yet it would be easy for her to lose the sympathy of the national audience, to sound too shrill a response to the peaceful common sense which Mr Callaghan so shrewdly projects. The Conservatives are on stronger ground on the economy. In late 1977 and early 1978 the Government have lost control of the money supply . . . As in 1972 and 1973 this has stimulated activity, temporarily cut unemployment, raised earnings above prices and, for the present, made the Government more popular . . .

There are contrasting strengths and weaknesses in the Labour position. They are now widely seen as the dominant party, primarily because the trade unions are seen as stronger than the business interest. Yet they are also seen as the party of high taxation, bureaucracy [14 Initiative and freedom] and trade union power itself [13 Government regulation in favour of individual], all of which are unpopular things. The performance of Government is thought to be improving, and Mr Callaghan is trusted and liked [5 Candidate reactions], but will not the whole experience of Labour Government since 1974 be remembered against them? [6 Government record and prospects].

Although these discussions start by reviewing issues the parties will stress, it is obvious from his comments that the writer considers they will also constitute the major issues of the campaign. As these are unusually compact reports, they form a clear example of how our procedures can be applied to estimate the balance of advantages between two parties. We carried through the analysis just after the second editorial appeared, at the end of May 1978: the results are presented in Table 3.1.

Table 3.1   *Summary Characterisation of Issues and their Effect for Anticipated British General Election of September–October 1978*

Specific issue	Issue type	Magnitude	Direction	Summed Net Effects Labour	Con-servative
Law and order	1 Civil order	Large (3)	+Conservative		
Personality of Mr Callaghan (present Prime Minister)	5 Candidate reactions	Large (3)	+Labour		
Inflation, unemployment, expenditure cuts 1975/6	6 Government record and prospects	Large (3)	−Labour		
balanced by					
Recent slowed inflation, increased real wages, firm government	6 Government record	Large (3)	+Labour		
Reduction of immigration	8 Ethnic	Large (3)	+Conservative		
Trade union power Excessive bureaucracy and taxation, restrictions on individuals' enterprise	13 Government regulation in favour of individual	Small (1)	−Labour		
	14 Initiative and freedom	Small (1)	+Conservative	+2	+7

Since we have already labelled issues as they appeared in the editorials, and they are so clearly identified there, there will be little controversy about the actual listing which takes up the first column of Table 3.1, nor in regard to the assignment of these specific issues to general types in column two. Once this assignment is made, the ascription of magnitude and direction are generally fixed. The only problem relates to the directions in which regulation and initiative should be seen as working – against Labour or for the Conservatives? In the second editorial 'high taxation, bureaucracy [14] and trade union power [13]' are all seen as acting negatively against Labour. But in the first the Conservatives are credited with raising individualism as an issue which should positively favour themselves. Since we normally assign direction in favour of the party the issue helps, unless there is a strong presumption to the contrary, we credit initiative and freedom to the Conservatives. Trade union power is mentioned solely as detracting from Labour appeals so we assign it negatively to them.

The only remaining decisions are in regard to candidates and government record.

On candidates, *The Times*'s discussion clearly viewed Mr Callaghan as a major attraction for the Labour Party; so we score his appeal as large and positive for Labour. Mrs Thatcher, leader of the Conservative opposition, is in an ambiguous and difficult position, which inhibits a strong personal appeal. Consequently we score her neither negatively nor positively.

Labour's record in government is viewed by *The Times* as having both negative and positive aspects. On the one hand, there is the background of recession and retrenchment, particularly during the middle period of the Labour term, from 1975 to 1977. On the other hand, there is the partial recovery and modest prosperity of 1978. Reflecting these two aspects of Labour's image we have divided our assessment of government record into two parts, which balance out as the discussion indicates that they should.

On the basis of the editorials, therefore, we reach a complete summary characterisation of the two parties' issue appeals from which we can see that the Conservatives enjoy a considerable advantage over Labour. By scoring 'small' magnitudes as one, 'medium' as two and 'large' as three (these numbers are the ones placed in brackets in Table 3.1 after the judgements of magnitude), we can add all the separate scores together, in order to put this judgement in a rough and approximate numeric form. This gives the Conservatives, with all issues anticipated as salient working to their advantage, and none against them, a high issue score of +7 compared to Labour's modest +2.

It is interesting that a high positive score for one party can emerge alongside a positive one for the other, albeit more modest. Competition is not always a case of a popular party confronting an unpopular one, but may involve relative degrees of popularity or unpopularity.

How correct did our characterisation of issues turn out to be? In the particular case of these editorials, and the implication that the balance of issue advantages lay with the Conservatives, the Prime Minister obviously agreed sufficiently to postpone the election. The polls, having given mixed results over the summer, concurred on assigning the Conservatives a lead after his decision. Short of being able to compare to the conclusions of Table 3.1 with actual election results, these seem reasonable grounds for accepting the validity of the diagnosis.

More generally, as we shall show below, the issue scores based on such reports predict votes in future elections, and explain them in past elections, rather well – indicating at least at a pragmatic level, that the crude scoring system applied to judgements of magnitude does not seriously distort the results. Why, however, should we make this particular equivalence –rather than, say, making 'large' = 5, 'medium' = 2, 'small' = 1, or any of the other sets of unequal intervals we might have devised? The brief answer is that either the alternative scoring systems are in practice equivalent to the one we have used, or when their performance is directly compared over all elections and countries, none gives better results and most give worse (see Appendix D). There seems every reason for proceeding with the simple 0, 1, 2, 3 scores – as long as we recognise, of course, that they simply constitute a useful approximation.

We do not ask readers to take the usefulness of this procedure on faith. Besides our explicit comparison with other systems in Appendix D, the plausibility of the results obtained while using it constitutes a continuing check on its validity. The relationships obtained with voting percentages, for the United Kingdom (Section 3.2) and for all twenty-three democracies (Section 3.3) form an immediate test.

In the context of a single election there is, of course, little point in assigning scores to issues, since one can reach the judgement that the Conservatives have the advantage without the aid of numbers. When it comes to saying how many votes their issue advantages will bring in, we need to obtain some idea of the relationship between issues and votes over the entire postwar period. If we want to make exact estimates of voting gains, from a knowledge of issue advantages, we must also relate issue scores, on the one side, to percentage votes, on the other, over all the elections so that we can state precisely the percentage by which vote will rise with a unit increase on issues. Earlier research provided some evidence on this (Chapter 1 above), but the question requires more systematic and comparative investigation.

3.2 Relating Issue Scores to Party Votes: The United Kingdom

The issue scores for each party in each election over the twenty-three democracies are given in Appendix B, and are based on the scoring system used in Table 3.1, that is, scores are assessed as three for a large impact issue, two for a medium impact issue, one for a small impact issue and zero for non-salient issues. We wish to estimate the effects of issues on party votes – how far do they contribute to raising or lowering the vote in successive elections? On the one hand, we have a single score for a party's issue attractiveness in each election, produced by adding the scores it accumulates on issues favourable to it, and taking away its scores on adverse issues. On the other, we have the actual record of vote in that election. To examine the relationship it is natural to set up a graph, in which issue scores, as one postulated cause of vote, form the horizontal axis, and party votes, dependent in part on issue attractiveness, form the vertical axis. An example of such a graph relating votes and issue scores for the two major British parties is given in Figure 3.1 below. Note that this does not cover the 1979 general election. The analysis and estimates reported in this chapter were produced by the beginning of 1978 and used for the future predictions of elections in Chapter 4 (covering 1977–9 and including the 1979 general election in Britain). Elections here only cover the period to mid-1977. Chapter 5 draws on the experience of the predictions and of subsequent elections to present revised final estimates.

Before we can draw substantive conclusions, several decisions need to be made about which groupings of parties and what figures for vote we wish to base estimates on. We could start, for example, by looking at the general relationship between party vote and issue scores for all countries and elections. Our interest is explicitly in a comparative theory and this procedure would produce a general estimate of the effect of issues on party votes.

The trouble is that it would produce a general estimate without providing any assurance that it fitted all parties (or any single party) very closely. We wish, after all, to obtain estimates that are as good an approximation as we can get to what is going in each individual country and election – not simply mechanical averages which may be misleading when applied to a specific time and place. This consideration points to starting at the bottom, with party-by-party analyses which can then be compared and, if compatible, put together, rather than with a grand slam at the most general level we can attain.

Secondly, we must decide what type of voting figures we wish to relate to issue scores. We could use raw figures or percentages. The percentages could be of votes cast for a party out of all those voting, or out of the total electorate (including non-voters).

Since electorates vary drastically in number, not only between countries but from one election to another within the same country, raw figures would not only be awkward to handle but positively misleading. Issues would be credited with sweeping increases in party votes, when these were actually caused by franchise extensions, population explosions or improved health measures. In regard to percentages, one advantage of our procedure, which derives issue scores for each party independently and separately, is that it should produce roughly equivalent estimates when related to either type of percentage. This is not to say that the estimates will be the same – they could not be identical, since party votes must take lower percentage values when non-voters are included in the base. But both types of estimate should be fairly easily translated into each other, once the numbers of those voting and of the total electorate are known.

It is more convenient to relate issue scores to party percentages of total vote, rather than to party percentages of the total electorate, for the following reasons:

(a) The vote percentages are more stable. If percentages are based on the total electorate, the parties will show a decline if non-voting increases, even though they both lose equally. Where percentages are based on total vote, however, they remain the same in this (fairly common) situation.

(b) Since electoral victory (or electoral gains, in a multi-party system) goes to the party whose voting percentage is higher than the other(s), it is in a sense this percentage we are directly interested in. Comparisons of relative party performance based on electorate percentages are often obscured by the non-voting fluctuations mentioned above.

(c) Reports of elections very often provide only the voting percentages, since this is what is important from the point of view of victory or defeat. While the other figures can be retrieved eventually (after considerable research in some cases), it is more convenient from the reader's point of view to have the analysis done with percentages of voters, since he can then apply the estimates to the figures most readily available if he wishes to extend the analysis to current elections.

For all these reasons we relate issue scores to vote percentages in the main analysis, which we report in the text. We have confirmed our conclusions through a duplicate investigation of electorate percentages, but our estimates of issue effects, and hence of basic vote, are given in terms of voting percentages.

We can now turn directly to Figure 3.1 which constitutes one example of the party-by-party relationships between issue scores and voting percentages, on which we base subsequent conclusions. In the figure each point represents the joint value, for each election, of a party's issue score and its percentage of the vote.

In this particular example the two major British parties are represented by points (the Conservatives by dots and Labour by circles) for the elections from 1950 to October 1974 inclusive. We are really analysing the relationship between issue scores and vote for each party separately. Since as it happens Conservatives and Labour in the United Kingdom fall within pretty much the same range of issue and vote values, we can conveniently put them together in the same graph. This renders the example more interesting and also illustrates how, where the separate party relationships are fairly similar, we can build up to a combined country estimate of the effects of issue on vote.

Certain broad conclusions can be drawn. It is indeed the case that a commanding position on issues is accompanied by relatively high voting percentages. For example, the Conservatives achieved their greatest issue advantage in 1959, when there was a popular Prime Minister (Macmillan) and considerable recent prosperity which had allowed some reduction in taxation. This election also produced (with that of 1955) their highest postwar vote. In both 1974 elections Conservative issue appeals reached their minimum (−4) and they also received their lowest shares of the vote.

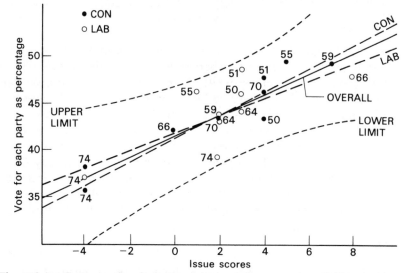

Figure 3.1   *Corresponding between major party issue scores and their percentages of the vote in United Kingdom elections between 1950 and 1974, with lines of best fit for Labour and Conservative parties, combined line of best fit and confidence intervals.*

Labour gained their second highest vote in 1964, this was also the election where they appealed most on issues. In February 1974 they seemed as unappealing as Conservatives and their voting percentage fell correspondingly to a mere 37 per cent.

Our approach thus passes its first check, in that votes do seem to increase with issue advantages. Moreover, the individual points form a fairly tight band and do not scatter all over the figure. It is not just the exceptional cases which correspond to expectations, but the middling ones too. These patterns do not in themselves provide exact estimates of the effect issues have on Conservative or Labour votes. For that we need to examine the average relationship between the two.

This can be represented graphically in terms of a line of best fit. In Figure 3.1 one dashed line best summarises the Conservative points and represents the average relationship between issue scores and votes for the Conservatives. The other represents this average relationship for Labour.

Now any straight line on a graph such as Figure 3.1 can be described by an equation:

$$Y = a + bX$$

In our case, Y is vote, X is the issue score and the two are related by b, the slope of the line. The intercept, a, is simply the value taken by the line when X is zero – that is, when the issue score equals nothing.

Thus b, the slope of the average regression line, constitutes a direct estimate of issue effects on the vote – the extent to which the party percentage of voters increases with each increment to its issue scores. These scores, of course, are only rough approximations. Nevertheless they are confirmed so far as they go by the plausibility of the relationships illustrated in Figure 3.1.

The intercept, a, provides an estimate of what vote the parties would receive in the absence of issues (or where positive and negative issue effects exactly counterbalanced each other to produce an overall score of zero). It is thus the most direct estimate of the Basic Vote parties would get in the absence of any issue attractions and we use it for measuring this in Section 3.4 below.

Slopes for the Labour and Conservative average lines are rather similar, as is the position of the lines themselves. These similarities imply that a general British average, based on all points in the figure, would be a good approximation to each of the separate party relationships. This overall relationship is represented by the solid straight line in Figure 3.1: it will be seen that it takes much the same path as the separate party relationships and that it genuinely passes near the middle of each set of party points. The slope estimate 'b' for this line (that is, the overall measure of issue effects for the United Kingdom) is 1·10, which falls roughly between, and reasonably near, to the estimate of 1·23 per cent for the Conservatives and 0·92 per cent for Labour. As only a few postwar elections have occurred, all these lines are based on a limited number of points and are strongly affected by extreme values such as most of those for the 1974 elections. This is unavoidable if one is to examine postwar results at all, but its effects are reduced as more countries are added to the analysis (see Section 3.3 below).

We have thus arrived at a country estimate built up from the separate party relationships and closely approximating them. This is the same procedure we apply to the general estimates over twenty-three countries which we obtain in Section 3.3. Before coming to these, however, we have to discuss a major complication which we can again illustrate with regard to the UK example. That is the question of how exact any of the estimates – either the party or the overall estimates – can be, when they are based only on a limited group of elections out of all those that have been and (more important) will be held.

The uncertainty attached to these estimates is represented first by the '95 per cent confidence interval' round the average lines for the party and country relationships shown in Figure 3.1. These are the slightly curving, dashed lines shown in the figure. They curve out at the ends since a wider range of possibilities exists for the true line at the extremities compared to the middle.

Of more immediate relevance for our purposes is the estimated slope of the lines – which, as we have said, provides the measure of how far party votes increase for a unit increase in the issue scores. We can also draw '95 per cent confidence intervals' round these values. Our estimates then become for Conservatives 1.23 ± 0.91 per cent, and for Labour 0.92 ± 1.70 per cent. In other words, the true value of issue impacts on the Conservative side could be anything from 0.32 per cent of the vote to 2.14 per cent, and on the Labour side anything from -0.78 per cent of the vote to 2.62 per cent. Should the increment to vote really be negative (each increment of advantage on issues loses votes), that would make nonsense of our reasoning. The same can be said for a horizontal line at 44 per cent of vote, showing no effect of issues.

In both cases it is the small number of cases and the concentration of most points close to the average which produces the very wide confidence interval, so that the possibility of estimating negative or zero vote gains will disappear as more cases are added. This is illustrated by the combined estimate obtained by putting Conservative and Labour cases together. This is a reasonable procedure given the similarity of the two party lines of best fit. The slope of the combined country line (1.10 per cent), based on both sets of party points has a confidence interval from 0.77 per cent to 1.43 per cent which covers much the same range of possible values as the parties', but excludes the possibility of negative or zero effects. This illustrates the greater stability of estimates based on larger numbers of elections which, in turn, points up the advantages of a comparative analysis of the type undertaken in Section 3.3.

3.3.   Issue Scores and Party Votes: The General Relationship

In extending our analysis to other democracies, we shall employ the reasoning illustrated in Section 3.2 with Britain, building up from party specific to more general relationships. Since we cannot, for reasons of space, report the separate analyses, we shall summarise results in the form of slope (i.e. issue) estimates for each of the parties considered. With the estimates of slope we shall also produce confidence intervals, and the greater the extent to which these intervals overlap, the less justification there will be for rejecting the possibility that the effect of issue on vote is the same for overlapping parties. Each party analysis rests on graphs similar to the UK ones illustrated in Figure 3.1. The slope estimates for socialist parties' 'average lines' (and for those of the 'reformist' US Democrats, Canadian Liberals and Irish Fianna Fáil) are summarised in Table 3.2, together with the range and upper and lower limits of probable true values within the 95 per cent confidence intervals surrounding them.

Table 3.2 shows that many of these intervals are rather wide. As with the United Kingdom, this stems from the limited number of postwar elections in each country. When we come to examine the effects of issues on votes with an adequate number of cases, as with the overall estimate for sixteen parties reported at the bottom of Table 3.2, the range of true values is immensely narrowed, to very acceptable limits (0·93 ± 0·10 per cent).

Table 3.2   *Estimates of Slope (i.e. Issue Effects) for Individual Socialist or Reformist parties in Each Country, and for most Socialist–Reformist Parties combined, with Ranges of Probable True Values about the Estimates*

Country	Estimate of Issue Effects %	Highest Probable True Value %	Lowest Probable True Value %
Australia	0·62	1·38	–0·14
Austria	1·38	1·87	0·89
Belgium	0·92	1·12	0·72
Canada	0·92	1·38	0·46
Denmark	1·21	2·03	0·39
Finland	1·12	1·36	0·88
Iceland	2·03*	2·69	1·37
India	0·55*	0·67	0·43
Ireland	0·81	1·15	0·47
Israel	0·87	1·13	0·61
Italy	2·30*	3·42	1·18
Japan	1·14	5·26	–2·98
Luxembourg	1·18	1·64	0·72
Netherlands	0·83	1·41	0·25
New Zealand	0·71	1·21	0·21
Norway	0·83	1·30	0·36
Sri Lanka	1·53	2·37	0·69
Sweden	0·67	1·05	0·29
Switzerland	0·37*	0·69	0·05
United Kingdom	0·92	2·62	–0·78
United States	2·08*	2·82	1·34
West Germany	1·22*	1·37	1·07
Overall estimate for sixteen parties	0·93	1·03	0·83

Note: The range of probable true values is that associated with the '95 per cent confidence intervals' discussed in the text. France is omitted as elections under the Fifth Republic are so few in number and each has been contested by different party combinations. As far as can be seen from French data, the overall estimate of 0·93 fits. Estimates marked with * were not used in the calculation of the overall estimate because they were inconsistent with it.

Despite the width of the confidence intervals a notable point is how few of the confidence intervals extend into negative values. Since a negative value implies that as a party gains on issues it loses votes, the possibility that some true values might be negative forms evidence against our hypotheses and procedures. The fact that only in three cases out of twenty-three is there a possibility of their appearing at all (in one case a very slight one), means that our explanation survives this check. This is in spite of the fact that no anomalous cases (outlying points or 'outliers' in regression terms) have been eliminated in the party-by-party analyses – where, with relatively few cases in each, they exert a disproportionate effect.

Since almost two-thirds of the slope estimates are reasonably similar, with substantially overlapping confidence intervals, there are strong grounds for suggesting a single general estimate to replace the estimated party values. This similarity is surprising and formed no part of the original hypothesis. To obtain such an estimate we extend the criterion of best fit to include the graphs for all parties except those where a general estimate would not be appropriate (that is, the Italian Communists, Indian Congress, German and Swiss Socialists, French left and US Democrats). In these exceptional cases, where the overall estimate is inconsistent with the individual party estimate, we take the individual party estimate as best. We include the Canadian Liberals and Irish Fianna Fáil in the general graph, since their slopes (though obtained through rather different coding procedures) resemble those for most socialist parties.

We cannot use unmodified issue scores and voting percentages to represent the general relationship on a single graph, simply because parties gain such varying shares of the vote (anything from 20 per cent to nearly 50 per cent). Instead we plot deviations from the individual party mean issue score and mean percentage vote. The points representing the conjunction of issue scores and vote in individual elections for all the parties involved in the estimate can now be superimposed on each other and related to an average line, just as was done for the British parties individually in Figure 3.1.

Naturally there are many more points on which to base the average line in Figure 3.2 compared with the British representation on its own. It is quite impressive to see how many cluster closely to the best fitting line and fall within the confidence intervals surrounding it. This provides additional reassurance that the line really approximates to individual party relationships, rather than providing a mechanical average. The slope itself – the general measure of issue effects for these socialist–reformist parties – is 0·93, with a confidence interval of ± 0·10, stretching from 0·83 to 1·03. The correlation coefficient is 0·75 implying that 56 per cent of the total variability is accounted for by issue scores.

We can proceed in exactly the same way for the bourgeois parties. Table 3.3 presents estimates for slope, that is, issue impact, with surrounding confidence intervals – either for individual large parties or for the 'bourgeois blocs' of smaller parties who tend to act together in government and which are especially prevalent in Scandinavia. In the case of India we have no estimate for the bourgeois side because the parties opposing Congress have always combined and redivided too much to provide the necessary continuity. The French right is omitted for the same reason as the French left – too few cases and changing combinations at each election.

Turning to the cases where relationships did appear and where consequently we could make estimates, we note first that the number where the lower confidence boundary is negative clearly exceeds that for socialist and reformist parties. In general, the 'variability', that is, the scatter of points about the average lines, for bourgeois parties is greater than for the socialist–reformist parties, and hence the confidence intervals are also wider. This is because the wider dispersion of sample points gives less confidence that the true values can be found within a small range.

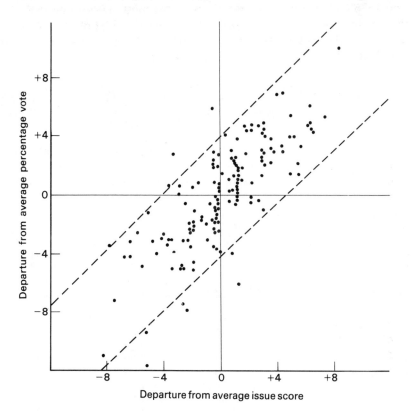

Figure 3.2 *Correspondence between normalised issue scores and normalised percentages of the vote for most socialist-reformist parties over postwar elections.*

The wider confidence intervals in Table 3.3 also overlap more than do those for left parties, however. Hence (with the exception of those omitted from Table 3.3, in any case), we can base a general estimate upon all parties – even US Republicans (and including the Progressive Conservatives from Canada and Fine Gael from Ireland). From the average relationship based on all these cases a greater variability in this relationship between issue scores and vote shares can be identified, concretely illustrated by the much greater dispersion of points round the average line and the increased numbers of outliers. Nevertheless, the majority of points still lie close to the line and within the boundaries of its 95 per cent confidence interval, so the average relationship genuinely fits most individual parties. The correlation coefficient is 0·50 implying that 25 per cent of the total variability is accounted for by issue scores. The slope of the average line (that is, our estimate for the cross-national impact of issues on the bourgeois vote) is 0·86, again ± 0·10, giving a range of probable true values from 0·76 to 0·96. Here, too, we uncover an almost one-for-one exchange rate between issue scores and percentage votes which applies to the great majority of the parties analysed, no matter what other variations exist in their cultural, institutional or historical context.

Table 3.3   *Estimates of Slope (i.e. Issue Effects) for Individual Bourgeois Parties in Each Country, and for All Bourgeois Parties Combined, with Ranges of Probable True Values about the Estimates*

Country	Estimate of Issue Effects %	Highest Probable True Value %	Lowest Probable True Value %
Australia	0·40	1·08	−0·28
Austria	0·56	1·04	0·08
Belgium	2·18	3·74	0·62
Canada	1·26	1·98	0·54
Denmark	0·36	1·24	−0·52
Finland	0·76	0·90	0·62
Iceland	1·12	1·38	0·86
India	–	–	–
Ireland	0·60	1·82	−0·62
Israel	0·80	1·04	0·56
Italy	1·63	2·67	0·59
Japan	1·29	2·09	0·49
Luxembourg	2·10	4·28	−0·08
Netherlands	0·19	1·95	−1·57
New Zealand	0·46	1·22	−0·30
Norway	−1·07*	1·71	−3·85
Sri Lanka	1·10	1·98	0·22
Sweden	−0·67*	0·67	−2·00
Switzerland	0·22	1·18	−0·74
United Kingdom	1·23	2·14	0·32
United States	1·31	1·79	0·83
West Germany	0·04	0·68	−0·60
Overall estimate	0·86	0·96	0·76

Note: The range of probable true values is that associated with the '95 per cent confidence intervals' discussed in the text. France is omitted as elections under the Fifth Republic are so few in number and each has been contested by different party combinations. The latter point is also true for the non-Congress parties in India. As far as can be seen from French data, the overall estimate of 0·86 per cent fits. Estimates marked with * were not used in the calculation of the overall estimate because they were inconsistent with it.

The confidence interval around the general estimate of issue effects for bourgeois parties thus covers much the same range as the one for socialist–reformist parties, while the sample estimates themselves are very close. There seems no strong support for the conclusion that bourgeois issues have different consequences for voting from socialist issues. This conclusion is reinforced by a glance at the individual party estimates in Tables 3.2 and 3.3 and justifies putting together all points included in the graphs to get a combined measured of slope and hence of issue impacts. The estimate for the combined line, not surprisingly, falls between the two general party estimates, at 0·89. The range of possible true values, at ± 0·07 (from 0·82 to 0·96), is narrower because of the much greater number of cases on which it is based.

This overall estimate of the slope falls well within the majority of party intervals, indicating that the data we have is consistent with a common value. This statement is deliberately less strong than saying that a common value is proven, since some of the intervals are very wide. But the clear impression from the tables is that the estimated effects are reasonably consistent. They are also consistent with the broad range of individual issue effects of 1·00 to 3·00 per cent identified by previous European research (Section 1.2, p. 10 above). For the United States, given also the different basis of coding, a combined country estimate of 1·85 per cent per issue increment for both Democrats and Republicans seems indicated by the elections under review. This also matches the higher range of individual issue effects, from roughly 1·5 per cent to roughly 6 per cent, which emerged tentatively from our review of American research (Section 1.1, p. 2 above).

This general convergence on a common range of values across countries and approaches is probably our most important and unexpected finding. Whatever the weaknesses of any particular method, the fact that they independently reach similar conclusions on different assumptions makes it hard to dismiss the result as a statistical artefact. It must be taken seriously as indicating that party appeals, under superficial differences, have much in common across a wide range of democracies.

3.4 Basic Votes

Besides being of interest for their own sake, our estimates of issue effects also aid analysis of another election phenomenon, the recurring levels of support which major parties can hope to retain from election to election. Our estimates indicate that only a minority of the votes going to a party can be attributed to the effects of campaign issues. Even in the exceptional case where it raised five or six salient issues, a party would gain only 10–12 per cent. As major parties commonly receive from 30 per cent to 50 per cent of the vote, it is clear that most of their support comes from other sources.

Moreover, when a party has a zero issue score (either because no salient issues relate to it or because advantages and disadvantages cancel out) the corresponding vote is still quite high (slightly over 40 per cent in the case of the major British parties in Figure 3.1). This vote which parties with zero scores attract independently of current issues, is what we term Basic Vote in subsequent discussion.

(i) Basic Vote and Normal Vote

Although it follows directly from our estimates the idea of a vote level round which parties oscillate regardless of the current campaign has obvious affinities to Philip Converse's well-known construct of the Normal Vote (Converse, 1966). Converse, in common with his fellow authors of the Michigan school of voting behaviour, postulates the existence of a lifelong attachment to party among most voters. This is not based simply on agreement with its policy stands but forms rather 'the individual's affective orientation to an important group-object in his environment' (Campbell *et al.*, 1960, p. 121). It can be measured empirically through survey questions such as: 'Do you generally think of yourself as a Democrat or a Republican? (If yes) How strongly (Democrat, Republican) do you feel? (If no) Do you feel closer to the Democrats or the Republicans?'. Answers to these questions permit the typing of respondents either as independents, or as strongly, or weakly, attached to one of the parties.

The point of measuring 'party identification' is that most of the time electors can be expected to vote in accordance with it – strong identifiers more consistently than weak. However, in any particular campaign, electors who disagree with their own party over issues may vote for the other side. Where current issues or candidates favour one party over the other, the aggregate effect is to pull voting levels away from those which might be expected from the distribution of party identification in favour of the advantaged party.

Converse proposed using this discrepancy as a measure of the strength and direction of short-term forces (that is, attractions of issues and candidates) in the election. This involved postulating the existence of a Normal Vote, which would be produced by electors voting in accordance with their party identification (with an adjustment for lower Democratic turnout) in a situation where short-term forces exerted no effect; or which would be produced by a balance of issue effects causing equal net defections to both sides, leaving overall levels the same as those which would occur in the first case.

The Normal Vote is, therefore, equivalent to the percentages of Democratic and Republican identifiers in the electorate, with allowance for a small differential turnout. It is also, as Converse points out, the level approached by party divisions of the vote in congressional elections at least up to 1960 (53 per cent Democratic, as compared to 54 per cent Democratic on Normal Vote estimates) (Converse, 1966, p. 27). Converse does not mention presidential elections in this connection. This is interesting given the equal alteration of US parties in the presidency from 1948 to 1976, which leads one to expect average percentages to tend nearer equality, as with our own estimate of Basic Vote below.

The Normal Vote is an analytical construct in the sense that actual election results may always differ from it. Since percentage votes over time tend to average out at 'normal' level, it does nevertheless constitute a measure of underlying party strength. Parties cannot forever count on being attractive to electors on campaign issues; thus the party which has a larger 'normal' following has a long-term electoral advantage. Since they possess more identifiers, the Democrats have been regarded as electorally dominant in the United States.

These analytic uses of the Normal Vote are shared by our own concept of Basic Vote. The two measures contrast, however, in that Converse first postulates the existence of an underlying partisan attachment ('party identification') and then uses deviations from the Normal Vote associated with this to measure the net strength of issues. We start at exactly the opposite pole, by first estimating the net impact of issues, and then removing it in order to measure the level of Basic Vote. For this reason, although our use of the construct is analogous to Converse's and obviously inspired by his reasoning, we give it a different name to emphasise its contrasting basis of measurement.

The Basic Vote has the advantage of applying comparatively – since we can relate issue scores to votes for almost all parties in the twenty-three democracies, we can readily find the vote corresponding to zero issue scores in all these cases. For some reason (perhaps doubts about the stability and meaning of party identification outside the US context), the Normal Vote has rarely been used cross-nationally (Budge *et al.*, 1976, chs 1, 3 and 6). Through the concept of Basic Vote we hope to fill this notable gap and to relate general analyses of elections more closely to the American analyses.

(ii) Why Study Basic Vote?

While the analogy with Normal Vote lends interest to an analysis of basic Vote, it is still strictly speaking unnecessary for calculation and prediction within our framework, since we can calculate relative change without it. Knowing the issue scores for a party in two consecutive elections we can simply subtract the first score from the second, multiply the result (for most parties) by 0·89, and add the resulting percentage to the per cent of votes received by the party in the first election. This gives the vote we expect the party to receive in the second election – which can then either be compared with the actual result if it is already known, or stated as a prediction if it lies in the future. Thus no additional estimate of a notional Basic Vote is required.

Why then should we wish to incorporate it within our approach? There are three reasons, in order of increasing importance:

(a)   Having a Basic Vote to suit all elections in a country avoids introducing the random effects of two particular elections into the prediction. As with issue effects, more stability is introduced when the baseline is calculated from a greater number of cases.

(b)   Of course, the fundamental strengths of the parties may be changing so that an invariant Basic Vote for all elections may be misleading. But how can we measure change in underlying strength, independently of issue advantages or disadvantages? Only through isolating some component which is not attributable to immediate issue effects. But this, of course, is precisely what Basic Vote is. Through the methods applied later in this chapter and in Chapter 5, we can also see if it remains the same, or rises or declines with time. If underlying change is taking place, we are on firmer ground in taking an exceptional previous election result as the baseline for prediction. Thus estimates of Basic Vote, even if we do not actually use them, still indicate which baseline we ought to take. They also indicate whether, in the long term, parties are gaining or losing support. Electoral volatility has received much attention recently, so we focus on this in Chapter 5, drawing on experience with predictions and on the revised estimates to which some of them give rise.

(c)   The most important reason for analysing Basic Vote, however, is for the sake of completeness. Any comprehensive explanation of elections needs to account (at least in broad terms) for the way in which all votes are cast, not only for those which contribute to net change. Admittedly, changing outcomes are the feature primarily demanding explanation – which is why we start from the campaign issues associated with them.

The type of voting which contributes to stability as well as change also requires explanation, however. Is it governed by completely different attitudes from those we have discussed in regard to changers, or can it be covered by the argument already developed? Do stable voters also group issues within the fourteen discrete types we have described? Do they too dislike proposals for change except when they provide immediate practical benefits. Do they associate these in the same way with the different parties? If so, why do they not also change votes in response to the campaign issues?

All these questions need to be answered before we have a complete explanation of elections. The idea of Basic Vote helps because its core must be formed by stable voters, even though it consists in part of random and counterbalancing changers. Estimates of its size thus put an upper limit to the numbers of stable voters predisposed towards particular parties. Discussions of why there is a Basic Vote at all and who provides it, help to clarify the motivations both of changers and stayers, thus contributing to the more complete explanation of elections.

(iii) Who provides the Basic Vote and Why?

Zero issue scores, indicating that neither party gains or loses from issues, may emerge for two reasons. Either no issues are present in the election – at least none which affect the particular party under consideration. Or parties are associated with both positive and negative issues which exactly balance out, leaving their overall score at zero.

Swiss federal elections very often lack national issues affecting any of the parties. In this case one can say that voting must be almost purely predispositional apart from transfers due to individual and idiosyncratic factors. Very few other elections lack issues entirely (see Appendix B). Even where none affect one of the competing parties or blocs, we cannot say that the vote on this side is entirely loyalist, since the gross (as opposed to net) changes produced by any issue will cause it to trade some electors with the other side.

Where zero issue scores result from a party balance of positive and negative appeals – the commonest case – Basic Votes will consist both of long-standing supporters of the party and of electors who have been pulled in and who were not partisan voters at the previous election and may well not be at the next. Changes of this kind at the individual level may well not affect the aggregate stability of Basic Vote. This is because one source of change – that due to idiosyncratic personal circumstances – can be treated as essentially random and counterbalancing from an overall point of view. Given the approximately equal sizes, there is no reason why idiosyncratic changers should favour one party rather than the other, or vary in total number over time.

Another source of change is issues. Each of the issue types identified in Table 2.1 (p. 28 above) has a net effect, in that it pulls more electors towards one party than it pushes further away from it. However, each does push certain electors away, and some of these end up with the other party. The gross change associated with issues can be far larger than the net change (Le Duc, 1977, pp. 311–39). Thus where issues are present in an election at all, some of the electors contributing to Basic Vote will do so on the basis of reactions to issues.

Why in this case can the overall percentage for Basic Vote remain constant? Because any increased intake of changers produced by larger numbers of issues is balanced by greater outflows of previous supporters in response to the same increase in issues. That is, the greater the number of issues the more influence they exert over long-standing supporters who, in the absence of these, would have continued to vote for their previous party. Since there is only a limited pool of electors from which both changers and loyalists emerge, any increase in the numbers of the former must be accompanied by a reduction in numbers of the latter. Exactly the same mechanism works here as is postulated by Converse for his Normal Vote, which remains at the same level whether no trade-offs of identifiers occur (all vote for their party) or if 25 per cent of identifiers on each side are traded.

Basic Vote remains stable because, internally, fluctuations over time in the proportions of long-term supporters compared to counterbalancing issue changers cancel each other out. This implies that we cannot estimate the proportions of loyalists to changers very exactly among those contributing to Basic Vote, since they vary between election and election. In any case, since our own procedures and estimates are geared to net change – the changes discernible at the aggregate level – rather than to change as such, they provide no basis for breaking down Basic Votes into their constituent parts. Since a solid core of loyalists provides an element round which the rest can cohere, we would guess that more than half of the Basic Vote is contributed by electors with a previous record of support for the party. A basis for estimate is provided by British panel data, where 54·3 per cent of all electors voted the same way in the consecutive elections of 1964, 1966 and 1970 (Budge and Farlie, 1977, p. 389).

Why should the three elements contributing to Basic Vote – that is, loyalists, idiosyncratic changers and (counterbalancing) issue changers, act the way they do? Have they different motivations from issue changers moving in directions specified in Table 2.6 (p. 50 above), whom we have primarily considered up to this point? Do they in particular divide the world into different issue areas from those in Table 2.1 (p. 28 above)? Do they have views about change other than that it ought to be opposed unless accompanied by concrete benefits; or do they link change less strongly and exclusively with socialist parties?

We see no reason to suppose they do. So far as loyalists are concerned, their consistent support for one party can be covered quite simply by assuming that their personal circumstances make one or some of the issue types we have distinguished of permanent and predominant interest to them, so that they are usually unaffected by issues salient in the election itself. One example would consist of electors in precarious personal circumstances for whom extensions of welfare and social services occupy their political attention to the exclusion of all else. For the rich, taxation and security have the same salience. Loyalists then need be viewed as no less issue-oriented than other electors, but simply as located in social positions which fixate them (quite understandably) on certain issues regardless of campaign stimuli, and therefore predispose them to steady voting for a particular party.

Idiosyncratic changers responding to special personal circumstances are also likely to view issues in the same way as other electors. Into this category would fall individuals marrying into different family backgrounds or moving to different areas where new contacts have different issue concerns from those encountered before, which provoke a change of voting support. We cannot treat such changes in aggregate except when they occur in unbalanced fashion and in large numbers, producing shifts in underlying strength (see Chapter 5 for an analysis of these). Normally, however, we should expect individual changes of this kind to balance out, producing no aggregate effect on Basic Vote.

The third contribution to Basic Votes comes from electors who do respond to issues salient in the campaign, but in opposite ways to those specified in Table 2.6. We are thinking here of electors who shift to bourgeois parties when socioeconometric redistribution comes up, or for whom nationalisation and extensions of government control are attractive policies that incline them to the socialists. In both cases they are a minority outweighed by a majority who shift in the other direction, but often a substantial minority, which is why the net gain to parties on the issues which favour them is so relatively small.

Obviously this type of issue changer is defined by his non-compliance with the directions assigned in Table 2.6. There is no reason to believe, however, that he does not view the world in terms of the discrete issue types listed in Table 2.1, or that he does not oppose change unaccompanied by immediate benefits. The likely explanation of his reaction is that he is in a social position where the impacts of issues differ from those affecting the general population. He may, for example, be in a particular branch of government employment where reductions in nationalisation would endanger his job; or in private employment where an extension of social services would threaten the firm. A member of minority ethnic or religious groups might well see immediate benefits in reforms which to the majority represent a threat. The general point, however, is that in complex societies general issues are unlikely to have the same effects on everyone: what most fear, some, because of their differing circumstances, will welcome – even though they use the same criteria of evaluation. Thus every issue will produce counterbalancing movements.

The general motivations we have attributed to individual electors thus cover all these cases, just as much as they apply to changers who move in the majority direction on issues. One implication, particularly in regard to loyalists, is that a party's issue endorsements in a campaign may have other purposes than simply the direct net gains they bring in votes. Failure to reiterate familiar partisan stands forcibly enough, over a series of elections, or even to provide some reassurance on issues whose net effects favour the other side, may cause some loyalists to doubt whether the issues of permanent concern to them will be better served by one party rather than the other, and thus produce long-term defections not accounted for by immediate issue effects. These will show up as changes in the Basic Vote of both parties, or blocs, as this is calculated over time.

This is one reason for comparing Basic Vote in different elections, as we do in Chapter 5. We have already noted, however, that it is difficult, if not impossible, for a party to acquire new issue stands or to shed old ones. Our investigation of party manifestos and platforms also indicates that parties, at least in Britain and the United States, actually do retain old emphases over very long periods (Budge and Farlie, 1977, p. 427). Long-term changes in Basic Vote are therefore more likely to emerge from other factors than issues – primarily from widespread socioeconomic change which suddenly extends the idiosyncratic individual transfers discussed above across the community and causes them to favour one of the parties disproportionately. Factors which might in this way produce long-term change are:

(a)   Fundamental social upheaval, such as widespread uprooting from old to new communities, loss of traditional friends and associates and acquisition of new ones. By breaking old ties and exposing individuals to new concerns, such movements might bring quite other issues into permanent salience, and thus produce irreversible changes of allegiance.

(b)   Personal crises which cause individuals to rethink their political position even if they do not shift geographically. An obvious example would be widespread economic crisis and depression, which through unemployment and insecurity prompt a re-evaluation of personal status and concerns (or prolonged affluence and prosperity, with opposite partisan effects).

(c)   Such rethinking could also be brought about by the physical impact of war or terrorism which might, in any case, bring geographical dispersal and personal crises into play.

Of course, many of these developments would also figure as salient issues and have a short-term impact on elections through the net transfers of votes they produced. This would only be the tip of the iceberg, however, if they were also operating directly to produce massive personal disruptions of the sort described.

Analysing the sources of Basic Vote tends to give the impression that it is an actual vote rather than a statistical construct. It is essential to stress again that even in situations where parties actually score zero on issues, Basic Vote is not a percentage they actually receive, but rather the percentage from which actual votes fluctuate under the impact of issues. As such it represents the best measure of underlying party strength, and of long-term trends which may be at work independently of the election campaign.

(iv) Estimating Basic Vote by Taking Away Issue Effects

We have defined Basic Vote as the percentage a party would receive, on the basis of the average relationship between its issue scores and vote, at an issue score of zero. Even though it may never have actually attained that value, we could still estimate the corresponding percentage on the basis of the regression line in a graph such as Figure 3.1.

There is one complication. Tables 3.2 and 3.3 present a wide range of estimates for the various parties, which give varying slopes to the average lines. Since most can be fitted by the general estimate of 0·89 per cent, we have used lines with that degree of slope where appropriate. This is an important qualification since it means that the estimated Basic Vote differs (though only slightly) from what it would have been had the original average line been used. For US parties we use the country estimate of 1·85 per cent; for Italian Communists their original estimate of 2·3 per cent; for the Indian Congress 0·55 per cent; for Swiss Socialists 0·37 per cent; and for German Social Democrats 1·22 per cent. For the Norwegian and Swedish bourgeois blocs, slope estimates were so low that they implied issues had no discernible effect on vote. The best estimate for Basic Vote in this case is their average postwar vote, as it is also for the German Christian Democrats.

France is a different case, because the line-up of socialist and bourgeois parties has differed at every election, the latter in particular attracting previously independent parties at every stage. The values for Basic Vote given in Table 3.4 for France thus relate only to the situation in 1978 when we made the prediction reported in Chapter 4, though the constant changes in underlying strength must be remembered in the discussion of long-term change.

Table 3.4 presents the percentage estimates of Basic Vote which we derive on the basis of these procedures, using the issue estimates made by early 1978 and the election data available to us at that time. Since these constitute the basis for the voting predictions of Chapter 4 – which in turn provide a crucial test for our approach – it has been necessary to present them separately here.

The Basic Vote figures in Table 3.4 are provisional. Detailed analysis of fluctuation over time is best left to Chapter 5. Suffice it to note that two estimates had to be given for West Germany and Austria, reflecting growing support for the Social Democratic parties there. In France the two ballots in legislative elections, separated by a week, involve different figures for Basic Vote between the first and second rounds.

We should also note a difficulty with the US estimates – 48·2 per cent for Democrats and 48·1 per cent for Republicans. These are very high. The US parties gain 1·85 per cent of the voters with each issue increment, and have gone up to +7 on overall issue scores (see Appendix B), though never simultaneously – a fact which in itself is responsible for the high level of the Basic

Vote estimate. Does this therefore open up the disquieting possibility that the US parties, if both received over 48·0 per cent, might end up receiving more than a combined 100 per cent of the votes?

Table 3.4   *Estimated Basic Vote for Major Parties/*Tendances *over Selected Postwar Elections in Twenty-Three Stable Democracies up to 1977*

Country	Left–Reformist Parties	Bourgeois Parties
Australia (Labour, Liberal–Country)	45·0	45·1
Austria (Social Democrats, People's)	(1) 39·8/42·1	43·1
Belgium (Socialist, Christian Social)	34·3	37·4
Canada (Liberal, Progressive Conservative)	38·9	33·9
Denmark (Social Democrats, bourgeois parties)	36·8	47·8
Finland (FPDU and Social Democrats; Agrarian and Conservative and Liberal)	44·9	42·0
France (Communist, Socialist, left–radical; Gaullist and Giscardiens)	(2) 42·3/40·4	38·2/48·3
Iceland (Independence)	–	39·1
India (Congress)	40·1	–
Ireland (Fianna Fáil, Fine Gael)	42·4	28·3
Israel (Labour and Allies, Likud and precursors)	46·3	24·6
Italy (Communists, Christian Democrats)	20·1	35·9
Japan (Japan Socialist, Liberal Democrats)	28·1	49·9
Luxembourg (Socialist, Christian Social)	34·3	33·0
Netherlands (P v. d. A (Soc.), Christian Democrats and precursors)	28·2	44·6
New Zealand (Labour, National)	43·6	45·2
Norway (Labour, bourgeois coalition partners)	43·3	48·4
Sri Lanka (SL Freedom Party, United National Party)	25·1	30·8
Sweden (Social Democrat, bourgeois coalition parties)	45·0	47·9
Switzerland (Social Democrat, bourgeois coalition partners)	25·5	56·6
United Kingdom (Labour, Conservative)	42·0	40·6
United States (Democrats, Republicans)	48·2	48·1
West Germany (SPD, CDU)	33·7/43·6	46·9

Note:
(1) Austrian pre/post 1960
(2) French First, Second Ballots
(3) German pre/post 1971

The danger does not exist in reality. The estimates of Basic Vote (and indeed of the relationship between issue scores and vote from which they derive) are not our own creation. The issues are thrown up by election campaigns and the relationship with actual vote percentages also emerges empirically. As it happens, no presidential election since the war has seen both parties gain on issues simultaneously. One loses while the other gains. Thus the sum of expected votes for both major parties always remains below 100 per cent. Had not issue gains by one party been accompanied, in practice, by issue losses for the other over the postwar period, our estimates of Basic Votes would also have been lower, so the two points are interconnected.

Why issue gains should always be accompanied by issue losses in the United States is harder to explain. Possibly again it has something to do with the peculiar nature of the presidential election, with its intense contest between two candidates. Under these circumstances it is perhaps hard for them both to make a positive impression. One has to cede ground to the other. Certainly this remains speculation and we have no systematic empirical justification for it. What has happened in the immediate past is, however, likely to happen also in the immediate future.

In this connection it is reassuring to note that an independent study of aggregate voting figures for presidential elections, based on entirely different methods from ours, ends up by estimating the Normal Vote for Democrats and Republicans in 1952 as approximately 48 per cent apiece (Flanigan and Zingale, 1974, pp. 72–3). This figure represents an adjusted mean of voting percentages over the previous five elections. With the exceptional number of evenly balanced presidential elections since 1952 (deviating elections more or less cancelling each other out in aggregate), these percentages do not change much for the entire postwar period. Their similarity to ours is striking and suggests that where estimation is based on presidential voting percentages rather than survey responses, some figure at the upper 40 per cent level is bound to emerge as the average, Normal or Basic Vote for each of the US parties in the postwar period.

Chapter 4

Predicting Elections

Having obtained estimates of Basic Vote and of voting gains attributable to issues by early 1978, we were in a position to make predictions of forth-coming elections. Given some reliable report of the issues which would dominate the campaign, we could code these into our categories in the way illustrated in Section 3.1 and from these estimate likely issue gains: then we could add or subtract them from Basic Votes to get the expected results. We had, in fact, started predicting outcomes earlier than this, from late summer 1977, using the individual country estimates available to us before completion of the comparative analysis. In all we made ten predictions between mid-1977 and mid-1979, which are reported below.

Prediction was important not only to check our estimates and assumptions as thoroughly as possible, but also to counter any doubts about the way in which our selection of past issues might retrospectively improve the fit between issue scores and vote. In preparing our basic data great care was taken to select issues in each election on the basis of reports made before voting (as much as two to three months before, if possible). In the case of smaller countries, however, reports of the campaign are often presented along with the voting figures. Moreover, even where this is not the case it is impossible, in spite of all precautions, to show conclusively that we have eliminated all knowledge of election history from the selection of issues.

This lingering doubt is not peculiar to our own research: it is a feature of all attempts to link two variables after the event. That is precisely why prediction becomes such a valuable test of the standing of a theory. Since the outcome here lies in the future it cannot influence our determination of the presumed influences upon it. A comparison of previously predicted figures with those which actually emerge later thus constitutes a necessary test of any theory to which it can be applied.

Conversely, because this permits the most searching test of validity, it is a great strength in any explanation to have the potential for making predictions. The very attempt to do so corrects internal weaknesses and inconsistencies, and since predictions are usually cast in numeric form they demand an exact specification of assumptions and a precise statement of conclusions which is still very rare in the social sciences. This is un-fortunate since even without the actual tests, a predictive theory with these characteristics is likely to provide a better explanation.

Only a few attempts at prediction of forthcoming election results have been made. Some have been based on computer simulation where *ad hoc* assumptions tended to overwhelm the workings of the underlying theory, and where the criteria of success are ambiguous (Pool *et al.*, 1965; Budge and Farlie, 1977, pp. 449–96). One attempt based on time-series equations relating change in real disposable income and in presidential popularity to congressional mid-term vote, predicted a Republican national percentage of 39·2 per cent two weeks before the election of 1974, which compared with an actual vote of 41·1 per cent (Tufte, 1975, pp. 812–25).

The discrepancy of nearly 2 per cent in this case provides one criterion against which to assess our (more extended) predictions. Another lies in the traditional test of seeing how much better the theoretical prediction does than some naïve forecast which would be made in total ignorance of any theory. Four types of naïve forecasting may be employed. Where forecast and actual results are truly quantitative in form, the mean value of the previous outcomes can be taken. Its success in specifying the next result may be compared with the success of the theoretical prediction: only if the latter comes nearer the actual result can it be taken as better.

An alternative form of naïve prediction is available where events are ordered in some way which relates the last outcome in the series to the next more closely than the others. This is, of course, likely to be the case with elections where in the United Kingdom, for example, outcomes in the 1974 elections are more likely to foretell those of 1979 than is voting in 1950. The superiority of the last result over the average cannot necessarily be taken for granted, so we shall compare the performance of both with that of our model.

Where outcomes are not quantitative in form, analogous forms of naïve forecasting are available. The first, corresponding to the mean in the previous case, is to predict that the next result will be what has happened most frequently in the past – that is, if a socialist party has won most elections in the series, we forecast a socialist victory in the next. However, in a changing situation it may be more efficient to characterise the next result by the last – that is, if a bourgeois party won last time it will be expected to win next time. Again both methods will be used in the comparison with our results.

In Section 4.2 we make systematic comparisons over all ten predictions made on the basis of our theory. Since we must specify how we arrived at the predicted figures, we first discuss them individually in Section 4.1. This also gives us the opportunity to evaluate their performance less technically, within the context of each country's politics. While we contrast theoretical with naïve predictions, we also consider more subtle points which cannot enter into a general, quantitative assessment – in particular, whether the anticipated showing of parties gives a good indication of the actual post-election situation, or not.

4.1 Individual Predictions of Election Outcomes

We present individual predictions in the order in which we made them.

Our first was for the Norwegian Storting election in mid-1977, and our last in March 1979 for the Italian general election. There is no theoretical or other reason for picking this particular two-year period, other than that the Norwegian election was the first to take place after we had developed our methods and collected data for prediction, and the Italian election was the last to occur before we completed the initial draft of the manuscript. We have not covered all elections which took place in our set of democracies within this period. We had to allow the Irish general election of 1977 to pass because we had not yet collected enough material on Irish issues to make estimates for it. The Finnish parliamentary elections of 1978 were, on the other hand, not reported in sufficient detail in the sources available to us. All other elections were covered.

Because we had not yet combined issue scores for most parties and run them against voting percentages to get the general estimate of 0·89 per cent, the first two predictions presented below (the Norwegian and Australian) are based on preliminary estimates of issue effects for each party, for post-war national elections only. They thus differ from those adopted subsequently in the light of the general comparative analysis. When we apply the general estimates to the issues identified before these elections, we get somewhat different percentage figures for anticipated voting. In our quantitative analysis we stick to the percentages actually produced in advance, even though they are obtained on a somewhat different basis from the others. In the more extended discussion in this section we do, however, consider how much better (if at all) our predictions would have been had the standard estimates been applied.

For the third prediction in the series – the French – general estimates were available before the election and were applied. However, owing to the shifting basis of the French government parties compared to previous elections, a special assumption about the former centrist vote had to be introduced which is not present in the other, straightforward cases. To a certain extent, therefore, the first three predictions could be regarded as preliminary or as standing on a rather different basis from the others. As a result our assessments of predictive success have been made not only for all ten predictions made on the basis of the theory, but also separately for the last seven, for which general estimates were available at the time and no special assumptions were made.

The procedure with all predictions was to base our characterisation of issues on newspaper or journal reports which appeared at least a month, and often earlier, before the election in question. Indeed, some of our predictions (for example, for the British and Canadian elections) were simply modifications of ongoing characterisations made at intervals over the previous years. In any case, reports were interpreted against the general background of issues identified for earlier elections and of our general diffuse knowledge of the country's politics. In the individual presentations made in this section, the major sources for the characterisation are cited:

these are the most recent and up-to-date assessments of the pre-electoral situation in the country under consideration.

Once issues were identified, the associated scores in favour of one or other party could be readily applied and percentage gains and losses calculated. These were added or subtracted to the appropriate Basic Vote (Table 3.4, p. 82 above) to obtain predicted voting percentages. Tables 4.1 to 4.10 summarise the actual calculations made before the election to get such percentages. These were then communicated to interested colleagues both orally and by letter. This was because experience with a previous prediction (*The Times*, London, 16 November 1977) indicated that published figures provoked discussion among party strategists themselves, thus running into the problem of self-fulfilling prophecies (Budge, 1973, p. 249).

The final percentages publicised in this way constitute our predictions, generated at points from one to three months before the election. It should be noted that the issues chosen as likely to be salient in the campaign were not necessarily those being discussed at the time of the prediction. They were rather the ones which we and the commentators thought most likely to be in electors' minds on the day they voted. The success of the predictions depends essentially on correct identification of such issues though they may be affected, of course, by underlying changes taking place in the Basic Vote.

Our predictions cover the national percentage of all those actually voting and not of all those qualified to vote. Although these may identify the party likely to form the next government in a two-party competitive situation, they will not necessarily do so (see the Canadian and New Zealand elections discussed below). This applies with even more force to multi-party situations. Nor do voting percentages bear any strictly determinate relationship to gains or losses in legislative seats. These depend not simply on how large a party's national support is, but also on where it comes from. Of course, if a party's support rises or drops quite drastically, or if it is already in a strong or weak position and seems likely to stay that way, inferences as to parliamentary and governmental strength can be made. However, our model does not extend that far; its reasoning and estimates relate only to aggregate votes in the general election.

It should also be remembered that the model applies only to national voting and does not cover regional variations within a country – interesting as these often are (in Canada or Norway, for example). Its assumptions and estimates could be modified for regional analyses but they would not then be the same as the national model we have constructed, which must operate on a whole-country basis.

With these caveats we are now in a position to cover the predictions made for ten elections in ten different countries. These are presented in the temporal order in which we made them.

(i)   *Norwegian Storting Election, 11–12 September 1977*

This was not the first election prediction we had actually constructed, the earliest being for a British general election expected after a vote of confidence in February 1977. Since the Labour government survived, the election failed to materialise. In contrast, Norwegian elections are held on a fixed four-year basis, so there was no doubt about the September election occurring.

Issues were identified on the basis of *The Times* (London) reports of 20 May and 19 July 1977. They are listed in Table 4.1. The final listing and scoring were done by 31 July 1977.

Table 4.1   *Issues Anticipated on 31 July 1977 to Influence Voting in Norwegian Storting Election 11–12 September 1977 with Associated Classifications and Scorings.*

Specific Issue	Issue Type	Magnitude of Impact	Direction of Impact	Issue Scores Labour	bourgeois
Government concessions in negotiations on fishing limits	3 Foreign relationships	Small (1)	–Labour	–1	
Inability of bourgeois parties to combine on common platform until just before election	6 Government record and prospects	Small (1)	–bourgeois		–1
Labour government's maintenance of reasonable prosperity and employment in world recession	6 Government record and prospects	Small (1)	+Labour	+1	
Expansion of oil-drilling in North Sea	12 Government control and planning	Small (1)	–Labour	–1	
SUMMED ISSUE SCORES				–1	–1

For Labour 1 increment in issue scores = 0.42% net
For bourgeois 1 increment in issue scores = 0.17% net
Predicted Labour vote = basic vote + issue effects = $45.14 - 0.42 = 44.7\%$
Predicted bourgeois vote = basic vote + issue effects = $48.20 - 0.17 = 48.0\%$

One or two peculiarities of Table 4.1 should be noted. First, the number of issues in the election is limited (only four, two of which deal with the general competence of government and opposition). This does not indicate that we have omitted issues which were actually influential. The average number of issue types salient in elections is generally low – approximately four, which is the number present here. Moreover, the average number of issue types over all postwar Norwegian elections is low compared with the United Kingdom or the United States (Table 2.2, p. 35 above).

Secondly, Table 4.1 is peculiar in that two issues are listed separately under government record and prospects. This forms an exception to the general rule that separate specific issues which fall under the same issue type will count only as one occurrence of that issue type. As noted, however, it does not make sense to lump together references to different parties under government record and prospects (nor to different candidates under candidate reactions) where quite different characteristics are being attributed to them. Hence we count references to different candidates or parties as constituting separate occurrences of these issue types, though repeated allusions to the same candidate or party will still only count as one occurrence. In Table 4.1 Labour is viewed in mildly positive terms for having preserved employment and reasonable prosperity, while the bourgeois parties are viewed rather negatively for their failure to form a convincing common front.

The other two issues redound against Labour, though they both carry only a limited impact. This again is not usual, since we normally count issues as working for the party which 'owns' them, rather than against the party which does not. In this particular case, however, both stem from particular actions or omissions of the Labour government with which the bourgeois parties had very little to do, and which they could not even promise to remedy, since binding agreements had already been made. So it seemed realistic to count them against Labour.

In retrospect our choice of issues seems realistic and justified by commentaries on campaign and results (*Keesing's Contemporary Archives*, 1977, entries under 'Norway Storting election'). The main un-expected event was a devaluation of the krone in the weeks before polling. This was explained through the financial strain imposed by a full employ-ment policy, which had already been covered in our assessment. Had we been able to anticipate the devaluation itself, we should still have arrived at the same assessment of the government's overall record, so its impact on our prediction does not seem to have been serious.

Having identified the issues in the table, their assignment to categories and scoring was fairly mechanical and, presumably, non-controversial in light of previous discussion. The summing of issue scores leaves both parties with a mildly negative score of -1.

Had we carried through our general analysis at the time of making this prediction, we should at this point have subtracted 0·89 per cent, the general estimate for the percentage equivalent of one issue increment, from the recomputed Basic Vote of 43·3 per cent for the Norwegian Labour Party (leaving aside the question of the bourgeois vote for the moment). At 43·3 per cent Basic Vote, minus 0·89 per cent on issue losses, this would have given a predicted vote of 42·4 per cent approximately. Our comparative analysis also indicates that the bourgeois vote continues at the same level unaffected by issue impacts. Thus our best estimate for any election is their mean vote over previous elections – which in this case is the same as one of the naïve predictors – 48·4 per cent. Table 4.1 incidentally suggests how it comes about that campaign issues do not affect the standing of the bourgeois parties. Their disunity and consequent lack of credibility as an alternative government are a permanent condition reflected in Basic Vote. The other issues tell for or against the 'natural party of government' – the Labour Party – rather than having much relevance for the permanent opposition. Thus the bourgeois vote *is* a Basic Vote composed mainly of loyalists with enduring policy concerns rather than one affected by net gains or losses on specific election issues.

If we had been in a position to make such estimates on the basis of issues identified before the election, predicting Labour as 42·4 per cent and the traditional bourgeois parties as 48·4, we should have almost anticipated the actual results – Labour 42·4 per cent, bourgeois parties 48·6 per cent. As it was, we had not got these estimates available and had to derive the ones actually used on regressions of issue scores against percentage votes for Norwegian elections only, which were based on a graph exactly like that shown for the United Kingdom in Figure 3.1 (p. 66 above).

This meant, of course, that we had to ground our conclusions about issue effects on a very limited number of cases – there were only seven postwar elections previous to 1977. With limited numbers the overall relationships can be very much distorted by an exceptional result, which pulls the line representing the average relationship to one side or the other, very far from what it would be if it simply passed through the middle of the remaining points. There is one such result in the Norwegian case: the Labour vote in the 1973 general election which had plummeted to 35·4 per cent under the tensions set in train by the referendum on entry to the Common Market. Since this vote is very much below what would be expected on the basis of corresponding issue scores, the 1973 result forms an 'outlier' which considerably steepens the slope of the average Labour line relating scores and votes, and thus materially increases the estimate of issue effects.

When we base estimates of issue effects on large numbers of cases, deviant cases of this kind can readily be included (as in our general comparative analysis in Figure 3.2, p. 71 above), since their ability to pull results away from the general average is reduced. For Norwegian elections on their own, however, we had to decide whether to allow our estimate for Labour to be transformed by this one case, or to base it on what had happened in all elections except for 1973. Since we are interested in general relationships rather than particular cases, we decided on the latter course.

Basing Labour issue estimates on the other elections gave a value of 0·42 per cent for the net gains or losses attributable to one issue increment. For the bourgeois parties (not having yet decided in light of comparisons with other countries that no real relationship existed), we estimated a very limited net change of 0·17 per cent. This was based on all the election results since no outliers cropped up in the bourgeois case.

These issue estimates also gave rise to slightly different values for Basic Vote compared to the ones in Table 3.4 (p. 82 above). Labour was put at 45·14 per cent and the bourgeois parties at 48·20 per cent. Subtracting 0·42 per cent and 0·17 per cent from these respectively gives 44·7 per cent and 48·0 per cent respectively as predictions for the parties' share of the votes. These were the figures actually reached at the end of July 1977, six weeks before the Storting election.

While these figures approach the actual voting returns (42·4 per cent Labour and 48·6 per cent bourgeois parties), they come less close than the figures reached (retrospectively) by applying our general estimates (or than the one we should have obtained for Labour by incorporating the 1973 result!). Since these constitute the prediction made before the election, however, we stick with them in our evaluation.

The anticipated figure for Labour is 2·3 per cent too high, and that for the bourgeois parties 0·6 per cent too low. This compares favourably with Tufte's error of 1·9 per cent in 1974, since his prediction was made only two weeks before the election compared to our six weeks. Perhaps not surprisingly, given the limited issue effects, one naïve predictor of the bourgeois vote performs more efficiently than the theoretical prediction. The mean vote over postwar elections is 48·4 per cent (only 0·2 per cent out); however, the last election result was 44·2 per cent (4·4 per cent out). In the case of Labour it is a major success of the prediction to anticipate that the election result would differ radically from the 35·3 per cent of 1973. But the mean vote over all preceding elections, at 44·3 per cent, still predicts marginally better. With naïve predictors, of course, the problem is always the choice, in advance, of the appropriate one.

The exact extent of divergences between the naïve and theoretical predictions is a matter for systematic assessment in the next section. Here we are concerned with the broader question of whether our advance characterisation gave a broadly truthful picture of the post-election situation, or whether it distorted this in such a way that action undertaken on its basis would have been inappropriate. A main reason for wishing to have predictions is, after all, the desire to anticipate and cope with future events, so in many ways this is the major criticism for predictive success.

In broad terms, the election saw the Labour vote recover spectacularly and the bourgeois vote remain tied to its old levels. Although it was the support given to the small parties of more extreme socialist persuasions which crucially determined whether the Labour government was to continue, our figures certainly indicated that the Labour Party itself would be revitalised and in much better shape to govern should it have the opportunity to do so (as it did). Since this was all correctly anticipated, our prediction for Norway emerges as qualitatively vindicated and broadly successful.

(ii)   *Australian General Election, 10 December 1977*

This election took place two years after the dramatic reversal of fortunes in which the then governor-general had dismissed the Labour leader, Whitlam (who had a majority of Lower House seats) in order to give Fraser, leader of the Liberal–Country Party coalition, the opportunity of calling an election which he won overwhelming (53·0 to 43·1 per cent of the votes). By September 1977 when a new election was in the offing, the government was generally considered to have failed in its pledge to produce greater prosperity, although it had reduced inflation to under 10 per cent at the cost of higher unemployment. In turn this had contributed to industrial unrest, which the government proposed to counter by legislation – a traditional tactic of the Liberal–Country Party when other issues are un-favourable (see Appendix B for the use made of this issue in previous elections). Encouragement for business to build up uranium mining to stimulate the economy was hotly opposed by environmentalists, who supported a five-year moratorium backed by strict government controls. The Prime Minister's abrasive style in putting forward these proposals and, in particular, the circumstances under which he had come to power made him the target of personal attacks by Labour supporters unprecedented even in Australian politics. However, his opponent Whitlam was still discredited by revelations of financial bungling and lack of central control in his own government, so neither of the leading candidates could be regarded as overwhelmingly popular. These issues are summarised and scored in Table 4.2 (they are extracted from the following reports: *Sunday Times*, London, 29 October 1977; *The Times*, London, 7 November 1977; *The Economist*, London, 24 September 1977).

In line with general comment, polls in October initially showed Labour leading by a small margin. This had changed to a comfortable lead for the government coalition in early December (*The Times*, London, 25 October, 19 November, 25 November, 27 November, 3 December 1977). Our final characterisation at the beginning of November showed both competitors as mildly unpopular and losing votes on campaign issues. While the coalition were predicted to win, the contest was viewed as essentially marginal – at least as far as first preference votes were concerned. The traditional tendency for second preferences to favour the Liberal–Country Party implied that the election as a whole would go in their favour once the additional votes were counted.

We were unable to take second preferences systematically into account, however, since voting percentages over postwar elections were reported in terms of first preferences only, in all the sources available to us. So our predicted figures related only to the initial distribution of votes – which essentially determines the outcome in any case. As with Norway, we had not got general estimates to work with and had to extract specific ones from the relationship between issue scores and (first preference) votes for

Australian postwar elections alone. Since we had no outliers, all were used in the calculation of effects. These estimates also produced 1 per cent lower figures for Basic Vote than the final general estimate. Substitution of the general for the specific estimates would, in the Australian case, hardly have changed the final prediction – only from 43·3 per cent for Labour to 44·1 per cent approximately, and from 43·8 per cent for the Liberal–Country Party to 44·2 per cent.

Table 4.2 *Issues Anticipated on 11 November 1977 to Influence Voting in Australian General Election 10 December 1977 with Associated Classifications and Scorings*

Specific Issue	Issue Type	Magnitude of Impact	Direction of Impact	Issue Scores Labour	L CP
Prime Minister Fraser's authoritarian style and provocation of party splits	5 Candidate reactions	Small (1)	–L CP		–1
Whitlam's unreliability and provocation of party splits	5 Candidate reactions	Small (1)	–Labour	–1	
Cost-of-living increases, unemployment, sluggish economy balanced to some extent by reduction of inflation to under 10%	6 Goverment record and prospects	Medium (2)	–L CP		–2
Uranium mining now *v.* 5-year moratorium	12 Government control and planning	Small (1)	+L CP		+1
Industrial disruption, strikes, laws to curb trade union activities	13 Government regulation in favour of individual	Small (1)	+L CP		+1
SUMMED ISSUE SCORES				–1	–1

For Labour 1 increment in issue scores = 0·62% net
For Liberal–Country Party coalition (L CP) 1 increment in issue scores = 0·40% net
Predicted Labour vote = basic vote + issue effects = 43·96 – 0·62 = 43·3%
Predicted L CP vote = basic vote + issue effects = 44·14 – 0·37 = 43·8%

In the event, the government parties won a clear majority of 48·0 per cent to 40·0 per cent on first preference votes on 10 December. The percentages anticipated in our prediction of a month before were slightly closer to the actual Liberal–Country vote than the previous result of 53·0 per cent. However, the mean Liberal–Country vote of 47·9 per cent almost precisely coincided with the actual result. In the Labour case the previous result was closer by 0·2 per cent than our prediction, though we in turn were closer than their mean vote of 45·9 per cent.

In general terms, although we did predict the winner, our characterisation of the election outcome is misleading in that it implied a close result from which whoever formed the government would not emerge with great authority or with any pretence to a strong popular mandate. Precisely the opposite happened. Whitlam was crushed and forced to resign as Leader of the Opposition and Fraser was triumphantly vindicated.

Our prediction went wrong not because issues were misidentified – no issues other than those listed in Table 4.2 actually emerged in the campaign – but because the 'erratic' issues which were identified were wrongly weighted. Fraser's firmness struck electors as authoritative rather than authoritarian, producing a large reaction in favour of the Liberal–Country Party, while Whitlam's unpopularity was even more massive than we had anticipated. This also spilled over into negative reactions towards Labour's previous governmental record. On the government side, its crushing of inflation also counted for more than we had thought (*The Times*, London, 12 December 1977). Amended in these terms, the retrospective issue scores of +4 to the Liberal–Country Party and –6 to Labour fit quite well. But of course they do so only with hindsight, after the event, and in this case our advance prediction fails.

(iii)   The French Assembly Ballots, 12 and 19 March 1978

A peculiarity of the voting system under the Fifth Republic is the holding of first and second ballots for Assembly seats (as, on a national scale, in the election of the President). Only candidates who win an absolute majority in the first ballot are declared elected. Otherwise, the leading candidates face each other in a second contest one week after the first. Retiring candidates' advice to their supporters as to who to vote for on the second round is thus of crucial importance. National inter-party agreements which affect that advice are similarly important, although (depending on the degree of cordiality between parties making the agreement) electors may be less disposed to follow it at some times than at others.

Voting patterns in the two ballots may differ profoundly, given the Frenchman's tendency to vote in the first with his heart but in the second with his head. Since the prospect of a victory for the left and especially of the entry of communists into government produces a threat of constitutional disruption, this implies that the right vote is likely to increase on the second ballot – the major reason for its restoration by de Gaulle in 1958.

A further complication in analysing French elections for this period is the changing composition of the major contestants. The government majority was originally largely Gaullist: by 1978, all parties of the centre and right had been attracted to a broad 'Giscardien' grouping, almost equal in numbers to the Gaullists with whom there was frequent bickering. On the other side, the Union of the Left, grouping Socialists, Communists and a small left radical party, had become less and less cohesive since 1973, culminating in a failure to adopt a common election programme in the autumn of 1977.

There were thus considerable internal divisions among both the main contestants in the election. This was not necessarily a disadvantage in voting terms for the Union of the Left, since the greater dissociation of Socialists from Communists might lead more electors to vote for them while Communist voting remained unaffected. Coupled with the government programme of rigid austerity and financial orthodoxy under the Barre plan, this led the left to hope for overall victory, and many outside commentators to predict this. The nominal leader of the Union of the Left, François Mitterand, retained popularity, matched to some extent on the government side only by the Gaullist Chirac (President Giscard having rather a neutral quality). The government commitment to massive nuclear development, recently dramatised by a pitched battle with counter-demonstrators, was the only independent question entering into the election. As with Australian uranium mining and Norwegian oil drilling, this conservationist issue falls under 'government control' since extensive regulation of business interests and direct implication of government in new areas are involved. The issues of the campaign and their anticipated effects were summed up on 20 January, for the elections two months ahead (Table 4.3) *The Times*, London, 12 December 1977, 4 and 13 January 1978; *The Economist*, London, 26 November 1977, 14 January 1978).

Extensive reporting of the campaign as it developed confirmed that these were the main issues. The week which elapsed between the first and second ballots merely saw a reiteration of the leading themes of the preceding campaign – compared to his predecessors, President Giscard markedly soft-pedalled the prospect of a breakdown should the left win. So we feel justified in assuming that issue effects on both ballots were the same. Since, however, the estimated Basic Votes for the parties, and their anticipated share of the old centre vote, differ sharply between the ballots, we have to make predictions separately, as we have in fact done at the bottom of the table.

The figures there demand explanation. The shifting nature of political alliances under the Fifth Republic, particularly on the right and centre, and the limited number of Assembly elections under that régime, make it difficult to get any precise estimate from French elections alone. A very wide variety of issue effects were compatible with the available figures. Since the general estimate of 0·89 per cent was quite as compatible as any others, and supported by the comparative analysis we had just finished in early January 1978, we had every reason for using 0·89 per cent as the difference made by one increment in issue scores. Using this as the slope of the line for both parties, we got figures for Basic Vote, the percentage supporting parties in the absence of issue effects, as 36·1 per cent for the

Union of the Left on the first ballot, and 40·4 per cent on the second ballot. Compared with this modest 4 per cent increase, the government Basic Vote shoots up from 32 per cent on the first ballot to 42 per cent on the second, in line with the great difference in attitudes between these election contests.

Table 4.3   *Issues Anticipated on 20 January 1978 to Influence Voting in French Assembly Ballots of 12 and 19 March 1978 with Associated Classifications and Scorings*

Specific Issue	*Issue Type*	*Magnitude of Impact*	*Direction of Impact*	*Issue Scores*	
				Left	*Government*
Chirac as defender of Gaullist legacy	5 Candidate reactions	Small (1)	+Government		+1
Mitterand as moderate reformer	5 Candidate reactions	Large	+Left	+3	
Unemployment, austerity balanced by signs of reduction in inflation	6 Government record and prospects	Medium (2)	–Government		–2
Socialist coolness to Communists	6 Government record and prospects	Small (1)	+Left	+1	
Nuclear development as opposed to environmental protection and moratorium	12 Government control and planning	Small (1)	+Government		+1
Incentives to free enterprise under Barre Plan	14 Initiative and freedom	Small (1)	+Government		+1

SUMMED ISSUE SCORES   +4   +1

For both parties 1 increment in issue scores = 0·89% net

First ballot: Predicted left vote = Basic Vote + issue effects + half of previous centre vote = 36·1% + 3·6% + 6·2% = 45·9%

Predicted government vote = Basic Vote + issue effects + half of previous centre vote = 32·0% + 0·9% + 6·2% = 39·1%

Second ballot: Predicted left vote = Basic Vote + issue effects = 40·4% + 3·6% = 44·0%

Predicted government vote: = Basic Vote + issue effects + previous centre vote = 42·2% + 0·9% + 6·1% = 49·2%

Basic Vote for the government is calculated for those parties in more or less close alliance with the Gaullists up to and including 1974. There is a complication, however, in that the Centre Democrats of Lecanuet joined the government in 1974 and fought the election of 1978 as part of the Giscardien Union pour la Démocratie Française. Their votes could not be included in calculations of the Basic Vote for the 'old majority' since they were a separate electoral force in all previous postwar elections, although certainly inclined to urge support for the government parties rather than for the left on the second round. Because of their independent centrist position and the probability that their following included voters of both right- and left-wing tendencies, the most plausible assumption was that their first ballot vote in the previous election (12·4 per cent) would divide evenly between the left and the government, providing each with an increment of 6·2 per cent independent of issue effects. This gives the predicted left vote for the first ballot as nearly 46 per cent, and the government vote as just over 39 per cent.

In the second ballot, the Centre Democrats had always ultimately favoured the right over the left. So we felt justified in adding the whole of their previous vote of 6·1 per cent to the Basic Vote on the government side. Together with their net gain on issues of 0·89, this gave a predicted government vote of 49·2 per cent, approximately, compared to the left's 44 per cent.

This prediction contrasted sharply with the reported results of numerous opinion polls, published in January, February and early March, which showed the left attracting most preferences (*The Times*, London, 18 January, 17 February, 20 February 1978). Since reports did not usually make the crucial distinction between intentions for first and second ballots, the general impression from the polls was that the Union would win the election.

In contrast, our prediction was that the left would win the first ballot and government parties the second. This anticipated reversal of fortune was the major focus of our prediction rather than the exact percentage figures (given the problems of making precise estimates for France).

As it turned out, our predicted first ballot percentage for the left came very close to the actual result (45·9 per cent compared with 45·2 per cent). This was closer than either the last election result (43·7 per cent) or the Fifth Republic mean (39·4 per cent). The prediction of 39·1 per cent for government parties was substantially lower than the actual 44·1 per cent, but still closer than the last election result of 38 per cent or the mean of 33·6 per cent. The main point is, however, the correct anticipation of the left's win on popular votes, albeit by a much closer margin than expected.

This victory, as predicted, was reversed on the second ballot. The government parties gained 50·5 per cent of the vote, as against our anticipated 49·2 per cent. Again this figure came closer to the result than either the previous election outcome (46·1 per cent) or general average (37·6 per cent). The Union of the Left gained 49·3 per cent of the actual vote, considerably more than the 44·0 per cent which we had expected (but again the predicted figure was closer than the last election result of 42·8 per cent or than the mean election result of 42·1 per cent).

Our theoretical analysis thus captured the dramatic reversal of fortune between the two ballots, but failed to anticipate the narrowness of the winning margin on both. Since the importance of this election lay in who won rather than what margin they won by, our ability to spot the winners is the significant aspect of this prediction.

Table 4.4   *Issues Anticipated on 30 May 1978 to Influence Voting in the Icelandic General Election 25 June 1978 with Associated Classifications and Scorings*

Specific Issue	Issue Type	Magnitude of Impact	Direction of Impact	Issue Scores Independence	Left
Termination of US Base at Keflavik, withdrawal from NATO	3 Foreign relationships	Small (1)	+Independence	+1	
Uninspiring leadership, lack of new ideas or leads in face of economic crisis	5 Candidate reactions	Large (3)	–Independence	–3	
40% inflation, wage freeze after prolonged recession, devaluation	6 Government record and prospects	Large (3)	–Independence	–3	
Need for measures against unemployment and price increases	11 Socio-economic redistribution	Large (3)	+Left		+3
SUMMED ISSUE SCORES				–5	+3

For Independence party 1 increment in issue scores = 0·89 per cent
Predicted Independence vote = Basic Vote + issue effects = 39·1% – 4·5% = 34·6%

(iv)   Icelandic General Election, 25 June 1978

This was the first of our 'standard' predictions, made with the comparatively based estimates shown in Table 3.3 (p. 72 above) and not involving special assumptions. Its peculiarity is that vote for the Independence Party is the only one predicted, since our analysis failed to fit issue scores to votes for the other parties. The general election took place against a background of economic crisis, with inflation running at the rate of 40 per cent a year. The ministers of the coalition government (Independence Party plus centrist Progressives) had proved personally uninspiring in the face of this immediate threat to living standards and to wages. The only other issue was the perennial question of evacuation of the Keflavik airbase by American forces and Icelandic withdrawal from NATO – a question which has generally favoured the Independence Party which wishes to keep both. Icelandic issues are generally limited in number and in nature owing to the small size and homogeneity of the population (see Appendix B): Table 4.4 lists and scores issues in the 1978 campaign

(*The Times*, London, 12, 16 and 26 October 1977, 30 May 1978), which turned out retrospectively as well as in anticipation to be the major ones in the election.

Our prediction shows a big dip in the Independence Party's vote, to 34·6 per cent, resulting from the country's problems and the failure of the government to face up to them. The slump is particularly evident in relation to the result in the last election, where the Independence Party had done well at 42·8 per cent of the vote, or in regard to its postwar average of 39·3 per cent. The actual result showed an even greater decline from these figures than expected – to 32·1 per cent. Our prediction thus performs substantially better than the naïve predictors and compares, over a period of three and a half weeks, with Tufte's error of 1·9 per cent over two weeks. The major point which anyone forecasting election outcomes would have wanted to know, was how disastrous the result might be for the largest (Independence) party. Our predictive model certainly informs him about that.

(v) New Zealand General Election, 25 November 1978

Like the Australian coalition, the New Zealand National Party had ousted the previous Labour government in 1975, piling up a large electoral majority in the process. It had likewise encountered adverse economic circumstances during its term of office, with unprecedented levels of unemployment. In 1975 Mr Muldoon, the Prime Minister, had attracted votes with the promise of firm leadership. His abrasive style, emphasised by displays of personal vindictiveness, had eroded this advantage to an extent to which he might be said to constitute a minor liability for his party. On the face of it the weak government position seemed a golden opportunity for Labour. Its performance remained curiously lack-lustre, however, apparently having lost the ability to formulate any convincing alternative to government policies. It was further tarnished by association with the trade unions, whose participation in a series of trivial strikes had provided the government with an opportunity to pass an Industrial Relations Reform Bill. These issues (*Australasian Express*, London, 20 October 1978) are summarised in Table 4.5.

Of this selection, the reduction in taxation did not figure much in the actual campaign. Labour and its leader, Mr Rowling, gained markedly in stature over the last fortnight, but from a critique of government policies rather than any advocacy of his own, leaving the situation described in Table 4.5 substantially unchanged. There was much discussion of one question not identified in advance – demands for more liberal abortion laws. As a religious-moral question this would have improved prospects for the National Party. There is some doubt, however, as to how salient it was to the electorate outside small vocal groups, and certainly no firm position was taken by any party which might have converted it into a question to be immediately settled by the election outcome (*The Economist*, London, 2–8 December 1978).

Table 4.5   *Issues Anticipated on 22 October 1978 to Influence Voting in New Zealand General Election 25 November 1978 with Associated Classifications and Scorings*

Specific Issue	Issue Type	Magnitude of Impact	Direction of Impact	Issue Scores Labour	National
Abrasiveness of Muldoon	5 Candidate reactions	Small (1)	−National		−1
Rise in unemployment 10–15% inflation, balance of payments difficulties balanced by general world depression, firm government	6 Government record and prospects	Medium (2)	−National		−2
Weak Labour opposition, no convincing plan for unemployment	6 Government record prospects	Medium (2)	−Labour	−2	
Trade union strikes, highlighted by Industrial Relations Reform Bill	13 Government regulation in favour of individual	Small (1)	−Labour	−1	
Reduction in taxation	14 Initiative and freedom	Small (1)	+National		+1

SUMMED ISSUE SCORES   −3   −2
For both parties 1 increment in issue scores = 0·89% net
Predicted National Party vote = Basic Vote + issue effects = 45·2 − 1·8 = 43·4%
Predicted Labour vote = Basic Vote + issue effects = 43·6 − 2·7 = 40·9%

This dramatically reversed the picture given by opinion polls of a comfortable majority for the government (45–47 per cent of the vote at the time we made our prediction). In fact the Labour Party secured 40·5 per cent of the popular vote to the National Party's 39·5 per cent, most of the remainder going to Social Credit, the third party. Our prediction (40·9 per cent) was thus very close to the Labour vote, more so than the last election result of 39·6 per cent or than the postwar average of 43·9 per cent. Although we had anticipated a decline from its previous 47·4 per cent, our prediction was still 4 per cent above the actual National Party vote. Moreover, we had incorrectly characterised the eventual winner (at least in terms of popular vote – the National Party gained most seats).

This disappointing result stemmed from underestimating the negative effects both of the bad government record and of Mr Muldoon. In the latter case, our prediction had taken a conservative course, reasoning that a man so popular in the last election could not lose his appeal so quickly. But this appears to be wrong. Neither did the existence of a recession elsewhere nor of extremely firm government render the experience of unemployment at home any more tolerable.

Table 4.6 *Issues Anticipated on 8 November 1978 to Influence Voting in Belgian General Election 17 December 1978 with Associated Classifications and Scorings*

Specific Issue	Issue Type	Magnitude of Impact	Direction of Impact	Issue Scores Social-ist	CS
Constitutional objections to French-language rights in peripheral Brussels communes	2 Constitutional	Medium (2)	–Socialist	–2	
Tindemans's popularity for achievements as Prime Minister in negotiating language settlements	5 Candidate reactions	Medium (2)	+CS		+2
Unemployment and economic recession	6 Government record and prospects	Large (3)	–Socialist –CS	–3	–3
Socialist split between French and Flemish wings	8 Ethnic	Large (3)	–Socialist	–3	
SUMMED ISSUE SCORES				–8	–1

For both parties 1 increment in issue scores = 0·89% net
Predicted Social Christian (CS) vote = Basic Vote + issue effects = 37·4 – 0·9 = 36·5%
Predicted Socialist vote = Basic Vote + issue effects = 34·3 – 7·2 = 27·1%

(vi) Belgian General Election, 17 December 1978

The depressed economic situation also constituted an important issue in the Belgian election a month later. The election was precipitated by the objections of the Flemish Social Christians to the proposed linguistic settlement, giving quasi-federal status to Flanders, Wallonia and Brussels, which had been worked out by a coalition of Christian Socials, Socialists and two minor parties since the general election in the preceding year. The objections were made to the constitutionality of awarding linguistic rights to French speakers in the Flemish communes around Brussels, and were aimed particularly at the Socialists. It was thought that Mr Tindemans, the popular Flemish Social Christian Prime Minister, had in fact raised the objections with the object of disadvantaging the Socialists in an election. They were vulnerable in part because of their incipient split into separate Flemish and French wings. Unusually, therefore, the constitutional and ethnic issues tell negatively against the Socialists, rather than for the

Christian Socials. Both parties also shared government responsibility for the gloomy economic record. Our judgements on these points are summarised in Table 4.6 (*The Times*, London, 12 and 29 October 1978; *The Economist*, London, 14 October and 4 November 1978).

Dominated, like all Belgian elections of the last fifteen years, by language and the economy, no issues of significance emerged unexpectedly in the campaign. The final result was 36·3 per cent for the Christian Socials –gratifyingly almost exactly what we had predicted, and closer even than the last election result (35·9 per cent) and the postwar mean (37·8 per cent). The Socialist result also resembled the last – 25·4 per cent compared with 26·4 per cent. Our prediction of 27·1 per cent was less close than this, but closer than the overall mean of 30·6 per cent. On the whole, therefore, the election seems well characterised by our forecast.

(vii) United Kingdom General Election, 3 May 1979

This had been seen as imminent since February 1977 and we had prepared a number of predictions at various times over the succeeding two years, one of which is illustrated in Table 3.1 (p. 61 above). By March 1979 the apathy or hostility of the Scottish and Welsh electors had removed devolution as an issue from the centre of the political stage and produced a breakdown in Labour's implicit coalition with the Nationalists. The government was defeated on a vote of confidence on Wednesday 28 March 1979 and a general election set for 3 May.

This all came at an unfortunate time for Labour which had just had to weather two months of strikes and industrial unrest. These had at one time threatened to bring the whole country to a standstill, and extensive picketing just on the borders of legality had also threatened the political fabric of the nation. Their record as a government in restraining inflation and restoring confidence over the previous four years had been seen by Labour strategists as one of their strongest appeals to the electorate, along with the reassuring image of Mr Callaghan, the Prime Minister. The apparent inability of the government to take decisive action during the unrest had also blunted this image, however, while giving Mrs Thatcher, Leader of the Opposition, a chance to project her own firmness and resolution. Moreover, the apparent strangulation of business by unions favoured the consistent themes urged by the Conservatives over the last four years – the deadening effects of controls, the undue powers of the unions and the need to extend freedom and incentives. The only counter Labour could make was to capitalise on widespread mistrust of the European Economic Community by its insistence on getting a better deal for Britain from the other members and from the Commission. (Based on a whole series of commentaries but immediately on the *Daily Telegraph*, London, January–March 1979. *The Times* did not appear over this period.)

These issues were clearly identified and classified in our final prediction

Table 4.7 *Issues Anticipated on 30 March 1979 to Influence Voting in British General Election 3 May 1979 with Associated Classifications and Scorings*

Specific Issue	Issue Type	Magnitude of Impact	Direction of Impact	Issue Scores Labour	Con- servative
Law on picketing, prevention of violence	1 Civil order	Large (3)	+Conservative		+3
Fair deal for UK from EEC	3 Foreign relationships	Small (1)	+Labour	+1	
Reassuring moderation of Mr Callaghan	5 Candidate reactions	Small (1)	+Labour	+1	
Firmness of Mrs Thatcher	5 Candidate reactions	Small (1)	+Conservative		+1
Collapse of Incomes Policy, vacillation by government during economic crisis, unemployment, inflation – balanced by previous success to summer 1978	6 Government record and prospects	Medium (2)	–Labour		
Creeping extension of bureauracy and regulations, semi-official regulatory bodies (quangos)	12 Government control and planning	Small (1)	+Conservative		+1
Powers of trade unions, need for reform	13 Government regulation in favour of individual	Small (1)	+Conservative		+1
High level of taxation needing to be reduced, increase in individual risk-taking	14 Initiative and freedom	Small (1)	+Conservative		+1
SUMMED ISSUE SCORES				0	+7

For both parties 1 increment in issue scores = 0·89% net of vote
Predicted Labour vote = Basic Vote + issue effects = 42·0 + 0 = 42·0 per cent
Predicted Conservative vote = Basic Vote + issue effects = 40·6 + 6·3 = 46·9 per cent

of 30 March 1979, presented in Table 4.7. They did, in fact, represent those which dominated the campaign. However, the actual percentages obtained by each of the major parties in the election itself were substantially lower than the ones we forecast; 36·9 for Labour and 43·9 for the Conservatives. The immediate reason for these depressed figures was the ability of the third party, the Liberals, to maintain a level of support (13·8 per cent) approaching that which they had obtained in the exceptional elections of 1974. The more fundamental reason, however, since the issues in Table

4.7 appeared in exactly the form and with the impact we anticipated, appears to have been a decline in the Basic Vote of both major parties to a level of about 38·0 per cent. We could not identify such a decline in our analysis of voting from 1950 to 1974 since the exceptional elections in that study constituted only the last two in the chain and the balance of the evidence was in favour of continuity. With three elections showing consistently lower levels of voting for the two main parties, and issues which on all the retrospective evidence seem to have been correctly anticipated giving predictions which are too high, the balance has shifted to indicating a fall in basic levels of support. Other investigations (notably Crewe *et al.*, 1977, pp. 129–90) have come to the same conclusion, independently and earlier, so we are not making out a special case here. (The point is followed up in Chapter 5.)

This implies that any future British prediction would start from Basic Votes of 38 per cent for Labour and Conservative. The present prediction, however, must be judged in relation to the figures advanced before the election. The 42·0 per cent anticipated for Labour is closer to the actual 36·9 per cent than the naïve average of 43·4 per cent, but less close than the previous election result of 39·3 per cent. With the Conservative vote of 43·9 per cent, on the other hand, the postwar average of 43·2 is closest, followed by our 46·9 per cent, with the last election result of 35·9 per cent wildly misleading if applied to the present result.

While polls conducted before and during the campaign concurred in giving the Conservatives a lead over Labour, those reported just after we made our prediction put the lead as high as 21 points (Conservatives 54·5 per cent, Labour 33·5 per cent). An average of all polls on 8 April, weighting for the number of interviews conducted by each, gave the Conservative lead as 13 per cent (*Observer*, London, 8 April 1979). Our prediction was noticeably more accurate in estimating the gap between the parties, and came closer to the percentages the parties actually received. In qualitative terms, therefore, our prediction charted the relative position of the major parties quite well and correctly anticipated that the Conservatives would have a clear but not an annihilating victory.

(viii)   Austrian General Election, 5 May 1979

This election took place at the end of two terms of Social Democratic government under Chancellor Kreisky, who had been instrumental first of all in abandoning the party's old doctrinaire commitments in the 1960s, and then in maintaining good levels of economic progress in the 1970s (all the more remarkable under conditions of world recession). Not only had the Chancellor maintained Austria's delicate neutrality between Soviet and Western blocs, but he had hosted various international meetings such as oil summits and the ratification of the Strategic Arms Limitations Talks, which had lent him added international lustre.

All this made it hard for the conservative People's Party to find a strong issue against him, apart from reiterating old fears about threats to free enterprise. There was one weakness in the Social Democratic position, however, which the People's Party was not in a good position to exploit. In a referendum on proceeding with nuclear development held at the end of the previous year and strongly backed by Kreisky, a majority had voted against. Since the People's Party had also backed the development they could not really turn this popular sentiment in their direction very effectively, but it did unquestionably detract from the socialist appeal.

These issues (*Daily Telegraph*, London, 22 March 1979; *The Economist*, London, 4 November 1978) are summarised in Table 4.8. As the campaign developed it seems likely that the support of the People's Party for free enterprise was so ingrained anyway that it may not have made much impact as a fresh issue. Also the government's achievement in maintaining relative prosperity should probably have been credited with a large rather than a small impact. Broadly speaking, however, the characterisation seems correct.

Table 4.8 *Issues Anticipated on 28 March 1979 to Influence Voting in Austrian General Election 5 May 1979 with Associated Classifications and Scorings*

Specific Issue	Issue Type	Magnitude of Impact	Direction of Impact	Issue Scores SD	People's
Consolidation of Austrian neutrality	3 Foreign relationships	Small (1)	+SD	+1	
Kreisky as world figure and firm leader	5 Candidate reactions	Large (3)	+SD	+3	
Relative economic prosperity in world recession	6 Government record and prospects	Medium (2)	+SD	+2	
Conservationist alarm at nuclear development	12 Government control and planning	Small (1)	−SD	−1	
Strong support for traditional free enterprise	14 Initiative and freedom	Small (1)	+People's		+1
SUMMED ISSUE SCORES				+5	+1

For both parties 1 increment in issues scores = 0·89 per cent net of vote
Predicted Social Democratic (SD) vote = Basic Vote + issue effects = 42·1 + 4·5 = 46 per cent
Predicted People's Party vote = Basic Vote + issue effects = 43·1 + ·9 = 44·0 per cent

Our prediction of 44·0 per cent for the People's Party was too high compared with their actual vote of 41·9 per cent (perhaps in part because of undue weight on the incentives issue), but not unduly so over a five-week period. Previous vote (42·8 per cent) would have predicted better but not their postwar average of 44·2 per cent. In spite of an accurate characterisation of the Social Democrats' issue position our anticipated 46·6 per cent was substantially below their actual 51·0 per cent of the vote – faring slightly better as a predictor than their postwar average (46·3 per cent) but again worse than the previous election result of 50·4 per cent. Polls reported in late March had also more accurately anticipated Social Democratic voting at just under 50 per cent of the vote (*Daily Telegraph*, London, 22 March 1979).

Because we do not seem to have gone wrong on issues, this underestimate suggests that Basic Vote for the Social Democrats is still increasing. It will be remembered that the Austrian Social Democrats are in fact one of the two cases where we recorded Basic Vote as changing in the postwar period (Table 3.4, p. 82). Taking the election of 1979 into account would have the effect of revising this estimate even more firmly upwards, to a level of 44–45 per cent.

In assessing the success of the present forecast, however, we have to stick with the figures actually produced before the election. We certainly identified the Social Democrats as the clear winner. However, the relative closeness of the result would either have left the third party, the Austrian Freedom Party, holding the balance, and counted by both the major groups as a coalition partner, or fostered a grand coalition between the major parties. Their absolute majority left the Social Democrats in complete charge, so qualitatively our prediction rather misrepresented the post-election situation.

(ix)   Canadian General Election, 20 May 1979

Like the British one, this election had been expected over a long period of time and came near to the end of the government's term of office. Economic recession had hit Canada very hard and the Liberal administration had been ineffective in dealing with it. Internally the government had been plagued by a high turnover of English-speaking ministers and some minor scandals, so it did not even confront the crisis with a credible display of cohesion. After ten years at the centre of Canadian politics, the Liberal leader and Prime Minister, Pierre Trudeau, had lost much of his former appeal and seemed to repel as many voters as he won over. The main issue favouring the Liberal Party was still their ability to stave off the threat of secession. However, the concessions which this policy entailed – notably bilingualism and a disproportionate flow of federal resources to Quebec –had fed resentments in the Maritimes and particularly the West, which played into the hands of the opposition Conservative Party. Related proposals to revise the British North America Act in order to 'repatriate' the constitution had raised fears as to the powers this might put into the government's hands and had been vigorously criticised during the previous summer, although the issue had been somewhat muffled during the winter.

These constituted the issues on which we based our prediction (from reports over a long period but immediately the *Daily Telegraph*, London, 27 February and 26 March 1979) (Table 4.9). In the actual campaign the personality of the two leaders loomed large: Trudeau acting very abrasively in the opening weeks but switching tactics in the last two to become more statesmanlike. Clark, the Conservative leader, had always appeared in the press and Liberal rhetoric as bumbling and inept. By limiting personal exposure he at least avoided any serious misadventure. Since both leaders seemed to repel as many electors as they attracted, we feel we were right to regard them as neutral factors in our prediction.

Table 4.9 *Issues Anticipated on 28 March 1979 to Influence Voting in Canadian General Election 22 May 1979 with Associated Classifications and Scorings*

Specific Issue	Issue Type	Magnitude of Impact	Direction of Impact	Issue Scores Liberal	Con-servative
Proposed 'repatriation' of constitution, amendment of British North American Act	2 Constitutional	Medium (2)	+Conservative		+2
Unemployment, inflation and government ineffectiveness	6 Government record and prospects	Large (3)	–Liberal	–3	
Threat of Quebec secession,	9A National unity	Large (3)	+Liberal	+3	
resentment in Maritimes and West of biculturalism and concessions to Quebec	9 Regional	Large (3)	+Conservative		+3

SUMMED ISSUE SCORES   0   +5

For Liberals 1 increment in issues scores = 0·89%
For Progressive Conservatives 1 increment in issue scores = 0·89% net
Predicted Liberal vote = Basic Vote + issue effects = 38·9 + 0 = 38·9% net
Predicted Conservative vote = Basic Vote + issue effects = 33·9 + 4·5 = 38·4%

An issue which did emerge, and which we should possibly have included, was Clark's promise of mortgage reliefs to home owners. The new constitution was absent as an issue in preliminary newspaper reports. Our inclusion of it was vindicated, however, by Trudeau making it a central campaign appeal (unwisely in our opinion, since it was likely to benefit the Conservatives rather than himself) (*Daily Telegraph*, London,

11 May 1979). So generally the issues in Table 4.9 do seem to have been correctly anticipated.

They also produced a good correspondence between prediction and actual voting. The actual Liberal vote of 40·0 per cent was quite close to our forecast of 38·9 per cent (and this was closer than either the postwar mean of 41·7 per cent or than the Liberal percentage in the preceding election – 43·2 per cent). We overestimated the Conservative vote (38·4 per cent compared to the actual 36·0 per cent, with both postwar mean of 35·1 per cent and previous result of 35·4 per cent closer). However, the error of 2·4 per cent is not unreasonable over a period of nearly two months – a Gallup poll at the beginning of May had Conservatives and Liberals tied at 41 per cent of the decided voters. Furthermore, the prediction gives a very accurate indication of the post-election situation, where owing to the accumulation of wasted Liberal votes in Quebec a narrow lead in popular votes is bound to give the Conservatives a plurality of seats (as did in fact happen). Our prediction also indicated that the third party vote would hold up, so that a minority government was likely. All in all this must be reckoned as one of our most successful predictions, both qualitatively and quantitatively.

(x) Italian General Election, 5 June 1979

The last prediction relates to Italy, where an election had been increasingly likely as polls showed the Communists losing support and Christian Democrats gaining it. This made the latter intransigent in denying Communist ministers a place in government as the price of their continued voting support which, in turn, made the formation of stable new coalitions impossible.

Outside political manoeuvring there seemed, however, little objective need for an election, the issues remaining the containment of terrorism, the great need for social reform in almost all spheres of life, the very mixed economic record of the government, and relationships with the Western Alliance should the Communists enter government. The Communists, who had seemed to offer a fresh and attractive alternative in the early 1970s, had lost much of their appeal as a result of implicit support for government manoeuvrings and compromises, although their Secretary, Berlinguer, remained an attractive figure. Table 4.10 presents these judgements (*The Economist*, London, 14 January, 14 October, 4 November, 16 December 1978; *Daily Telegraph*, London, 9 February and 22 March 1979), which were confirmed by the course of the campaign – generally agreed to be unexciting so far as the major parties were concerned.

This is reflected in the actual votes. Far from gaining the 4·5 per cent that polls had indicated, or even the modest 1 per cent we had credited them with, the Christian Democrats actually lost a small amount, dropping from 38·7 in the previous election to 38·1 per cent. The last result was thus a better predictor than our theory in this case, although the postwar average of 40·4 performed more poorly.

Table 4.10 *Issues Anticipated on 28 March 1979 to Influence Voting in Italian General Election 5 June 1979 with Associated Classifications and Scorings*

Specific Issue	Issue Type	Magnitude of Impact	Direction of Impact	Issue Scores Communist	CD
Containment of terrorism	1 Civil order	Large (3)	+CD		+3
Relations with NATO should Communists enter government	3 Foreign relationships	Small (1)	+CD		+1
Pragmatism of Berlinguer	5 Candidate reactions	Small (1)	+Communist	+1	
Modest economic recovery balanced by economic crisis and austerity 1972–7	6 Government record and prospects	Neutral (0)			
Need for social reforms	11 Socio-economic redistribution	Large (3)	+Communist	+3	

SUMMED ISSUE SCORES   +4   +4

For Communists 1 increment in issue scores = 2·30% net
For Christian Democrats (CD) 1 increment in issue scores = 0·89% net
Predicted Communist vote = Basic Vote + issue effects = 20·1 + 9·2% = 29·3%
Predicted Christian Democratic vote = Basic Vote = Basic Vote + issue effects = 35·9 + 3·6 = 39·5%

We were, however, out by less than a percentage point so far as the Communist vote was concerned (29·3 compared to an actual 30·4 per cent). Their postwar average (25·7 per cent) fell well below the present result, and their previous result was much too high (34·4 per cent).

Our prediction thus anticipated correctly the substantial fall in Communist support, and the relatively better performance of the Christian Democrats. Effectively, therefore, it also captured the leading features of the post-election situation – one of no change, in which Christian Democrats continued to dominate government, and Communists to form a bloc too large to be ignored.

Out of the ten predictions described, we should, in broad qualitative terms, judge seven to be reasonably successful and three – the Australian, New Zealand and Austrian – to be rather misleading. Certainly these are not unqualified failures (just as some of the others are not an unqualified success). Depending on the criteria used, different aspects of the prediction may be emphasised. Here we have concentrated on the overall characterisation of individual outcomes: in Section 4.2 we carry out a more rigorous comparative evaluation.

Seven out of ten is certainly a reasonable success rate if it is upheld on further evaluation. Table 4.11 summarises the information about individual predictions on which we have based the qualitative assessments and which is evaluated systematically and comparatively below.

4.2   A Comparative Evaluation of Predictive Success

We have already specified the four naïve methods of prediction generally compared with theoretical forecasts where there is no pre-existing theory against which to measure success. These are, for continuous 'measured' data, the mean of past outcomes or, where these are ordered, the last result. For 'qualitative' 'unmeasured' data the corresponding methods are to use the result which has occurred most frequently in the past, or (again) the last result.

None of the naïve methods emerges as clearly best when used retrospectively to characterise outcomes in the past. Each works better for some countries and parties than for others. We have accordingly measured the success of our theoretical predictions against that of each of the four methods, over all the elections we are dealing with. Some basic information necessary to make this comparison has already been given in Table 4.11. This is expanded in Table 4.12, which compares the discrepancies between predicted and actual results over twenty-one cases for our theoretical prediction, the overall mean vote in previous elections, and the last election result. There are twenty-one such deviations reported in the table, since for Iceland we consider only one party (the Independence Party) but for France we have first and second ballots, which in a quantitative comparison we have no choice but to consider as separate cases.

It is useful to look for a pattern in the overall deviations, since a consistent bias towards either overestimating or underestimating would indicate the presence of some systematic error in our theory. The easiest way to check is to calculate the mean of the deviations in column five to see how far it departs from zero – which is the value it would assume if errors on either side of the actual result tended to balance each other out. The mean of deviations for our theoretical prediction actually approaches zero (0·20), demonstrating that there is no major systematic bias.

As it summarises the extent to which, overall, our predictions diverge from the true figure, this mean should be compared with the corresponding means for the naïve predictions, to see how much closer to zero it is than they are. Our figure of 0·20 compares reasonably well with –0·06 for differences between the overall previous mean and actual results, and with

Table 4.11   Predicted and Actual Outcomes over Ten Elections July 1977–June 1979

Election	Polling Date	Date of Final Prediction	Parties/ Tendances	Theoretically Predicted % of Vote	Actual % of Vote
Norwegian Storting	September 1977	31 July 1977	Labour	44·7	42·4
			Bourgeois	48·0	48·6
Australian general election	10 December 1977	10 November 1977	Labour	43·3	40·0
			Liberal-Country Party coalition	43·8	48·0
French Assembly first ballot	12 March 1978	20 January 1978	Government Parties	39·1	44·1
			Union of the Left	45·9	45·2
second ballot	19 March 1978	20 January 1978	Government Parties	49·2	50·5
			Union of the Left	44·0	49·3
Icelandic general election	25 June 1978	30 May 1978	Independence	34·6	32·1
New Zealand general election	25 November 1978	22 October 1978	Labour	40·9	40·5
			National	43·4	39·5
Belgian general election	17 December 1978	8 November 1978	Socialists	27·1	25·4
			Christian Socials	36·5	36·3
United Kingdom general election	3 May 1979	30 March 1979	Labour	42·0	36·9
			Conservative	46·9	43·9
Austrian general election	5 May 1979	28 March 1979	Social Democrats	46·6	51·0
			People's	44·0	41·9
Canadian general election	20 May 1979	28 March 1979	Liberal	38·9	40·0
			Progressive Conservative	38·4	36·0
Italian general election	5 June 1979	28 March 1979	Communist	29·3	30·4
			Christian Democrats	39·5	38·1

−0·12 for discrepancies between the present and previous election result. The fact that neither of the other means departs very far from zero demonstrates, however, how well we can manage in the field of elections by using an a-theoretical prediction. Of course, the advantages of theory are not primarily predictive, but rest rather on the enhancement of knowledge which it provides. Where this is combined with even a slightly better forecasting performance, it is preferable to blind extrapolation.

The small mean deviation might be produced by larger deviations on both sides cancelling out, rather than by a genuine reduction in error. However, a scan over individual figures in the last three columns of Table 4.12 shows that any such effects are more likely to be working on the side of the naïve rather than of the theoretical prediction. The largest deviations from the theoretical prediction are the Australian Liberal–Country Party's underestimate of 4·2 per cent (on first preference votes); the French underestimate of 5·0 for government parties on the first ballot and 5·3 per cent for the minority party on the second ballot; 4·4 per cent for the Austrian Social Democrats; and the overestimate of 5·1 per cent for British Labour. Individual deviations are both more frequent and more marked for the naïve predictors. This is not only evident from a comparison of specific cases, but from contrasting the extent to which the individual errors differ from their means.

If, on the whole, the individual deviations of predictions from the true score vary more about their mean for the theoretical prediction compared with the naïve predictions, the standard deviation of the former ought to be larger than the standard deviation for the latter, and vice versa. In fact the standard deviation for the theoretical prediction is smallest at 2·88, followed by that for the last election result (4·77), with the standard deviation for errors associated with using the overall mean being largest (5·00). Differences in this measure are in fact larger and more impressive than they are for the means; this shows that our theoretical reasoning consistently gets estimates closer to an overall, limited, mean error than do the naïve predictions. Similar results are obtained for the mean squared error – the extent to which estimates vary round a notional zero error.

How far is the better performance of the theoretical predictions based on results from Norway and Australia, where general estimates were not used, and on the two French ballots, where special assumptions about the fate of the centrist vote were added to the predictive model? In fact our predictive performance was slightly worse in these cases (a mean error of −1·4 compared to the overall 0·20, and standard deviation of 3·12 compared to 2·88). Thus inclusion of the first three cases represents a conservative element in our evaluation and does not unduly boost our success rate.

So far we have concentrated on comparisons using percentage differences. For some purposes it may be more important to predict the winner – or at least the party which obtains a plurality of the vote. Our theoretically based prediction correctly identifies the leading party nine

Table 4.12 Deviations between Anticipated and Actual Result for Theoretical and Naïve Predictions over Ten Elections

	Percentage Party Vote Predicted:				Deviation of Predictions from Actual Result for:		
	From Theory	From Overall Mean	From Last Election Result	Actual Election Result	Theoretical Prediction	Mean Prediction	Last Election Prediction
Norwegian Labour	44·7	44·3	35·3	42·4	+2·3	+1·9	-7·1
Norwegian bourgeois	48·0	48·4	44·2	48·6	-0·6	-0·2	-4·4
Australian Labour	43·3	45·9	43·1	41·0	+2·3	+4·9	+2·1
Australian Liberal–Country Party coalition	43·8	47·9	53·0	48·0	-4·2	-0·1	+5·0
French government parties first ballot	39·1	35·8	38·0	44·1	-5·0	-8·3	-6·1
French Union of the Left first ballot	45·9	39·9	43·7	45·3	0·6	-5·4	-1·6
French government parties second ballot	49·2	39·2	46·1	50·5	-1·3	-11·3	-4·4
French Union of the Left second ballot	44·0	42·1	42·8	49·3	-5·3	-7·2	-6·5
Icelandic Independence Party	34·6	39·3	42·8	32·7	1·9	6·6	9·9
New Zealand Labour	40·9	43·9	39·6	40·5	0·4	3·4	-0·9
New Zealand National	43·4	45·4	47·4	39·5	3·9	5·9	8·9
Belgian Socialist	27·1	30·6	26·4	25·4	1·7	5·2	1·0
Belgian Christian Socials	36·5	37·8	35·9	36·3	0·2	1·5	-0·4
UK Labour	42·0	43·4	39·3	36·9	5·1	6·5	2·4
UK Conservative	46·9	43·2	35·9	43·9	3·0	-0·7	-8·0
Austrian Social Democrats	46·6	46·3	50·4	51·0	-4·4	-4·7	-0·6
Austrian People's	44·0	44·2	42·8	41·9	2·1	2·3	0·9
Canadian Liberals	38·9	41·7	43·2	40·0	-1·1	1·7	3·2
Canadian Progressive Conservatives	38·4	35·1	35·4	36·0	2·4	-0·9	-0·6
Italian Communists	29·3	25·7	34·4	30·4	-1·1	-4·7	4·0
Italian Christian Democrats	39·5	40·4	38·7	38·1	1·4	2·3	0·6

times out of ten (again, we have nothing with which to compare the Icelandic Independence Party, and have to count the two French ballots as different trials). Prediction from the most frequent leader in the past has seven successes out of ten; and from the last election result, eight successes out of ten. Again our theory leads, but narrowly, over the extrapolations. If only the elections based strictly on our comparative estimates are included, our approach has five out of six successes; and both naïve extrapolations have four out of six. Again the narrower comparison produces essentially similar results.

Both individual qualitative assessments of our predictive success and the general quantitative comparison with two kinds of extrapolation show that a better forecast can be made using our approach than by using other available methods. The improvement in accuracy is slight but it is real – and in a field where extrapolation produces such good results, any improvement is hard to achieve. Predictive success is less of a recommendation for the theory than its ability to explain and relate disparate election phenomena over a wide area. Nevertheless, it helps demonstrate that the explanation actually works, and provides further grounds for accepting and applying it.

Chapter 5

Electoral Volatility

The foregoing estimates and predictions were made before summer 1979 when we completed the draft manuscript. In the two years until final revision in September 1981, elections have been held in most countries – which substantially adds to the limited number of postwar results.

The working of our predictions also points to the need for some revision in earlier figures. We have therefore taken the opportunity of updating estimates to mid-1981 and tidying up data sets on which they are based. This has involved checking all figures and correcting a few inaccuracies which crept into our 1978 analysis: but principally starting with the elections of 1950 or as soon as possible thereafter. To have different starting points except where it is unavoidable (West Germany, Japan and Sri Lanka) produces accidental differences between the country analyses.

Revising estimates on the basis of a rather different data set also tests how stable they are. The question of stability was tackled inferentially through the use of confidence intervals in Chapter 3, but another test is the similarity between earlier and later estimates once the data base changes (Section 5.1 below).

Once revised estimates have been made in light of later knowledge we can go on to check the voting effects attributable to individual types of issue, rather than simply relating overall issue scores to vote as we have done up to now (Section 5.2). Having confirmed that they are broadly in line with expectations, we can proceed to substantive investigation of a central election phenomenon – voting change and electoral volatility (Section 5.3).

5.1   Revised Estimates

Once we have modified data sets starting with 1950 or the election immediately following that date (apart from Sri Lanka), and including all elections up to July 1981, analyses can be carried out along the lines described in Chapter 3, Sections 3.2 and 3.3 (pp. 63 and 68). That is, issue scores are related separately to vote for each party or bloc in each country. These give rise to slope estimates – which measure issue effects – as in Tables 3.2 and 3.3.

In the exploratory analysis of Chapter 3 we were particularly concerned to use individual party estimates and confidence intervals rather than a global estimate of an overall slope and tests for inconsistency, in order to be certain that there was a genuine similarity of issue effects over all countries. It was too easy at the preliminary stage to come up with an average effect and impose it on the individual party data, rather than letting it emerge from the analysis. Now, however, we are much more certain of the overall similarity of issue effects. So we can simplify by focusing Table 5.1 on the question of whether the estimated slope for each overlapping party is consistent with (*a*) no issue effects at all, or (*b*) with the overall issue effect obtained by using one least squares estimate of the slope from all the data.

Table 5.1　*Estimate of Slope (i.e. Issue Effects) for Individual Socialist–Reformist Parties over Period 1950–81*

Country	Estimate of Slope b	Standard Error of Slope b	Consistent with a True Slope	
			b=0?	b=0·96?
Australia	0·7	0·25	No	Yes
Austria	1·5	0·39	No	Yes
Belgium	0·9	0·10	No	Yes
Canada	0·9	0·14	No	Yes
Denmark	1·1	0·34	No	Yes
Finland	1·0	0·12	No	Yes
France*	–	–	–	–
Iceland	1·1	0·67	Yes	Yes
India	0·5	0·06	No	No
Ireland	0·8	0·19	No	Yes
Israel	1·5	0·37	No	Yes
Italy	1·8	0·72	No	Yes
Japan	0·7	0·89	Yes	Yes
Luxembourg	1·2	0·23	No	Yes
Netherlands	1·2	0·39	No	Yes
New Zealand	0·7	0·25	No	Yes
Norway	0·8	0·17	No	Yes
Sri Lanka	0·7	0·66	Yes	Yes
Sweden	0·7	0·19	No	Yes
Switzerland	0·4	0·16	Yes	No
United Kingdom	0·9	0·32	No	Yes
United States	2·1	0·55	No	Yes
West Germany	0·7	0·77	Yes	Yes

*France omitted from all averages
Average slopes:

Overall socialist parties	0·91	Omitting India and Switzerland	1·02
Overall parties	0·87	Omitting India, Switzerland and Scandinavian bourgeois parties	0·96

Since we now have reason to believe in the existence of a single value for the issue effects, it is of some interest to test the null hypothesis that the issue effects are constant for all socialist parties and for all bourgeois parties. A single, overall test of this equality is provided by an analysis of variance into components due to overall slope, variation in slopes between countries and the residual variance about the individual lines of best fit. The results are very reassuring. For bourgeois parties the single slope is highly significant (an F-ratio of 67·7 based on degrees of freedom $n_1 = 1$, $n_2 = 118$), the variation between slopes is not significant at the 10 per cent level (F-ratio of 1·44 based on degrees of freedom $n_1 = 17$, $n_2 = 118$), and the residual variance is 15·64 giving a standard deviation of 4·0 units per cent. For socialist parties the results are even more reassuring. The corresponding F-ratios for a single-slope estimate and variation between slopes are a highly significant 173·0 and non-significant 0·9 with a residual variance of 8·23 giving a standard deviation of 2·9 units per cent. This analysis of variance quantifies the impression gained from the individual graphs that prediction is more difficult for bourgeois parties.

Table 5.2   *Estimate of Slope (i.e. Issue Effects) for Individual Bourgeois–Reformist Parties over Period 1950–81*

Country	Estimate of Slope b	Standard Error of Slope b	Consistent with a True Slope	
			b=0?	b=0·96?
Australia	0·5	0·31	Yes	Yes
Austria	0·6	0·24	Yes	Yes
Belgium	2·2	0·78	No	Yes
Canada	1·4	0·36	No	Yes
Denmark	–0·6	1·13	Yes	Yes
Finland	0·7	0·16	No	Yes
France*	–	–	–	–
Iceland	1·0	0·15	No	Yes
India*	–	–	–	–
Ireland	0·1	0·39	Yes	Yes
Israel	0·9	0·22	No	Yes
Italy	0·6	0·47	Yes	Yes
Japan	1·0	0·13	No	Yes
Luxembourg	2·1	1·09	Yes	Yes
Netherlands	0·1	0·89	Yes	Yes
New Zealand	0·5	0·39	Yes	Yes
Norway	–1·4	1·13	Yes	Yes
Sri Lanka	1·9	1·59	Yes	Yes
Sweden	–0·9	0·79	Yes	Yes
Switzerland	0·2	0·48	Yes	Yes
United Kingdom	1·2	0·15	No	Yes
United States	1·4	0·29	No	Yes
West Germany	0·3	0·39	Yes	Yes

* France and India omitted from all averages

Average slopes:

Overall bourgeois parties	0·81	Omitting Scandinavian parties	0·90
Overall parties	0·87	Omitting India, Switzerland and Scandinavian bourgeois parties	0·96

When looking in detail at the individual graphs the evidence is sparse in some cases and the results are individually consistent both with zero issue effects and with the overall effect. Since we are not now checking the reality of the effect, we consider as negative results only those definitely inconsistent with the overall estimate. Table 5.1 is analogous to Table 3.2 in presenting estimates of issue effects for socialist and reformist parties (though based on the updated and revised data set). It differs in form by giving the estimate with its standard error and the results for checks of consistency with two natural null hypotheses. Is the issue effect zero, and is the issue effect the same as the overall estimate? The really important question is whether the confidence interval extends to cover the revised general estimate of issue effects (now 0·96 per cent per increment in issue scores as compared to the previous 0·89 per cent). In the case of socialist–reformist parties, all but two have intervals consistent with 0·96 per cent. Only the Swiss Socialists and Indian Congress are consistent with zero but not with the general estimate. In these cases the estimates of 0·37 per cent and 0·55 per cent are retained. The wider variability of values for bourgeois parties, which is as evident in Table 5.2 as in the analogous Table 3.3, means that all individual estimates are compatible with the general figure of 0·96.

This now fits both US Democrats and Republicans. On the other hand, the individual estimates for these parties are both on the high side. In view of the indications from other research and from our earlier analysis that issues have more effect in the United States than elsewhere, future predictions should still use a higher estimate, of the order of 1·70 per cent. Apart from Switzerland and India, and the Scandinavian bourgeois parties (Danish now as well as Norwegian and Swedish), the general estimate can be employed throughout. It gives a range of issue effects, from roughly 1 per cent for a small impact issue to 3 per cent for a large, which is also consistent with values obtained using other assumptions on different data (Chapter 1 above). Its closeness to the earlier estimate of 0·89 per cent testifies to the stability of both.

Generally individual country estimates are quite similar between the earlier and later analysis, as can be seen by comparing Tables 3.2 and 3.3 (pp. 69 and 72) with Tables 5.1 and 5.2. When substantial differences occur, they are generally associated with smaller numbers of elections where omission or addition of a set of results makes a considerable difference; or with long-term growth and decline in party support (see Table 5.5, p. 126 below). As no allowance has been made for this in our estimates it can affect individual values quite considerably. Here again the general estimate is more stable and reliable because it is based on larger numbers and is relatively unaffected by particular party changes. Hence we shall use this estimate in our remaining analyses, including the investigation of changes in Basic Votes (Section 5.3). Before coming to that, however, we wish to check the effects attributed to each type of issue more closely than we have hitherto been able to do.

5.2   Voting Effects of Individual Issue Types

In setting up Table 2.6 (p. 50 above) we assumed that different issue types exerted 'large' or 'small' effects, with one type (constitutional issues) exerting 'medium' effects. There were also erratic issues – candidates and government record – whose impact could vary from small to medium to large, depending on circumstances. For the United States, Canada and Ireland we postulated related effects, but rather different impacts for some types of issue. Note that these weights are assigned in terms of the number of votes likely to be affected by the issue, not in terms of varying impacts on the individual. On the contrary, each elector is likely to weight all the issues important to him equally as one, and to decide his vote in terms of the party which scores highest over the equally weighted issues (see Section 2.1, p. 22 above).

For the aggregate analysis we scored a non-salient issue as zero, and among salient issues a small impact as one, medium as two and large as three. This procedure is supported by an analysis of alternative scoring systems (Appendix D) and also by our success in relating the summed scores for each party in an election to the corresponding vote.

Strictly speaking, however, both these checks simply relate overall issue scores to votes. This supports the scoring we have assigned to individual issue types so far as it contributes to the overall scores. None the less the results could have been achieved despite weighting some particular issue type wrongly, particularly if it were consistently balanced by wrong weighting of another type.

It is important to check all assumptions if we can. It would be unsatisfactory to have the overall working of the model dependent on detailed scoring errors. Moreover, a comprehensive explanation of issue effects should be concerned with the answers to questions similar to the following. What is the general effect of law and order as an issue? Which party benefits and by how much? Answers to these questions are of great importance for evaluating party strategies in the next chapter.

If possible, we should not base such answers simply on the overall success of our issue scores but examine the effects of the issue types themselves. In particular, we should see if their observed effects are consistent with the impact we attribute to them. We cannot rely on the data from any one country, since it is too limited; instead we base estimates on the data we combined to produce the general estimate of 0·96 per cent.

We have explored the deviations of the actual percentage vote from that predicted by the issue score and the general estimate 0·96 rather than the individual party estimates. Dividing these deviations into groups corresponding to the differing score values for a particular issue type in each election, ignoring the values for the others, enables us to check whether the deviations vary systematically from issue type to issue type or from one point on the scoring scale to another. For example, if the true effect of a particular issue type was 0·5 rather than 0·96, then the predicted vote would be on average 0·46 per cent high when the issue score was +1, 0·92 per cent high when the issue score was +2. Again, if the dependence on issue score was not linear, the per cent vote for an issue score of +1 could be underestimated and for an issue score of +2 could be overestimated. If, on the other hand, the adjustments reflect actual issue impacts reasonably well, the deviations will show a similar pattern no matter how we may position them in terms of the prediction variables. In particular, they should centre around a zero or near-zero average. In effect we make an adjustment for the effect of issues other than the one studied by using the general estimate 0·96 and then we explore whether this 0·96 is suitable for the issue type studied.

A systematic search of the subsets of deviations produced by partitioning in turn on the scores of each of the issues showed that for all except government record and prospects the deviations fell into subsets consistent with zero means – demonstrating that our scoring system characterises these issue types quite accurately.

The case of government record is interesting, particularly since it appears to tie in with the econometric research into issue effects cited in Chapter 1. For this reason, and also to illustrate the general procedure, we reproduce deviations and tests for this issue type in Table 5.3.

Table 5.3   *Average Deviations between Observed Per Cent Votes and those Predicted by Overall Estimate*

Issue Score		Number of Elections	Average Deviation	
Bourgeois	+3	17	−1·43	(2·40*)
	+2	4	−2·85	(1·52)
	+1	14	2·11	(1·66)
	0	45	−0·36	
	−1	13	0·72	(0·98)
	−2	5	−0·02	(0·04)
	−3	39	0·27	(0·38)
Socialist–Reformist	+3	16	0·02	(0·02)
	+2	12	−0·25	(0·56)
	+1	10	0·23	(0·31)
	0	61	−0·82	
	−1	9	2·36	(4·56**)
	−2	6	2·74	(2·77*)
	−3	23	0·57	(0·69)

* Significant at 5% level
** Significant at 1% level

As government record and prospects may take on scores of zero, one, two or three depending on circumstances, all of these are shown in the table. Such scores may be assigned negatively or positively, to either the bourgeois or socialist–reformist party. All these cases are examined separately, and the number of times each occurred is also reported. For each case the table reports the average deviation of observed vote from actual vote, and applies a t-test to check whether the deviations have a mean that differs significantly from zero (the t-values are shown in brackets).

By examining the deviations at each scoring level in turn the procedure checks for curvilinear effects, in the sense that the average deviations for a score of one, a score of two and a score of three might differ significantly from the ratio 1:2:3. No such effects appeared for other issues (where, of course, the range of scores was much less, particularly for those with fixed rather than erratic effects).

In the case of government record, however, there are significant t-values at the scores of +3 for bourgeois parties and at −1 and −2 for socialist–reformist parties. It seems from this that bourgeois parties do not benefit as much as we predicted from a good record or prospects in government, and that their opponents suffer less than expected from a poor record or promise of performance. This recalls the asymmetrical effects identified by Bloom and Price (1975) (p. 3 above), where governments were punished for a bad economic record but not significantly rewarded for a good one. Our finding interestingly refines this by suggesting that effects also differ between parties. Bourgeois parties are punished for a bad record but not proportionately rewarded for a good one. Socialist–reformist parties experience a reverse effect where they get credit for a good record or prospects and tolerance for bad performance or bickering when in opposition.

This asymmetry is readily interpretable given bourgeois parties' attempts to present themselves as the business party able to deal with affairs efficiently (Table 6.1 p. 132 below). They may, as a result, be judged more critically on performance than socialist parties, which are not expected to be so efficient. The link between this and findings from a different approach with other data represents another element of continuity in research.

One has nevertheless to treat the figures as suggestive rather than final. They are embedded in over sixty comparisons so an occasional highly significant result is to be expected. Rather than indicating that the scores should be changed for this issue type, they can be taken as a caveat, when coding, not to be overimpressed by good bourgeois records or prospects in government, nor by a poor record or internal divisions for socialist or reformist parties. No other issue type produces such caveats or any other indication that the assigned scores are inappropriate, so the judgements summarised in Tables 2.6 to 2.9 can be taken as retrospectively validated.

5.3 Voting Fluctuations and Electoral Volatility

Now that our estimates both of broad party issue appeals and of the effects of individual issues have been broadly confirmed and updated, we can apply them to an important substantive investigation. This is the question of whether parties have been gaining or losing support at an increasing rate over the last ten or fifteen years. Concern over this point has been, sharpened by certain spectacular events, particularly of the late 1960s and early 1970s. These involved a seeming transformation of some party systems (e.g. Belgium, India); a mushrooming of new parties (e.g. Denmark, Norway, United Kingdom); a decline of some established parties (e.g. Japan, Italy, Netherlands); and a general growth and consolidation of socialist alternatives (e.g. Canada, France, Italy, West Germany, Austria).

Some of these developments have proved transitory, as in India and Japan, where the dominant parties have re-established themselves, or in Italy where the Communist growth has been checked. Elsewhere, however, electoral change seems to continue at a quickening pace, as in France where the Union of the Left has broken into government or in Britain where a significant third party has formed through the alliance of Social Democrats and Liberals. So the question remains as to whether a fundamental change is occurring in the basis of party support, at least in many countries, or whether these are temporary realignments which do not challenge earlier orthodoxy on the underlying stability of Western party systems since the 1920s (Lipset and Rokkan, 1967).

Most studies of these developments have measured volatility through differences in the percentage vote received by each party in consecutive or successive elections (e.g. Børre, 1980). No other measure which has been employed seems more sensitive to change in overall party balance (Pedersen, 1980).

Certainly percentage differences are ideal for the descriptive task of pinpointing elections and parties which have witnessed major voting shifts. They do not tell us very much, though, about the point of real concern: what do these shifts portend? Are they, as suspected, part of a continuing haemorrhage of loyal supporters out of some parties into others, or out of parties altogether? Or are they just more marked short-term fluctuations which will right themselves eventually, leaving core support untouched? Depending on the answer one is more or less optimistic about long-term prospects for existing parties.

As our approach makes precisely this distinction between short-term fluctuations due to 'normal' issue effects, and levels of underlying support expressed through the Basic Vote, it provides a way of differentiating them and particularly for discovering whether underlying party strengths have been affected by recent voting shifts. The relatively good fit between estimates and observed votes over the postwar period eliminates a third possibility – that electoral volatility might invalidate some of our assumptions based on the earlier postwar period and appear in discrepancies between actual results and those expected on the basis of our explanation. We can therefore examine the extent of volatility within our framework and particularly in terms of the distinction between issue effects and Basic Vote.

The term 'volatility' is a borrowing from the physical sciences (like the idea of 'short-term forces' themselves which is analysed in Chapter 7, Section 7.2, p. 149 below). It refers to the ease of transition of a substance between one state and another – liquid to gas, for example. The equivalent in the case of elections seems to be the speed of transition of support from one party to another.

From one point of view the ease of transition of support can be related to the impact of issues. As Tables 5.1 and 5.2 show, some party electorates respond more extensively than others to the prominence of issues. Actual estimates vary a good deal, of course, but since most can be fitted by the general figure of 0·96 per cent it is better to use this in comparisons and to contrast the parties to which it applies with, on the one hand, those where the response to issues is obviously lower and those where it is markedly higher.

The parties whose voters are least affected by issues are the Swiss Socialists and Indian Congress. Issues probably affect fewer electors than elsewhere on the Swiss bourgeois side as well, since the actual estimate of effects there is very low: it is covered by the general estimate because of the wide confidence interval. Swiss electors' responsiveness is obviously affected by the institutional context. The very wide autonomy enjoyed by individual cantons leaves most issues to be fought out and settled at local level. Partly as a consequence, the national government has been conducted by a coalition of the main parties, including Socialists, since the First World War. Since national elections hardly affect the composition of government and major issues are lacking, it is hardly surprising that electors respond sluggishly.

In India there is a definite reaction to issues, but the size of the issue effect is still only half of that found overall. This is most probably due to social factors such as the vast size of the country and electorate and strong caste and regional differentiations which limit knowledge of national initiatives.

It seems likely that the impact of issues is greater in the United States, where our suggested estimate is almost double the general one. The greater impact of issues here is due, first, to the position of the United States as a world power, affected much more strongly by foreign events which elsewhere pass over electors' heads; and secondly to the social composition of the US electorate, much less rooted in particular places and groups than Europeans or Asians. As a result issues are mediated less through continuing social preoccupations leaving electors less fixated on a particular topic and more prone to respond to events of the campaign. Issue consequences are, in any case, objectively more marked. All these points are reflected in the different basis of coding for the United States (Table 2.7, p. 52 above).

Voting changes produced by issues are not confined to the greater or lesser impact of a single issue. They may also be affected by the number of macro-issues which become salient in any one campaign. We have already seen that countries vary quite considerably on this (Table 2.2, p. 35 above). Switzerland has few or no issues at national level and the northern Scandinavian countries only a limited number. The United States and India are among the countries where large numbers of issues normally emerge.

The countries with least short-term volatility are those where issues have a limited impact anyway and where few or no issues come to prominence in national elections. Switzerland is the archetype. In contrast, big percentage differences between successive party votes should open up where more electors respond to issues anyway, and where more issues tend to become important. The archetype here is the United States.

There are intermediate cases, the most interesting being perhaps India. Here individual types of issue have a more limited impact than elsewhere, but on the other hand more issues become prominent. This accounts for the considerable ebb and flow of support towards the Congress Party over the years. Britain represents a case where single issues have the same impact as in other countries but where there are many more of them.

Even where striking percentage changes in party vote appear, therefore, analysts should be wary of attributing them automatically to shifts of underlying strength. In countries like India and the United States they may well stem from the normal working of electoral competition. Large percentage changes in voting support will be more likely to reflect basic change for electorates with average or low sensitivity to issues, and medium or low numbers of issues becoming prominent in the election.

It is, of course, volatility in its other sense (loyalists becoming floating voters or supporters of other parties) that is the real focus of current debate. A measure of the stability of underlying support is provided by our estimates of Basic Vote. This is defined and measured as the percentage of votes a party would attract with zero issue scores. While Basic Vote normally includes issue changers traded reciprocally with the other party, it comprises an even higher proportion of loyalists voting regularly for the party. As there is no obvious reason for the number of reciprocal changers to alter, any change in Basic Vote should reflect losses or gains of loyalists and hence measure fluctuations in underlying support for the party (see Section 3.4, p. 73 above).

Since this is a topic of major current concern, both academic and practical, it deserves careful examination. Our revised estimates provide a basis for examining changes more subtly than before. Previously we measured Basic Vote as percentage of votes corresponding to zero issue scores on the average line relating issue scores to votes over all postwar elections. The slope of the line was 0·89 per cent where that general estimate fitted the party under examination – otherwise it was the individual estimate. Where two parallel lines seemed to fit the observations better than one, and they corresponded to different temporal sequences of elections, we had an indication that Basic Vote had changed over time. But this pattern emerged only for the Social Democrats in Germany and Austria (Table 3.4, p. 82 above).

While proceeding this way produces reasonable results, it does represent the imposition of an average despite variation in individual results. The bias is against detecting underlying change. Still defining Basic Vote as the percentage obtained without net issue advantage (i.e. at zero issue scores), we can obtain an alternative estimate for each election simply by taking the percentage of votes attributable to issue advantages away from the actual vote the party obtained (or adding it on where issue effects were negative). This will give a different estimate for each election, of course. But where such estimates are very similar we can attribute the limited variation to error round a stable underlying figure. Where they differ sharply, and particularly where they dip or rise between two or more sequences of elections, we can infer that some kind of basic shifts are under way.

Table 5.4   *Basic Votes of British Conservatives and Labour 1950–79*

	Conservatives			Labour		
Year	Actual vote received %	Estimated Basic Vote for election year (actual vote – issue vote) %	Difference between postwar average Basic Vote (42·0%) and estimate for election year %	Actual vote received %	Estimated Basic Vote for election year (actual vote – issue vote) %	Difference between postwar average Basic Vote (42·0%) and estimate for election year %
1950	43·4	39·6	–2·5	46·1	43·2	1·3
1951	48·0	44·2	2·1	48·8	45·9	4·0
1955	49·7	44·9	2·8	46·4	45·4	3·5
1959	49·4	42·7	0·6	43·8	41·9	–0·1
1964	43·4	41·5	–0·6	44·1	41·2	–0·7
1966	41·9	41·9	–0·2	48·0	40·3	–1·6
1970	46·4	42·6	0·5	43·1	41·2	–0·8
1974 (a)	37·9	41·7	–0·3	37·2	41·0	–0·9
1974 (b)	35·8	39·6	–2·4	39·3	37·4	–4·6
1979	43·9	37·2	–4·9	37·0	37·0	–5·0

The procedure is illustrated in Table 5.4 for the United Kingdom. This is typical of the individual tables produced for this analysis for separate parties and countries. For both Conservatives and Labour we give their actual vote in the election; the percentage obtained by subtracting from this the percentage attributable to issue advantages or disadvantages (at the general rate of 0·96 per cent of votes to each increment); and finally the percentage difference between this estimate of Basic Vote, specific to the election, and the average Basic Vote over all postwar elections. For both Labour and Conservatives this is 42·0 per cent.

The average Basic Vote figure comes reasonably close to the election-specific estimates for the Conservatives, except for the last two elections of the 1970s (with a slight underestimate for the 1950s). In the case of Labour, the general figure underestimates for the 1950s, fits fairly well from 1959 until the first election of 1974 and overestimates underlying support for the most recent two. The decline of loyalism within both major UK parties in the 1970s is well attested. Less obvious is the slip in support of 1959, linked to the resurgence of the Liberals in that year.

Table 5.5   *Changing Basic Votes in Twelve Postwar Democracies*

Country	Bourgeois Parties		Socialist–Reformist Parties	
	Dates	%	Dates	%
Austria	1955–9	40·0	1953–9	40·4
	1962	42·6	1962	42·0
	1966–79	43·0	1966–71	43·5
			1975–9	45·9
Belgium	1950–61	42·8	(1950–78	34·41)
	1965	36·4		
	1965–78	33·8		
Denmark	1950–66	45·9	1950–66	39·7
	1968–71	52·7	1968–71	37·1
	1973–9	30·5	1973–9	33·6
France	1958–78	50·9	1958–62	45·6
(second ballot)	1981	38·5	1967–73	37·6
			1978–81	45·6
Ireland	1948–57	22·9	(1948–81	41·82)
	1961	30·8		
	1965–81	32·2		
Israel	1949–65	22·6	1949–65	46·4
	1969	26·7	1969	49·1
	1973–81	27·8	1973–81	40·2
Italy	1948–68	38·6	1948–68	22·1
	1972	37·8	1972	23·4
	1976–9	34·7	1976–9	28·6
Japan	1958–67	52·1	1958–67	29·0
	1969	49·5	1969	24·3
	1972–6	43·4	1972–6	19·9
	1979–80	49·6	1979–80	24·8
Netherlands	1946–63	49·4	1946–63	29·6
	1967	47·5	1967	26·5
	1971–81	32·7	1971–81	25·9
New Zealand	1951–60	47·0	1951–60	45·0
	1963	43·3	1963	43·7
	1966–78	41·8	1966–78	42·0
United Kingdom	1950–9	42·8	1950–9	44·1
	1964–74 (a)	41·9	1964–74 (a)	40·9
	1974 (b)–9	38·4	1974 (b)–9	37·2
West Germany	1957–72	41·6	1957–69	34·6
	1976–80	47·5	1972–80	43·1

Tables 5.5 and 5.6 summarise results of all the individual analyses, giving estimates of Basic Vote for different periods where it has changed during the postwar period (Table 5.5) and giving a general postwar estimate for the countries where it seems to have remained unchanged (Table 5.6). Only in Ireland has Basic Vote for one party, Fianna Fáil, remained stable while that for the other (Fine Gael) has built up. The only other case of party differences is Belgium where the Christian Socials have declined in terms of underlying support while the Socialists have remained more or less stable. This might be thought surprising as the actual vote for both parties fell by about 10 per cent in the mid-1960s and has since stabilised at a lower level. Why then the contrast in Basic Vote? It is explained by the peculiarly adverse effect of recurrent linguistic and communal issues on the Socialist appeal. These consistently drag down their vote in every election without its decline having to be explained by a reduced Basic Vote. Substantively, the implication is that if linguistic and regional controversies could be settled, Socialist support would revert to former levels very quickly, while the Christian Socials would remain as they are.

Table 5.6   *Stable Basic Votes in Thirteen Postwar Democracies*

Country	Bourgeois Parties %	Socialist–Reformist Parties %
Australia	43·0	44·5
Belgium	–	34·4
Canada	33·2	38·7
Finland	41·4	44·2
Iceland	36·0	–
India	–	38·7
Ireland	–	41·8
Luxembourg	34·3	33·5
Norway	45·1	43·6
Sri Lanka	32·9	29·9
Sweden	46·5	44·5
Switzerland	57·0	25·9
United States	48·0	47·8

The fact that parties in most countries vary together in terms of Basic Vote, points to reciprocal influences which changes in the base of one party seem to have on the other. Or possibly the joint variation indicates that both are responding to the same societal trends. This accounts for the fact that periods of stable Basic Vote often seem to correspond to each other, within the two parties or blocs in a country. One would expect one party to gain long-term support when the other loses it. Often, however, they seem to lose or gain together, as in the United Kingdom in the late 1970s or in

Japan and New Zealand. Most commonly, the losses reflect an electoral entry by third parties who gain at the expense of both major contenders.

Another aspect of change is that it often works itself out over two or three elections, leaving outcomes in the middle of the series transitional between one period of relative stability and another. Hence we have often included a separate estimate for a single election in Table 5.5 because putting it with either the earlier or later period would distort the averages.

The major turning points in postwar elections have been identified as the late 1960s and early 1970s – associated with the protests and new political movements of that time. This is true for such countries as the Netherlands and Italy. But in many countries the turn of the 1950s also seems to witness change, as in the United Kingdom, New Zealand, Ireland, Belgium and Austria. In some cases change has been continuous and this is reflected in larger numbers of adjusted estimates – as for the Austrian Social Democrats and the British parties.

Table 5.5 demonstrates that long-term changes have been occurring in many parties over the postwar period – in twenty-two out of the forty-four we have studied, or roughly half. In cases like Japan, alterations in support have not altered the fundamental basis of the system. As the Liberal Democrats have declined so have the Socialists, so the former remain clearly predominant. But this cannot be said of any other country in Table 5.5. In these countries changes in long-term support have clearly made one side rather than the other predominant in government (as in Austria, France and West Germany) or made the system more seriously competitive (Ireland, Italy and Israel, for example). Electoral volatility in terms of shifting long-term support is widespread and has important consequences.

That said, a slight majority of systems and parties have not experienced basic change – including some which were thought to have, such as India. The estimate for the United States still attributes to the major parties a monopoly on long-term support, in line with our earlier findings and those of Flanigan and Zingale (1974). The findings broadly suggest that change and stability are always with us and not just a phenomenon of the late 1960s and 1970s. Certainly the impact of new issues and some shifts in Basic Vote had dramatic effects on election results at that time, over many countries. But less concentrated changes are also evident over the whole postwar period and in many cases have not worked themselves out. These conclusions suggest that there is no period during which some parties have not experienced underlying shifts of support, quite apart from the (occasionally severe) impact of short-term election issues.

Chapter 6

Party Appeals

Taking our theory of issue effects as broadly supported by existing evidence, we can apply it to the second major concern of this study – the campaign performance of political parties. Do parties always make the issue appeals which most benefit them? Or do they sometimes act in ways which decrease their vote?

These are questions we could not answer until we had some kind of external criterion against which to assess party behaviour. Failing this, we could only assume that election strategists – rational men, interested in gaining office without sacrificing too many of their principles – adopt the best means to this end. Thus the policy stands they take could not be evaluated but only accepted as the best available under the circumstances.

Given independent knowledge of how electors react to issues, we are not bound to accept practical judgements as automatically best. We can, for example, judge that where a socialist party emphasises the law-and-order question to a more marked extent than its bourgeois competitor, it is acting to depress rather than to increase its vote. There may, of course, be good, non-electoral reasons why it should choose to do this, but so far as increasing votes is concerned, such a stand is inefficient.

This qualification does point to a limitation on the use of our theory for evaluating party actions. Many factors shape a manifesto other than election considerations. Ideology may override tactics, simply because financial and activist support could not be guaranteed any other way. Or the actual state of the world may make certain issues unavoidable (as indicated by the relationship between objective developments and issues in Tables 2.3 and 2.4, pp. 36 and 39 above). Faced with a problem of obvious and wide concern, a party can lose credibility and thus votes, even among consistent supporters, if it fails to give it due consideration. This may be the case even although the topic crops up in an area more favourable to its rival than to itself.

Thus the guidelines provided by our theory of electoral responses cannot be pushed to an extreme. We cannot maintain that a party ought not, under any circumstances, to mention issues favourable to its rival. Were party leaders completely insulated from external events and from the need to appeal to ideological supporters as well as to electors, complete silence on certain topics might indeed prove the optimal tactic. Approaches to this situation occur in some local US elections. Normally, however, both constraints exist and rule out a blanket omission of any important problems. Party leaders themselves may prefer to voice thoughts about these, rather than winning office without popular support for the policies they think are right (Budge and Farlie, 1977, pp. 158–62).

Our theory can, therefore, provide only a partial and not a complete criterion for evaluating campaign strategies, since the vote gains and losses associated with the various issue types constitute only some of the rewards and penalties deriving from a policy position. Nevertheless we can make clear judgements about some aspects of party behaviour. It may not be inefficient for a socialist party to mention law and order when there is extensive crime on the streets. According to our findings, however, issues of this type produce a net benefit to bourgeois parties. Therefore the socialist party would make a mistake if it raised the issue gratuitously, when crime did not constitute a problem, or if it emphasised the topic more than its rival.

It is hard to say when crime constitutes an important objective problem. We can stipulate, however, that (a) the socialist party should not raise the question when bourgeois party(ies) do not – its omission by the traditional supporters of order surely indicates that the objective problem is not overwhelming; (b) the socialist party should not emphasise the question *more* than the bourgeois party(ies) – due consideration to satisfy supporters that it takes the matter seriously is one thing, a positive pushing of disadvantageous issues is quite another. It is, therefore, the relative emphases of parties on topics which favour or disfavour them, rather than their selection in isolation, that we investigate below. In Section 6.1 we examine manifestos and platforms to see whether the issues which parties most emphasise in practice are indeed the ones which should be singled out for the purpose of maximising party votes. In Section 6.2 we discuss the best vote-winning strategies for socialist and bourgeois parties. Since the issues which win votes are also ones to which parties have a traditional attachment (otherwise they could not be credited with 'owning' them), a further important conclusion is that vote-winning and ideology are not necessarily in conflict.

6.1   Issue Areas Emphasised in United Kingdom Manifestos and US Platforms

Where we could check our ideas about issue impacts against evidence from twenty-three countries, we are limited in our assessment of party strategies to only two – the United Kingdom and the United States. Our investigation of the way in which parties use issues is moreover limited to only one type of statement which the parties make – their national programme and statement of policies for the election – termed in Britain the party manifesto and in the United States the platform (on which the party 'stands' during the campaign).

The contrast in scope between the investigation of electoral impacts, on the one hand, and electoral strategies, on the other, reflects differences between the regular appearance of comprehensive reports of election campaigns in accessible publications and the scattered, partial and decentralised compilations of party literature. Efforts are under way to list and analyse manifestos or their equivalents in the countries we are dealing with (Budge and Robertson (eds), forthcoming). However, the only quantitative materials currently available are those deriving from the UK and US documents (Robertson, 1976; Budge and Farlie, 1977, pp. 421-3).

The geographical and cultural limitations this imposes on conclusions are serious. The United Kingdom and the United States are competitive two-party systems operating in a legal and cultural milieu which contrasts with much of the rest of the world. However, preliminary results from the comparative investigation do seem to indicate that party strategies are comparable, though they may differ in some details. The United Kingdom and the United States also contrast on important institutional and electoral features, so a check in the one case is not simply a replication of the other. The electoral impact of issues seems to differ more between the United Kingdom and the United States than between the UK and the multi-party countries. For these share a socialist–bourgeois form of party competition while the United States deviates considerably from this norm. This is at least as important a difference as the number of parties, so the tendency of strategists to employ selective emphases is being checked under significant variations of political practice, even in these two cases.

Neither manifestos nor platforms are, of course, the only documents produced by parties during a campaign. There are also newspaper releases and statements, television addresses and interviews, and the literature emanating from individual candidates for constituency consumption. Many of these represent individual pronouncements rather than authoritative party statements, though they are usually linked by a common point of view. The unique characteristic of the central policy documents – the manifesto or platform – is that they are authoritative. They are the only campaign statements made on behalf of the party as a whole rather than in the name of a particular candidate or group. Certainly they reach many fewer people than, say, a television address. On the other hand, the persons whom they influence are the opinion makers and publicists, those responsible for commentaries and interviews, and headlines. So their role in shaping the party campaign is very great.

To discover the policy areas emphasised by parties, we compare counts of sentences within each manifesto/platform, for each of the clusters into which they group. Or rather, since these documents differ considerably in length (from one and a half printed pages to over eighty, in the case of recent US platforms), we compare the percentage of all references within each group. The clusters are those already listed in Table 2.1 (see p. 28 above) as the general topics covered by these documents – which correspond to the macro-issues identified at electoral level.

Table 6.1 gives the average (mean) percentage devoted to each broad topic by the individual parties in the United Kingdom and the United States for the modern period – interwar as well as postwar in this case (limitations of time and resources have precluded coding here the enormous US platforms for 1976 and 1980). The table also reports the average percentage devoted to the topic by the two parties combined. The latter (in the third and sixth columns) gives an indication of the different preoccupations of politicians in the two countries. The most striking contrast lies in the strong emphasis given to social services in the United Kingdom – almost three times that given in the United States.

Table 6.1   *Mean Percentage of Sentences Devoted to Each Broad Area of Policy by UK Major Party Manifestos 1924–79 and US Party Platforms 1920–72*

	Percentage of Sentences Devoted to Each Area of Policy by:					
Areas of Policy	*Labour* %	*Con-servative* %	*Both* %	*Democrat* %	*Republican* %	*Both* %
Empire/special foreign relationships	2·00	5·50	4·41	1·23	1·49	1·36
Regionalism	1·05	4·24	2·64	3·62	4·13	3·87
Freedom	0·34	2·00	1·04	3·14	4·46	3·80
Enterprise	1·49	8·23	4·46	2·53	3·85	3·19
Democracy/ constitutionalism	3·41	3·11	2·69	3·62	3·65	3·63
Controlled economy	12·16	1·02	6·59	0·87	0·26	0·56
Economic planning	7·45	1·53	4·49	0·35	0·32	0·34
Regulation	1·89	3·11	2·50	5·18	2·23	3·71
Labour groups	3·80	1·89	2·79	5·12	3·84	4·48
Agriculture	4·02	5·19	4·61	9·55	8·51	9·03
Veterans	0·32	0·81	0·57	2·14	2·58	2·36
Other minority groups	1·02	1·40	1·21	2·12	3·28	2·70
Culture	2·02	1·80	1·91	0·16	0·10	0·13
Decolonisation	2·09	1·06	1·57	2·38	2·05	2·21
Economic stability	8·32	6·56	7·44	5·45	4·02	4·74
Protectionism	1·10	3·88	2·49	1·25	2·75	2·00
Productivity	4·31	3·89	4·10	1·07	0·94	1·00
National effort	0·10	0·31	0·20	0·79	1·02	0·90
Social justice	4·30	0·81	2·29	3·59	2·15	2·87
Technology	2·34	3·37	2·86	3·97	3·30	3·63
Conservation	1·33	1·31	1·32	5·63	4·38	5·00
Military	1·65	3·32	2·49	4·35	6·58	5·46
Government performance	1·85	7·12	4·48	8·68	11·92	10·30
Incentives	1·02	3·82	2·42	1·40	2·12	1·76
Peace	3·90	3·43	3·67	4·33	4·08	4·21
Social services	18·09	15·87	16·98	8·01	5·04	6·52
Internationalism	9·20	6·04	7·79	4·17	3·23	3·70

The main interest of the table relates to partisan differences within each country. Looking at the UK parties (columns 1 and 2), we see that many of the differences reflected in issue scorings also emerge in terms of differential emphases on manifesto topics. Thus the Conservatives stress the Empire, regions, freedom, incentives and enterprise considerably more than Labour. They are also disposed to pay more attention to farmers and the military. The Labour Party, on the other hand, heavily emphasises economic control and planning (as opposed to the Conservative preference for regulation), supports internationalism more and advocates the importance of labour groups and social justice (in contrast to Conservative neglect of this topic). Above all, Labour emphasises the social services – devoting to them more than twice the references than are received by any other area of policy.

All this conforms to the ideas about selective emphasis and party 'ownership' of issues discussed earlier. There are certain breaks in the pattern, however. Economic stability is stressed more by Labour than by Conservatives, but this is because it includes a high proportion of references to unemployment. Farmers are also mentioned more by Labour than labour groups! And although Labour stress the social services more than Conservatives, the topic is still given more than twice the references devoted to any other over the set of Conservative manifestos.

The other obvious contrast between the parties is on government performance, to which Conservative manifestos devote almost as much attention as they do to enterprise, and Labour very little. Perhaps the Conservative and related parties' presentation of themselves as the 'businesslike' party accounts for the different reactions of electors to socialist and bourgeois parties on government record and prospects (Chapter 5, Section 5.2 and Table 5.3, pp. 119 and 120 above). Republicans also stress this area more than Democrats, although the difference here is less than in the United Kingdom.

This is true generally. While the same more or less expected contrasts hold for Democrats and Republicans as for Labour and Conservatives, the percentage gap between partisan references is smaller. To illustrate this, one need look only at headings pertaining to free enterprise and collectivism: enterprise itself, incentives, freedom, controlled economy and economic planning. Given the support of both US parties for an uninhibited free enterprise system, the very muted differences in these areas are, of course, understandable. It is noteworthy, however, that the differences which exist do go in the expected direction – Republicans making marginally more references to these points than Democrats.

However, contrasts between the US parties seem sharper (given the overall lower number of references) in regard to social services – probably because the question of their extension has been more sharply controverted. And on other topics central to US politics – regulation, for example, compared to the question of government control discussed earlier, or protectionism – party emphases are more evident than in the United Kingdom.

Pointers to differences between the parties and thus to the major foci of competition emerge quite clearly from Table 6.1. Nevertheless, comparisons here can hardly be final, since they stem from aggregations of references over fifty years. For more definite conclusions we must review references separately, for each party in each election.

We cannot present all such references here. A table with $14 \times 2 \times 27$ percentage entries (for the United Kingdom alone, not counting the United States) is too complex. A simplified solution is suggested by the widely varying level of percentage references reported in Table 6.1 and, in particular, by the fairly large number of topics that group less than 3 or 2 per cent of sentences in all (an extreme example is national effort, which figures in only one-fifth of 1 per cent of sentences in UK manifestos and in less than 1 per cent in the United States). Many of these are mentioned only incidentally, if at all, in most manifestos. Topics which parties want specially emphasised are surely those which received greater emphasis, which we can take operationally as over 5 per cent of mentions (practically identical with the ten most often-mentioned topics). Within this group we can distinguish those receiving more than 10 per cent of references which parties must wish to be particularly noticeable.

Table 6.2 lists these leading topics from each UK party's manifestos since 1924. These are presented very directly, simply by reporting all topics which received more than 5 per cent of sentence references in each manifesto and distinguishing those which attracted more than 10 per cent. The last row of the table gives the number of topics heavily stressed by Conservatives or Labour which were also heavily stressed by the rival party. Although it is dangerous to rely to much on this, it does summarise one aspect of the information presented there.

While there are several avenues to explore, a major finding which positively leaps out of the table is the heavy stress placed by both parties on the social services and to a lesser extent on internationalism – particularly, in the latter case, for the postwar period. These always fall among the topics mentioned simultaneously by the two parties and often constitute the only topics common to both party manifestos.

Internationalism not only includes references to co-operation between nations, but also to international organisations such as the United Nations and the European Economic Community. It thus includes aspects of foreign affairs which no party could easily ignore and to which, because of their importance, they must make some reference. This accounts for their common focus upon the subject and illuminates again the constraints imposed by objective factors upon the party documents: whatever has significant and continuing effects cannot be consistently ignored.

The same reasoning holds true for the social services, at least in part. Because of the large percentage of the national product consumed by these,

Table 6.2   Topics Most Heavily Emphasised in UK Party Manifestos (1924–79 Inclusive)

Date of Election	1924	1929	1931	1935	1945	1950	1951	1955	1959	1964	1966	1970	1974	1974	1979
Policy Area:															
Empire/special foreign relationships	C*	C	C*	C	C	C		C							
Regionalism									C		C	C	C	C	C
Freedom															
Enterprise					BC*	C*	C*			C	C	C	C	C	B
Democracy/constitutionalism												L			
Controlled economy	L*	L*	L*	L*	L*	L*	L	L*	L	B	L	L	L	L*	L*
Economic planning		L*	L*	L	L*	L	L				L	C	L	B	
Regulation											C	C			
Labour groups	L*		L*	L											
Agriculture	C*	B	C*	C*	C	L									
Minorities	C														
Culture										C					
Economic stability		B*	C*	B*			L*	L*	L	L	BL*	L*	L*	L*	L
Protectionism	C	C*	BC*						C						
Productivity	L					L					B	B	L		
Social justice							L	L*	L		L				L*
Technology					C					B					
Military					C					L					
Government performance	C*	C*													
Incentives						C	C		C*				C	C	C
Peace	B*			BL*	L										C*
Social services	B*	B*	B*	B*	B*	B*	BL*	B*	B*	B*	B*	B*	BL*	BL*	B
Internationalism	L	L*	B*	L	L	L	B	L	B	B	BC*	B	B	BL*	B
Total Topics															
Conservative	5	5	4	6	6	5	4	3	5	6	6	6	5	6	7
Labour	4	5	6	6	6	6	5	6	6	6	6	6	4	5	6
Common	1	3	1	4	2	1	2	1	3	4	4	3	2	3	3

Note: Topics marked with C, L, B occur in over 5 per cent of sentences in Conservative, Labour, or both manifestos respectively. The presence of topics occurring in over 10 per cent of sentences is indicated by an asterisk, C*, L*, B* except for the few cases where one manifesto mentions the topic in 5–10 per cent of sentences and the other in over 10 per cent of sentences. In these cases the manifesto with the larger percentage is separately indicated by either BC* or BL*. All topics not marked or not mentioned occur in less than 5 per cent of the sentences in both manifestos.

as well as their immediate effects on the lives of most of the population, the Conservative Party cannot avoid mentioning them: to omit them altogether might constitute a more effective way of drawing them into the election than discussing them with reference to incidental waste and inefficiencies, which go some way to neutralising the pro-Labour effects they might otherwise have on voters.

Nevertheless it is a tribute to the power of social issues – the one strong electoral card on the side of socialist parties – that even the party which stands to lose is forced to mention them. One may query whether, for electoral purposes, the Conservative Party does not in fact make too much of this question. Certainly, it does give social services less coverage than Labour – a mean percentage of 16 per cent of sentence references compared with 18. Nevertheless, the amount and consistency of attention that it pays to them is extraordinarily high and it might be to their electoral advantage to play them down rather more – as the US Republicans have succeeded in doing until recently.

The other topics listed in the table appear much less frequently and thus give more scope for selective strategies aimed at ignoring rival strong points and pushing one's own. Amongst these the ones which appear (almost entirely on the Labour side) are the controlled economy and economic planning – not a wise electoral strategy if our assumptions about electoral reactions are correct, since these are issues likely to lose Labour votes. Both sides are concerned with economic stability (though Labour more so), while the Conservatives have naturally emphasised incentives, enterprise and freedom. They also stress the Empire and the nexus of Commonwealth and colonial relationships.

However, the main interest of these other themes from our point of view lies less in the number of times they recur than in how often they differentiate the points of view voiced by the parties. Here the figures in the last row of the table – summarising the proportion of leading themes shared by the parties – prove quite instructive. They show that apart from the 1960s and 1935, when the parties shared as many as two-thirds of their major topics, the common topics have been social services and internationalism. On all other matters the manifestos have tended to talk past each other, thus upholding our general expectations and confirming the strong partisan differentiation already observed (Budge and Farlie, 1977, p. 425).

Both parties seem inclined to stress the same number of major themes in their manifestos, in spite of the Conservatives potentially having a wider range of favourable issues to draw upon (Table 2.6, p. 50 above). However, this and other questions about partisan tactics are probably best considered after bringing in the US evidence.

Generally speaking, the proportion of topics which Democrats and Republicans mention simultaneously is about the same as in the United Kingdom (compare the last row of Table 6.2 with that of Table 6.3).

Table 6.3   Topics Most Heavily Emphasised in US Party Manifestos (1920–72 Inclusive)

Date of Election	1920	1924	1928	1932	1936	1940	1944	1948	1952	1956	1960	1964	1968	1972
Policy Area:														
Empire/special foreign relationships			R											
Regionalism									B					
Freedom					R	R	R	R				R*		D
Enterprise	R		D		R	B		R				R		D
Democracy/constitutionalism				D	D*	D								
Regulation			D		D									
Labour groups	D	B*	D	B*	B*	B*	R	D	R	BR*	D			
Agriculture	D		B*	B*		B*	B	B	BD*	BR*	R		R	D
Minorities														R
Decolonisation										R				
Economic stability		R		BD*	D*	D	D	R					D	D
Protectionism		R	R		R									
Social justice	D	D											D	D
Technology		D	B							B	D		B	
Military	B*	B*				R	R*		BR*	B	R*	BR*	R	R
Government performance		D	R	B*	B*	R*	R*	R	R*	B	D	R*	R	B
Conservation		R						D	D	B	B	D	D	R
Peace						D	D	D		R	D	D	D	R
Social services							D*		D	D	BD*	BD*	B*	BD*
Internationalism	D	R		R	D		D*	B		B	B			
Total topics														
Republican	2	6	6	5	5	5	5	6	5	5	6	5	5	6
Democrat	5	5	6	5	6	5	5	5	5	6	6	5	5	6
Common	1	2	3	4	2	2	1	2	3	3	4	2	2	2

Note: Topics marked with D, R, B occur in 5–10 per cent of sentences in Democrat, Republican, or both manifestos respectively. The presence of topics occurring in over 10 per cent of sentences is indicated by an asterisk, D*, R*, B* except for the few cases where one manifesto mentions the topic in 5–10 per cent of sentences and the other in over 10 per cent of sentences. In these cases the manifesto with the larger percentage is separately indicated by either BD* or BR*. All topics not marked or not mentioned occur in less than 5 per cent of the sentences in both manifestos.

However, the striking concurrence of UK parties on the same two topics in every election is absent from the US table. In the prewar period, certainly, both stressed government performance on almost every occasion. While this topic also comes into most postwar campaigns as well, it is less emphasised. Agricultural groups and their needs are also stressed throughout – but again more heavily in prewar than in postwar elections. In the postwar period, social services come to the fore for both parties, but are more heavily stressed by Democrats.

What concurrence appears between the US parties is thus due less to a permanent fixation on certain topics than to a common selection of topics for a particular campaign. This tendency must not be exaggerated. Only very rarely (in 1932 and again in 1960) are a majority of topics emphasised by one party also stressed by the other. Selective emphases predominate in most elections.

So far we have concentrated analysis on what the parties themselves say. This is of relevance to election outcomes only if what they say actually gets through to voters. An important question before discussing the optimal tactics for parties is, then, the correspondence between the salient issues of an election and those emphasised in manifestos or platforms.

Since we have grouped manifesto topics under different types of macro-issue (Table 2.1p, 28 above), we can count the number of such topics (out of all those heavily emphasised by each party in each election) which correspond to the issue types salient in the election: and conversely we can report the proportion of salient issue types which correspond to manifesto topics. Table 6.4 shows that the correspondence is strong over the postwar period.

The different ways of looking at the relationship are not equivalent. If the question is, how many issues salient in the election correspond to topics emphasised in the manifesto or platform, we reach very positive conclusions. Only in one election (Britain, 1955) is the proportion less than a half, and generally it ranges from 60 to 75 per cent. Even this is artificially depressed by the fact that candidates' personality or background often ranks as a salient issue which by its nature cannot find a parallel in the manifesto. The choice of candidate is, however, as much a strategic decision of the parties as the topics stressed in their pronouncements. If we take candidates into account with the manifestos, salient issues correspond almost entirely to the issue emphases and personalities selected by the parties.

On the other hand, when we reckon the proportion of manifesto or platform topics which correspond to salient issue types, we find that this is generally lower. A range of topics is emphasised out of which some find an echo in the general campaign but some do not. In the United Kingdom these numbers are generally equal: about half the topics emphasised, on average, correspond to issues. In the United States this proportion is lower, generally between a quarter and a half.

The asymmetry between issues corresponding to manifesto or platform

Table 6.4   Correspondence between Topics Most Heavily Emphasised in Postwar Manifestos and Platforms and Salient Issues in the Election Campaign

United Kingdom

| Date of election | Proportion of manifesto topics corresponding to salient issues | | | Proportion of salient issues corresponding to manifesto topics |
	Labour	Conservative	Total	
1950	3/6	2/5	4/10	3/6
1951	5/5	3/4	6/7	4/6
1955	1/6	0/5	1/10	1/3
1959	4/6	3/5	5/8	4/5
1964	4/6	2/6	5/8	5/7
1966	5/6	4/6	6/8	4/5
1970	3/6	3/6	3/9	4/6
1974 (Feb)	3/4	2/5	4/7	4/7
1974 (Oct)	4/5	2/6	4/9	4/6
1979	3/6	4/6	6/9	4/7

United States

| Date of election | Proportion of manifesto topics corresponding to salient issues | | | Proportion of salient issues corresponding to manifesto topics |
	Democrat	Republican	Total	
1948	3/5	4/6	6/9	4/6
1952	1/5	2/5	2/7	2/4
1956	1/6	1/5	2/8	2/4
1960	3/6	3/6	3/8	3/4
1964	2/5	1/5	2/8	3/5
1968	2/5	3/5	4/8	3/5
1972	2/6	2/6	4/10	3/6

Note: Topics most heavily emphasised are those reported in Tables 6.2 and 6.3 as receiving over 5 per cent of sentence references. Since parties often stress the same topics, neither the top nor base number of the 'total' proportions ar necessarily the sum of the corresponding numbers in the separate parties.

topics, and topics corresponding to issues, gives a clue to the dynamics of the relationship between manifestos and issues. If parties could respond to electors' preferences by stressing those topics, and only those topics, which they knew were of general concern we should expect practically all topics mentioned to relate to issues: which they do not. The alternative conception, more compatible with the general view we have taken of the electoral process, is that parties cast around for issues favourable to themselves which will produce some resonance among electors. In that case, we should expect the topics they select not to have an automatic guarantee of resonance. Sometimes they will provoke popular concern and interest, and sometimes not. This is certainly the kind of effect which appears in Table 6.4. The result supports the view that party emphases bring issues to the fore, rather than simply reflecting issues already prominent among electors.

On the other hand, we have already noted that politicians do not have a completely free hand in producing only those issues favourable to themselves. The existence of competing parties, and of non-electoral constraints, force them on the whole to relate their cues to real problems in spite of possible short-term vote losses (the best example being Conservative and Republican concern with social services). Objective circumstances first spark off discussions in party pronouncements (slanted one way or another to favour the authors) which then – in some but not all cases – stimulate interest and concern among electors to create a salient issue.

In Table 6.4 we look at the proportion of topics corresponding to issues separately for each party), and for both combined, where the proportion is reckoned out of all topics stressed by the party), and for both combined, where the proportion is reckoned out of all the independent topics stressed by the two parties. Since as we have seen (Tables 6.2 and 6.3) parties often stress the same topics, the total number of independent topics is less than the sum of those stressed by each party. The proportion of topics corresponding to issues does not diverge much overall from the proportions inside each party. Nor does there seem any clear movement to greater or less correspondence over time.

The main import of Table 6.4 is that manifesto and platform emphases are not isolated from the rest of the election campaign. There is a strong correspondence between the topics featured there and the salient issues which shape election outcomes. Placing emphases where they will bring in most votes constitutes an important part of the strategist's task. It also forms a practical problem which will be considered in Section 6.2.

6.2   Using Issue Emphases to Gain Votes

It would be presumptuous on the basis of new research to advise the whole-sale alteration of party appeals, if this flew in the face of what generations of politicians have found effective. In this sense the investigation of what parties actually emphasise, in the last section, constitutes an essential element in our diagnosis here. Had politicians' actual practices directly contradicted our theory we would have been led to query its adequacy rather than contradict the unanimous judgement of experienced practitioners.

As it turns out, however, what the parties actually do conforms broadly to what we would advise them to do anyway. By and large, they do emphasise areas more favourable to themselves and play down those which are unfavourable. There are some cases, however, where this rule seems not to be applied to the full, and these offer scope for marginal adjustments based on theoretical considerations. The outstanding cases are those of the British Conservatives' (and to a lesser and more recent extent of the US Republicans') stress on social services; of British Labour's determined concentration on economic control and planning, and of the US Democrats' proclaimed commitment to internationalism and peace.

No one would maintain that these goals were undesirable in themselves. It is, as we have noted, a characteristic of each type of issue to have an obvious and desirable goal attached to it. The problem from the point of view of campaigning is that a rival party may appear as the obvious candidate to effect that goal and thus attract votes whenever it becomes salient. To emphasise the topic in the campaign enhances the chance that it will become salient. For it to be stressed unduly by the party which stands to lose may be evidence of a sincere commitment, and good for all sorts of non-electoral reasons, but must be weighed against the immediate loss of votes.

Our advice can be based only on election considerations because we have no criterion to offer within other areas. From the point of view of attracting votes, however, it seems desirable to modify these emphases. Certainly it might be unwise to abandon them completely. Complete silence on services which consume a very large share of the National Product, or on an obviously important and desirable goal like peace and international co-operation, could lead to a rival making great capital out of the obvious lack of concern, and thus ultimately to a greater salience of the issue in the campaign than it would have had under the present treatment. Similarly, any public abandonment by the Labour Party of longstanding commitments would be widely noted. While this might prove electorally beneficial it would also be certain to touch off factionalism and inner conflicts which could be used to cast doubt on Labour's ability to govern (turning the contested issue of government record and prospects against Labour).

There is no point in substituting one adverse issue for another. Hence adverse topics which have figured prominently in the past should not be completely or drastically abandoned: simply have the emphases reduced. Conversely the rival who stands to benefit should increase his emphasis – as the Democrats have obviously been doing with social services.

Politicians themselves have not, of course, been blind to these points. Many revisionists have sought to turn socialist parties towards a more resolute concern with welfare and away from economic control. Gaitskell's attempt in 1959 to revoke Labour's commitment to nationalisation is well known, and we have noted the electoral benefits of Brandt's reformist policies for the West German SPD and of Kreisky's for the Austrian Social Democrats. What our theory additionally provides is a systematic justification for these attempts in terms of their enhancement of the socialist parties' electoral position, and an explanation of how this occurs.

Similarly, there is strategic sense in the right's contention that bourgeois parties should not simply echo socialist welfare goals. The remedy is not, however, as the extreme right often urges, to oppose them outright but to direct attention from them to almost any other area of concern.

These suggestions for marginal change in the way parties have defined their positions in past campaigns all add up to an overall conception of the optimal electoral policy for each party. This is easiest to define for socialist parties, because of their restricted choice of favourable issue areas. They have no alternative but to emphasise socioeconomic redistribution in some form, whether as extensions to public housing and education, improvements in pensions and labour conditions, better social services, or a concern with social justice. While pushing this as much as possible they must, if they are to win, combine this fixed appeal with attractive candidates and an effective attack on the other party's government record. To maximise their chances they must also present themselves as a party with reasonable government prospects (avoiding internal factionalism, for example) and if possible 'capture' the area of foreign relations.

The bourgeois parties' best reply to this is, at the very least, to be competitive in terms of government record and prospects, and candidates. Their other choices are more complex, since the range of possible favourable issues is much wider. Civil order (increasing crime, or any kind of subversion or disruption) provides them with a topic of continuing concern to the average citizen. The existence of large immigrant populations in most countries, and the effect of these on ethnic relationships, also provide bourgeois parties with a powerful counter to redistributive appeals. This can be reinforced by stressing the importance of traditional standards, which are seen as threatened not simply by foreigners but by the whole ethos of the permissive society. Provided that three or even two of the issues of government control, regulation of cartels (including trade unions) in favour of individuals, freedom and initiative can be brought into debate, bourgeois parties can benefit substantially and might even gain by making them key issues of the election.

Optimal bourgeois strategies might, therefore, centre on civil order, or ethnicity, with traditional morality as a back-up. Or under a full-blooded commitment to free market ideology they might group attacks on controls and proposals for regulating trade unions with prospects of greater freedom and incentives. A mixed strategy of stressing the last three topics, along with law and order and immigration, might be best of all, since it would safeguard against either set of issues failing to attract attention.

The US Democrats are in a similar position to socialist parties in being heavily dependent on redistribution (in some shape or form) as an issue. However, they will derive additional benefits if ethnic interests and relationships are brought into play. Moreover, questions relating to the regulation of cartels and monopolies should also attract votes. Choosing a key issue to emphasise is thus more of a problem for Democrat tacticians than for socialists. Social welfare questions, however, recur more regularly and reliably than ethnic issues, while the impact of trust-busting is relatively small. So the choice of fixed issues is not, in practice, very different for Democrats; they should generally aim at emphasising social welfare even when they are alert to windfall benefits accruing from the other two.

In terms of erratic issues, it is perhaps even more vital in the United States, given the concentration of power in the presidency and the popular focus on a race between individual nominees, to present the party favourably in these areas if it is to win. Having an incumbent President is a decided advantage, but it is not final, since the record of his administration may weigh against his party whatever his personal record of competence and reliability. Possession of an attractive alternative candidate may, in these circumstances, give the opposition an edge which will be consolidated if they can get the volatile farm vote on their side. (In the United States and Canada, unlike other party systems, the urban–rural issue does not favour any one party – a situation recognised by strategists on both sides if the prominence of agriculture in both parties' platforms is anything to go by.)

While they have numerically less issues 'fixed' in their direction than bourgeois parties confronting socialists, the Republicans have the advantage of having annexed foreign affairs – in the United States a large impact issue, and moreover a fairly constant anxiety. Because of these characteristics it seems to have the capability of balancing redistribution on the Democrat side, particularly if Republicans can also raise questions of military and defence.

Freedom and initiative are also natural appeals for Republicans to make, but have the disadvantage of constituting only a small impact issue. The Democrats have taken over the question of regulation and offer only a small target on government control, so this cluster of issue types is not really, in the final analysis, of great value to Republicans. Nor are constitutional or regional questions very likely to become salient in elections – the most that can be hoped for is an occasional windfall benefit. The most promising alternative to foreign affairs is civil order – since it encompasses questions of crime and policing which are a perennial concern among low-income voters normally attracted to the Democrats.

Looking back at Table 6.3, it is in fact surprising that the Republicans have not emphasised peace, and law and order much more. They are, after all, topics on which they could hardly lose. In combination with appeals to farmers, a reasonable candidate and a mediocre government record on the part of the Democrats, they appear to constitute an optimal policy package.

Why should parties not stress all the issues which favour themselves, without making any kind of prior selection, but simply relying upon circumstances to let some of them achieve prominence? This might be an attractive alternative if it carried no costs. However, the finding that voters become more confused with increases in the number of issues on which they base their decision (Chapter 1, Section 1.3, p. 14 above) indicates that costs do exist. Each issue which is additionally stressed attracts further electors into the party but may also leave more electors undecided. The more issues are stressed, the greater the risk of some unfavourable aspects of party policy being revealed, and hence of the issues in combination pushing out more people than they pull in. We need only assume that this point is reached fairly quickly, to see that it limits the optimal number of issues any party should stress. An implicit awareness of the risk of confusing electors explains why in practice parties do not shower them with diverse appeals, but concentrate their emphases on five or six topics (Tables 6.2 and 6.4).

Besides the capacity of electors, other constraints limit the number of issue appeals. One is that for the programme to have plausibility and to achieve a response, issues must relate, even if distantly, to some real problem. It is unlikely that more than five or six of the topics it is possible to raise actually correspond to real or even perceived current problems.

The third constraint relates to the inability of most of the mass media to sustain a complicated and inter-related argument bringing in large numbers of topics. The nature of the presentation usually requires the repetition of broad simplified themes, so that five or six are about all that can be accommodated.

These factors in combination powerfully enforce selective emphases on the framers of party programmes – along with their own biases towards certain topics in preference to others. In practice, no more than six topics receive over 5 per cent of references in any election (Tables 6.2 and 6.3). In the case of socialist parties (and to some extent of Democrats and Republicans, too), the limitation is explained – only this number favour them, in any case. For bourgeois parties selectivity is not enforced in this way so the choice of issues becomes a crucial element in their success – giving greater scope to the imaginative and innovatory politician than exists among socialists.

Election advantages are often seen, particularly in socialist parties, as conflicting with principle – forcing the adoption of policies which the party was created to oppose. By stressing the indelible association of particular parties with certain policy positions, our theory helps eliminate clashes between ideology and immediate electoral advantage. Party ideologies affirm traditional positions inside the issue areas we have identified. These are so embedded that it is no use a party striking postures other than those adopted before. It will simply not be believed. In pursuing immediate electoral advantage, party strategists should not alter traditional stands. They should simply emphasise those which are electorally popular. This is all they can do in a democracy anyway – and it seems, in a muddled way, the course pursued by most parties over the last half century. Electorally unprofitable goals can be advanced by a different route, through building up grass-roots support and a large Basic Vote permanently committed to the party which, in the end, might secure it continuing dominance within the political system.

Chapter 7

General Theory

7.1 Recapitulation

The implications of the theory we have proposed are best considered after it has been restated and viewed as a whole. In Chapter 2 we identified our leading postulates as (a) electors' simplification of political complexities into fourteen autonomous issue types; (b) their dislike of proposals for change, except where they bring immediate and obvious benefits; and (c) identification by a majority of electors of certain (bourgeois) parties with opposition to change in most areas and of certain (generally socialist but sometimes reformist) parties with overall promotion of change.

These assumptions represent a marked simplification of reality. No doubt many electors at various times look at other aspects of issues than their promotion of change. On some occasions change, even without immediate benefits, may be welcomed by the majority – in the case of a patriotic war, for example. Nevertheless, one has only to start citing counter-examples to appreciate that these occur infrequently and in exceptional circumstances, and consequently that generalisations are best based on electors' suspicion of change rather than spontaneous acceptance of it.

The most likely alternative to change as a general criterion for evaluating issues are anticipated benefits. Most general analyses of voting behaviour do indeed adopt a 'rational choice' approach whereby electors are supposed to weigh the benefits against the costs of a particular line of action and decide to vote for it only if the balance is positive.

It is, however, difficult for electors to make any estimates of these at all, let alone to calculate them realistically. No policies can be spelt out in the detail required for real evaluation of the consequences – even governments, for all their statistical forecasting and policy papers, usually fail in this. So how can the ordinary elector succeed? Let alone that in an uncertain national and international environment, the main problems which will actually face the elected party are not even discussed at the election. (Difficulties of calculation and their consequences for electoral decision processes are analysed in Budge *et al.*, 1981; Budge and Farlie, 1977, ch. 5.)

In order to decide, the ordinary elector must simplify the decision. He has one obvious baseline against which to measure proposals – that is, his current personal situation which in the countries we are dealing with is usually not intolerable. He can ask of each issue which comes to his attention: will action in this area improve my immediate situation? Or will it impose change with no guarantee of personal benefits – only the prospect of unrequited costs which experience with urban renewal, economic reconstruction, and so on, has taught me to expect? In the latter case, he will not bother with detailed calculations of even medium-term effects, but will decide against the proposal without further ado.

Because of the difficulties of calculating long-term benefits, many rational choice approaches recognise the existence of information costs which incline electors to vote as they have done in the past unless some drastic change takes place, in which case they re-evaluate their position. In this reformulation any direct calculation of costs and benefits has receded into the background – more so, in fact, than in our theory. For the vast majority of electors will simply vote on the basis of habit and tradition, whereas we see them all as making (simple) calculations centred around their present situation and distrust of proposals for altering it (Budge and Farlie, 1977, chs 3–7 *passim*).

A further way in which voting decisions are simplified is by ignoring parties' detailed proposals in each area, and crediting them with consistent and enduring attitudes. However reformist and interventionist a bourgeois party may have become in comparison with its own position in the past, it is unlikely to go further than the contemporary socialist opposition. Hence to oppose change one votes bourgeois and to promote it one votes socialist. In particular situations this strategy may, in practice, produce the opposite of what is intended – the British Conservatives, for example, have in certain instances undertaken more sweeping measures of control than Labour might have done (for example, the creation of a British Broadcasting Corporation in the 1930s and of an enforced incomes policy in the early 1970s). In general, however, the Conservatives and their analogues elsewhere are less likely to institute large-scale change than the socialists, otherwise they lose their entire ideological rationale. As a general strategy over all elections and issues, voting Conservative to oppose change and Labour to promote it is more likely to be right than to be wrong. It has the advantage, moreover, of being applicable to future contingencies. Given that these – to an equal or even greater extent than issues debated at the election – will dominate the life of the government, it is obviously better to select a party which will broadly decide future policies along the lines you want than to choose one which has only a slight utility margin on current election issues.

Electors' simplification of their voting decisions along these lines provides the key assumptions for a comparative theory of election outcomes. Where there is a socialist–bourgeois competition the divergence between the parties' general attitudes to change is so clear that it forms the obvious criterion, regardless of particular circumstances in each country. The fact that the latter differ does not really, in light of electors' reductionism, constitute an argument against the applicability of a general theory. To insist that the impact of issues must vary with circumstances, and be estimated separately and independently for each election situation, is to maintain that electors, in so far as they vote on issues, make laborious special calculations. But this is impossible for them (Budge *et al.* (eds), 1976, pp. 370–92; Budge and Farlie, 1977, pp. 176–81).

Either electors simplify voting decisions on some kind of generally applicable basis, or they do not decide by reference to issues at all. Since outcomes change rapidly without a corresponding upheaval in social circumstances, there is no alternative to assuming that at least some electors react to issues. Once that conclusion is reached, the change criterion is the simplest to apply.

Although we have developed this argument primarily in regard to a socialist–bourgeois type of party competition, analogies can be found in other party systems – usually in terms of confrontation between a reformist and more conservative party. Party contrasts are less clear, possibly making it harder to decide on the basis of attitudes to change. But within different issue areas the implications of change for electors can be specified (as in Tables 2.7 to 2.9, pp. 52–6 above), so broadly similar decision-making processes seem to operate to those which exist where a socialist party is present.

The other way in which electors can simplify their decision-making is by grouping specific issues into broad types, which can then be assigned to one party or the other on the basis of the consequences of change. Of course this assignment can proceed only on the further simplifying assumption that actions directed towards one issue type do not affect any of the others. Even governments have got to proceed more or less on this basis, even though they pay lip service to interconnections, so it is perfectly understandable why electors could draw sharp boundaries between the various areas and refuse to allow that policy effects spill over into other areas.

To sum up, our whole picture of electors' decision processes is dominated by the necessity for them to simplify, in order to reduce complex political realities to manageable form, while still retaining some contact with their own personal preferences and with party ideologies. Moreover, in the form we have adopted it ties in naturally with other research into voters' decision processes – particularly with that of Kelley and Mirer (cited in Chapter 1, Section 1.3, p. 14 above). Their 'decision rule' for individual voting decisions was for electors to subtract the number of negative from the number of positive evaluations of each party and then vote for the party which had the largest positive evaluation. The most natural way to envisage electors making up their minds within our formulation is to see them as adding up pro- and con-attitudes to parties on the basis of the issue types salient to themselves at the time of decision. Probably each issue type would count as one, as in Kelley and Mirer's rule. (The *individual* decision processes of electors should not, of course, be confused with our *aggregate* procedure for adding up differently weighted issue scores for each party – these relate to numbers of electors likely to be affected overall by the issue type, not to its degree of importance for individuals.)

Kelley and Mirer's findings also apply at the macro-level, however, in that the confusion caused to the individual confronted by too much information about the parties is likely to muddle outcomes if it occurs on a large scale, that is, if too many issue types are introduced into the campaign. In fact, various constraints seem to prevent the number of salient types from rising above a limited level calculated not to cause general confusion – one of the constraints being an appreciation by party strategists of the need to emphasise only a limited number of key themes.

At the party level this theory of elector reactions clarifies the analysis of optimal strategies. If it is supplemented by the well-attested hypothesis (Robertson, 1976, pp. 93–105; Budge and Farlie, 1977, pp. 424–30) that politicians seek to gain votes except where these will not help them to win, we can actually predict how parties will campaign under given circumstances. The typology of issues and characterisation of their effects, based on our earlier postulates, then enables us to predict what success a given set of campaign emphases will enjoy – and, perhaps of more importance, to explain why it enjoys the success it does. The complete theory thus provides an explanation of elections at the two main levels of voters and politicians, which has a number of interesting implications. We develop these in the context of the formal statement in Section 7.2.

7.2 Propositions

Table 7.1 presents the theoretical assumptions which we have just discussed as a series of explicit propositions. These are verbal rather than mathematical in form because the conditions which must be stipulated for a fully mathematical theory to apply in this area are so stringent that they certainly cannot be met by our subject matter (and possibly not by any that can conceivably be developed). Moreover, verbal propositions are more accessible to the general reader, while still providing a strict and testing way of summarising a theory, since most ambiguities which slip into a general discourse are mercilessly exposed. Hidden postulates must also be explicated, since otherwise the chain of reasoning presented in the propositions remains incomplete. Thus Table 7.1 is as direct and full a statement of our theory as we can make it.

Since we have just been over the ground, we simply relate each assumption to the general argument unless some special feature calls for further comment. Assumptions 1 and 2 specify the division into fourteen issue types more precisely than we have done hitherto, separating and emphasising the point about action on one type not involving others. Assumption 3 generalises Kelley and Mirer's finding about the greater inconsistency of individual electors who evaluate the parties on a large number of points. This consequence for individual decision-making will be enhanced when more issue types are introduced by parties and other agencies into the general campaign. Here widespread individual confusion will render the electorate as a whole less predictable. To avoid this, party strategists will be strictly selective about the themes they introduce into the campaign (see Assumption 9, p. 152 below).

Table 7.1   *General Assumptions of the Theory of Election Outcomes and Party Competition*

---

1   Electors evaluate political issues in terms of their location in one of fourteen self-contained issue types (specified in Table 2.1, p. 28 above).
2   Electors do not see action on one of these issue types as involving consequences for any of the others.
3   Above a certain threshold (probably six or seven), the introduction of more issue types into a campaign leads to confusion in electors' voting decisions.
4   The only aspect of an issue type relevant to electors' voting decisions is the prospect for personal change associated with it.
5   Electors dislike proposals involving the prospect of change except where change brings immediate and obvious benefits.
6   The majority of electors associate socialist parties with proposals for change irrespective of their detailed policies on each issue type, except in regard to their candidates, foreign policy and immediate record/prospects as a government.
7   Electors direct their vote according to the overall partisan balance of issue types salient to them at the time of the election.
8   Party leaders publicly emphasise issue types which produce favourable net switches of support – more so where such switches will alter the election outcome than where no alteration will be made.
9   The number of issue types emphasised by each party is limited:
   a   by the perceived possibility of confusing electors (see Assumption 3);
   b   by the need to stress a majority of issue types related to externally given problems;
   c   by the inability of the mass media to stress more than a limited number of types at one time.

Assumptions 4 and 5 carry the importance of change for the political evaluations of electors to its logical conclusion, by stipulating that the only aspect of an issue type relevant to voting is the prospect for change associated with its saliency. This is an admitted simplification, but then to make any kind of practical decision the actual complexities have to be simplified to some extent, and electors are hardly more prone to do so than parties or governments.

Similarly Assumption 6, on electors' invariant association of socialist parties with proposals for change over most issue areas, is justified on the grounds that bourgeois parties are, in general, less likely to intervene or innovate, whatever may be the case at particular times or in particular instances. Certain qualifications in this exact statement of the case need to be noted, however. It is the majority of electors who make this association.

We have already pointed out when discussing the Basic Vote that majority shifts in one direction are partially offset by minority shifts in the other, precisely because some electors may associate the socialists with opposition to specific changes. This may stem from exceptional personal circumstances, as when the voter is a government employee whose livelihood depends on continued state expansion. We need only stipulate that a majority make the association between socialists and change, because we are dealing with net switches of support rather than with all types of electoral movement.

The second qualification in Assumption 6 is that socialists are not necessarily associated with change on the 'erratic' issue types (see Table 2.6, p. 50 above, for further specification of these). Socialist candidates may gain votes (like Callaghan or Schmidt) precisely because they are known as moderates opposed to the radical ideas of some of their colleagues. Similarly, electors may vote for a continuance of prosperity under a socialist administration. In these areas the immediate impact of circumstances and of what candidates and governments are actually doing is so great as to shake fixed ideas about party attitudes. In the other issue areas, however, the impact of government action is more obscure, and the parties are more bound by ideology to consistent forms of action. So invariant ideas about party attitudes are both more realistic and less likely to be refuted by a government taking uncharacteristic measures. These distinctions between erratic and fixed issues have, of course, been made throughout our discussion: Assumption 6 merely codifies them.

In Table 7.1 we concentrate on the situation of electors under a socialist–bourgeois type of party competition, because this is the most general case. If we included the reformist parties in Canada, Ireland and the United States, we should need to make separate statements for each country about issue types where the party was, or was not, associated with change. To avoid unnecessary detail we omit them here, particularly since specifications have been made in Tables 2.7 to 2.9. However, it is immediately apparent how the formal statements could be extended to these systems. The specification of erratic issues apart, all the assumptions apply to the 'reformist' party systems as much as to the socialist.

Assumption 7 in the form in which it appears here is a more general statement of Kelley and Mirer's decision rule for electors – leaving deliberately open the precise way in which the overall partisan balance of salient issue types is calculated. Most likely it is by weighting them equally and adding algebraically, as Kelley and Mirer found. Since we ourselves do not depend on going into individual processes of decision to determine the overall result, we do not need to commit ourselves to a specific process. Although Assumption 7 generalises Kelley and Mirer's rule, something like it follows from our assumptions about the overall election process. If electors do decide how to vote by evaluating the issue types which are important to them, they must have some relatively simple way of aggregating them so as to select the more congenial party over the whole set. So Assumption 7 is not an afterthought to our other reasoning but a necessary part of it. For the majority of electors the same issue type(s) will be salient all the time and they will always support the same party. These electors constitute the major element in the Basic Vote. Changes in outcomes are produced by a minority who, for whatever reason, respond to campaign issues and thus contribute to net shifts of support between parties.

Assumption 8 follows closely on this – if party leaders are concerned to gain votes at all, given the decision processes just described, they will emphasise issue types which produce favourable net switches of support. We know that democratic parties must be concerned to win votes, since even where coalitions are formed an increase in seats will enhance bargaining power. There are situations, however, where this does not happen (for example, where a dominant party is so firmly entrenched that no real alteration in the government situation can occur under any realistic election outcome). Under two-party competition, increasing votes ceases to be a consideration where a party is bound to win or lose anyway. In both cases, leaders will be more concerned to emphasise topics congenial to activists and fellow members rather than to electors as a whole – either to avert blame by maintaining purity in the case of defeat, or simply allowing ideology, to which they are also attached, to take over when it can without producing undesirable electoral consequences.

Assumption 9 reiterates the point (related in part to Assumption 3) that strategists, particularly in bourgeois parties, must be selective if they are to attract and not confuse voters. The constraints emerge not simply from the nature of electoral reactions, but also from considerations of plausibility and effective communication.

Implications of these general assumptions are stated in Table 7.2. They do not include all the possible consequences which might be derived from our reasoning, but only the most important. The relationship of these statements to the assumptions in Table 7.1 does not entail implications in any formal logical sense, since the deductions would change if other substantive concepts were substituted for the ones actually used. On the other hand, the deductions we make are not illogical, in the sense of infringing established rules of logical argument. Except in a few cases, however, logic does not narrow down possible implications only to the one stated. It is our substantive reasoning which does this. The number(s) of the specific assumption(s) which lead to each implication are accordingly bracketed after it.

All the implications stated in Table 7.2 are, of course, familiar from previous discussion – they are just worded more exactly. Implication 1 makes the obvious connection between the numbers of electors affected by an issue type and the size of its effect on votes. Implication 1a allows for the variation in effects associated with the erratic issue types. Implication 2 and its related statements (2a, 2b, 2c) make similar points in regard to the partisan direction in which issue types act. If change produces immediate benefits, it will (by Assumptions 5 and 6) favour the socialists: otherwise it reduces their support or increases that enjoyed by the bourgeois parties. If we accept that only in the case of socioeconomic redistribution does change bring immediate benefits, this will form the only set of specific issues which favour the socialists (2a); in the case of erratic issues change may bring immediate benefits and so it may favour the socialists, or may not (2b); where any other issue type is salient socialists lose out and bourgeois parties gain (2c). None of this is new, but the implications do draw our previous reasoning together and state it as unambiguously as possible.

Table 7.2 *Implications of the Theory of Election Outcomes and Party Competition (from the General Assumptions in Table 7.1)*

1   The size of the net voting switches produced by the saliency of a particular issue type in an election varies with the number of electors who feel themselves affected by policy changes associated with it (Assumptions 1, 2, 4; see Tables 2.6 to 2.9 (pp. 50–6) for rankings of issue types in terms of the numbers affected by associated changes).

1a For certain issue types, notably government record and prospects and candidate reactions, the number who feel themselves affected varies with circumstances. Hence the size of the net voting switches produced by their saliency varies from election to election (Assumptions 1, 2, 4).

2   The partisan direction of the net voting switches produced by the saliency of a particular issue type in an election is determined by the extent to which change associated with that issue type produced immediate benefits (Assumptions 1, 2, 4–6).

2a The only issue type where proposals for change always bring immediate and discernible benefits for the majority of electors is socioeconomic redistribution. Hence the saliency of this issue type always improves the electoral support of the socialist party/*tendance* relative to the bourgeois party/ *tendance* (Assumptions 1, 2, 4–6).

2b For foreign relationships, candidate reactions and government record and prospects, the evaluation of whether change brings immediate benefits varies with circumstances. Hence the party whose electoral position is improved by the saliency of those issues varies between elections (Assumptions 1, 2, 4–6).

2c For all other issue types change does not bring immediate and discernible benefits for the majority of electors in a situation where a socialist party/ *tendance* competes with a bourgeois party/*tendance*. Hence the saliency of these issue types always improves the electoral position of the bourgeois party/*tendance* relative to the socialist party/*tendance* (Assumptions 1, 2, 4–6). For a specification of the issue types associated with this effect, see Table 2.6 (p. 50). For their effects in other party systems see Tables 2.7 to 2.9 (pp. 52–6).

3   For many electors a particular issue type or combination of issue types may always be salient, regardless of the issues emphasised in a particular campaign (Assumptions 1, 2, 4–7).

3a Since such electors always vote for the same party/*tendance*, they contribute to a Basic Vote which persists at a level independent of issue gains or losses in a particular campaign (Assumptions 1, 2, 4–7).

Table 7.2 (*continued*)

4 Counterbalancing switches between voting blocs also contribute to a Basic Vote which persists at a level independent of issue gains or losses in a particular campaign (Assumptions 1, 2, 4–7).

5 In order to improve their electoral position socialist parties/*tendances* competing with bourgeois parties/*tendances* should stress socioeconomic redistribution only, out of the issue types which have a 'fixed' direction (Assumptions 1, 2, 4–7; cf. Implication 2a).

6 Over a series of elections, socialist parties/*tendances* competing with bourgeois parties/*tendances* do stress socioeconomic redistribution more, and other 'fixed' issue types less (Assumptions 1, 2, 4–8).

6a This tendency is more marked in competitive elections and less marked in non-competitive elections (Assumptions 1, 2, 4–8).

7 In order to improve their electoral position, bourgeois parties/*tendances* competing with socialist parties/*tendances* should stress a combination of civil order, ethnic or moral-religious issues, together with opposition to controls, regulation and/or support and incentives (Assumptions 1, 2, 4–7; cf. Implication 2c above).

8 Over a series of elections, bourgeois parties/*tendances* competing with socialist parties/*tendances* do stress such issue types more, and socioeconomic redistribution less (Assumptions 1, 2, 4–8).

9 In order to achieve their maximum overall vote, major parties/*tendances* should, in addition to emphasising the previously specified 'fixed' issues, endeavour to make government record and prospects, foreign relationships and candidate reactions favourable to themselves, or at least unfavourable to their opponents (Assumptions 1–7; cf. Implication 2b above).

9a Government record and prospects, foreign relationships and candidate reactions are stressed more by major parties/*tendances* in competitive than in non-competitive elections (Assumptions 1–8).

10 The number of issue types emphasised by each major party, and salient in the campaign, is limited (Assumptions 1–3, 7–9).

The magnitude and direction of election change having been covered, we now turn to the elements of stability in the results. Implications 3 and 3a make the point raised above in regard to Assumption 7, that many electors will always vote on the basis of the same issue type(s), regardless of which enter into the campaign. By consistently voting for the same party they contribute to an underlying level of support (which we have called the Basic Vote) which is unaffected by the events of a particular election. Since a minority of electors may well make different associations between parties and political change compared to the majority (Assumption 6), they may cause counterbalancing shifts of support which also contribute to Basic Vote (Implication 4).

The remaining implications relate to party strategies, both in the sense of recommending what parties should do to gain votes (on the basis of the first seven assumptions of Table 7.1, stipulating electoral reactions) and in the sense of specifying what they actually do (by adding in the modified office-seeking hypothesis, Assumption 8). Implication 6a is a consequence of the distinction drawn in Assumption 8 between party behaviour in competitive elections when it is worthwhile modifying emphases to draw in votes, and in non-competitive elections when it is not. It has not been tested directly in this discussion but seems to find support in previous research (Robertson, 1976; Budge and Farlie, 1977, pp. 428–32). The implication applies to socialist but not bourgeois parties, since the optimal election strategy for the latter is also one they favour ideologically. However, we should expect both types of party to make a special effort to capture erratic issues in a competitive situation (Implications 9 and 9a). Implication 10 rounds out the discussion of strategies by spelling out the consequences of Assumptions 3 and 9 for the number of issue types introduced into the campaign.

All the implications in Table 7.2 are drawn for a socialist–bourgeois type of confrontation, since the assumptions from which they derive dealt exclusively with this. With a few necessary changes, however, they can be made to apply to the exceptional situations – all the essential specifications for these have, in any case, already been made in Tables 2.7 to 2.9.

Although in a sense these implications represent a spelling out of the consequences of the general assumptions, they are also stated at a certain level of abstraction. The most interesting findings from our previous analysis came when we actually scored issues in terms of their magnitude and related the summed issue scores to party voting percentages. To do this we had to make the operational assumptions which appear in Table 7.3.

Table 7.3 *Operational Assumptions for the Theory of Election Outcomes and Party Competition*

---

1 The numbers of electors who react as expected to the saliency of an issue type, and hence the magnitude of the net voting switches (see Implication 1, Table 7.2) can be measured by assigning 0 for non-saliency, 1 for relatively small effects, 2 for medium effects and 3 for large effects.

2 Individually, electors may switch votes in any direction in response to the altered proposals for change produced by the varying saliency of issue types; but imbalanced changes in aggregate support (where numbers switching in one direction overbalance numbers switching in the other) occur only between major parties/*tendances* and third party voters/non-voters, not between major parties/*tendances* directly.

3 Hence scores for and against major parties/*tendances* on each salient issue type in an election can be summed algebraically to give an overall issue score for both major parties/*tendances* for each election. This reflects the extent of their overall support on the basis of a commitment for or against change over the various issue types, and by extension, the size of the net voting switches to and from them.

These are further spelt out in Appendix D. The first relates to the equivalence between rankings of magnitude and the simple scoring system we have employed. The second is the crucial postulate which allows us to add major party issue scores independently of each other: that is, the assumption that switches between major parties in response to the saliency of an issue type are balanced, so that net transfers take place only between other voters and the major parties. The scanty evidence on this point is mixed, but certainly compatible with the hypothesis that such transfers occur in most cases. In conjunction, these first two operational assumptions allow us to sum scores over all issue types for the two major parties or *tendances*, to provide a measure of their overall campaign appeal – the procedure summarised in Operational Assumption 3.

Table 7.4   *Applications of the Theory of Election Outcomes and Party Competition (Using the Operational Assumptions in Table 7.3)*

1   Overall issue scores for each major party/*tendance* in each postwar election for (a) each party, (b) each country, (c) sets of countries, can be plotted against corresponding voting percentages to estimate an average relationship between increments in issue advantages and vote gains/losses (see Figure 3.2, p. 71).

2   Over most countries and major parties/*tendances* there is a standard relationship: a unit increase in issue scores produces 0·96 per cent increase in net vote (and conversely for a unit decrease in issue scores) (see Chapter 5, Section 5.1 and Tables 5.1 and 5.2, pp. 115, 116 and 117: these also give individual estimates for exceptional cases.

3   The percentage vote for each major party/*tendance* at an issue score of zero gives an estimate of Basic Vote – the enduring percentage which it can attract in the absence of overall issue effects (see Tables 5.5 and 5.6, pp. 126 and 127, for such estimates).

4   By characterising issues in advance of the election, net vote percentages which will be gained or lost on issues can be calculated and added to/subtracted from Basic Vote to give a prediction of major party/*tendance* support in the next election (Chapter 4).

5   Using the quantitative estimates of issue effects and Basic Votes, exact specifications can be made of net gains and losses accruing from the rise, or deliberate introduction, of each issue type into the election campaign (see Chapter 5, Section 5.2, p. 119).

This renders possible the types of analysis carried through in the major part of the book. These are summarised in Table 7.4. The basis for all our estimates were the graphs of issue scores against voting percentages described in Application 1. The most striking finding of the analysis – that substantively similar issues produce similar gains and losses in votes across most countries – is summarised in Application 2. The generation of estimates of Basic Vote is covered in the third statement of Table 7.4. These then provide a basis for genuine predictions which combine Basic Vote estimates with estimates of issue effects calculated in advance of the election (Application 4). Diagnoses and advice for party strategists can be based on these quantifications of the electoral effects of various policies (Application 5).

7.3 Relationships with Rational Choice Theory

Formalising the explanation provides an opportunity to relate it to other theories more systematically than before. This section concentrates on differences and similarities between our formulation and 'rational choice' approaches to elections, which form the most systematically developed body of theory in the field at the present time. At many points in the previous discussion we have made explicit, or implicit, references to such theories which seek to treat politics analogously to economics, with voters as consumers of various 'public goods' seeking to maximise the supply of those they prefer, and politicians as entrepreneurs trading votes against promises to meet certain preferences (and thus, ultimately, to gain office). Within this framework electors are expected to choose the party whose policies concur most closely with their preferences, and politicians are expected to locate policies nearest the preferences of the largest grouping of electors. Both electors and parties are usually represented as points in single- or multi-dimensional space, constituted by the various public policies they endorse. As parties move towards a position that commands the largest voting bloc, they will 'converge', that is, agree on policies.

This picture of elections gives rise to the theoretical problem that the content may have no conclusion other than an arbitrary or imposed one, in that equal proportions of electors can have rankings of preferences over policies or parties, such that each can always get a majority over its rivals (the so-called 'paradox of voting'). This problem remains unresolved, as does the practical one of applying the theoretical formulation directly to voting behaviour. (For a comprehensive review see Budge and Farlie, 1977, chs 3–5.)

Despite these difficulties, rational choice theory has become a dominant paradigm in the field of election studies, certainly to the extent of providing an overall interpretation for the econometric models and findings on policy voting, which we discussed in Chapter 1. Why therefore have we chosen to break away from this approach in favour of the one we have applied?

In one sense, of course, we have not broken away, in that our theory makes voters and politicians just as 'rational' as any of the others. We have departed from the usual tradition, however, in attributing to electors a more specific criterion of choice between parties than the general stipulation that they vote for the party closest to their own (uncharacterised) preferences. General rational choice theory refuses to specify electors' preferences for fear of losing generality, while paradoxically proving overspecific and restrictive in terms of politicians' goals. Attainment of office is quite probably the main goal of many US politicians who lack a clear ideology attaching them to specific lines of policy. (Even in the United States, however, it is clear that presidential candidates maintain their party distinctiveness.) Where ideology is salient, however – that is, in most other democracies – the achievement of policy goals is more important than office.

Obviously this contrast is not absolute. Policy goals cannot be achieved except through office, and in order to gain it, as we have seen, policy emphases may be modified to some extent. Policies are not likely to be totally reversed in order to gain office, however, since their attainment is what makes office worthwhile in the first place; without this prospect, it would become an empty shell.

The modified office-seeking hypothesis (Table 7.1, Assumption 8) recognises this point by postulating that leaders are more likely to try to appeal to electors when they think this affects their chances of office than when they feel it does not. The whole conception of party competition in terms of which this assumption is stated differs radically, however, from the one developed in mainstream rational choice theory. Instead of parties confronting each other with different policies on the same issues, we have parties talking past each other about different issues. Electors, in turn, are viewed as making invariant judgements as to which parties are best in most issue areas, and voting for parties in terms of the saliency of the issues they 'own' – quite a different picture from one of electors judging parties in terms of last-minute adjustments of policy and their own divergent preferences on the same issue(s).

Where electors react in this way, without preference rankings being involved (because there are no competing preferences), the paradox of voting ceases to be a problem. Convergence, the other major concern of rational theories, similarly loses most of its content since it becomes a question of parties emphasising the same issues rather than agreeing on the same policies. Since one of the main assumptions behind spatial representations of rational choice theory is that all parties take a position on all issues, our conception of a strategy where the whole object is not to mention some policies is equally corrosive of traditional representations of 'pure policy space' (for a review of these see Budge and Farlie, 1978).

The theory, therefore, must be regarded as having developed out of rational choice rather than falling into the mainstream of that approach. Our reason for ascribing more specific criteria for electors' choice, centred around their personal situation and the threat of change, and leading on to the ascription of specific partisan effects to most issue types, is scepticism about the possibility of ever applying these substantively empty models directly to empirical data. Paradoxically, the existence of a highly abstract general mathematical theory which cannot be operationalised seems positively to encourage unrelated investigations of particular election situations. These can always be imprecisely interpreted in rational choice terms and thereby pass as related and cumulative, whereas at the level of data-based research they do nothing to validate each others' estimates or to produce a reliable stock of comparative knowledge. The kind of *a priori* ascription of substantive preferences to electors, which we have made, whose validity can then be checked over a wide variety of elections in terms of observable consequences, seems the best way to create a viable theory which can actually be applied in detail to real situations (for an intermediate position see Budge *et al.*, 1981).

7.4 Prescriptive Implications

In our introduction we pointed out that an improved descriptive explanation was essential to justify elections as a guarantee of government responsiveness, since we could not argue convincingly that they provided such a guarantee unless we knew how election processes really functioned. Our descriptive formulations have strong bearings on prescriptive theory and may ultimately shape our political stands just as much as moral imperatives.

Returning first to the major question of responsiveness raised in the introduction, our analysis certainly upholds the contention that electors' concerns are reflected as issues in the election campaign. Since such issues correspond broadly to the topics given heavy emphasis in campaign documents, they will find their way into government programmes provided that parties once elected do retain some of their campaign commitments. This is a moot point at present – so important that it will form the focus of our next research. There is scope for optimism in our election theory, however. The issue types whose saliency secures a party (or *tendance*) election are ideologically congenial to it, otherwise it would never have been trusted by the electorate to carry through the obvious course of action. So a government response is likely because of ideological imperatives as well as election considerations.

We have shown that parties are elected on a balance of salient issue types. As a result they may pursue actions some of which electors evaluate negatively (as well, of course, as taking what action they please on questions not brought up in the election). However, the fact of being elected means that on the majority of issue types deemed important by electors they will take an approved line, and this guarantee of a rough overall correspondence between changing electoral desires and government actions is all that has ever really been claimed for democracy.

Whether parties manage to convert the topics they initially raise into issues of concern to electors, or whether party propaganda responds to emphases already there, is again debatable. Possibly both processes occur, or possibly the parties focus and sharpen concerns that already exist in a vague form. Even on the most adverse assumption, that parties do raise topics first and thus shape electors' perceptions of saliency, one cannot characterise the process as completely manipulative or wholly circular (that is, parties determining the salient issues which they then act upon as governments, ignoring electors' 'real' preferences). For one thing, salient election issues seem to refer to real problems (Tables 2.3 and 2.4; pp. 36 and 39; Table 7.1, Assumption 9). For another, only some manifesto and platform emphases become salient issues: a process of selection is at work, not uncritical digestion of party appeals (Table 6.4, p. 139). This would argue for electors reacting to parties in an autonomous manner, picking up those suggestions which are relevant to them and ignoring others.

By suggesting also that loyal voters who support the party under most circumstances are also rationally evaluating and pursuing their own interests, in terms of the issue(s) of permanent importance to them, our theory also disposes of the suspicion that parties can do what they like with their own supporters. Their changes of direction on other policies are, on the contrary, tolerated because they are marginal to supporters' interests. The workhouse donkey might be elected if he ran in the party colours, but only if he continued basic party commitments. Can anyone doubt that abandonment of social welfare programmes by a socialist party would be followed by a major flight of adherents? Or that espousal of complete state ownership by bourgeois parties would carry similar results for them? Loyal electors on this view are voting for the party which will act as they wish in the unforeseen contingencies which dominate the life of governments – a highly rational approach which avoids costly and inconclusive calculations.

Our theory therefore views electors as voting understandably and sensibly on policy-based grounds, and parties and governments as sensitive to their views. The detailed process whereby this comes about is explained through the typology of issue types and characterisation of the partisan direction and magnitude of their impact. Of the assumptions underlying these, the hypothesis that electors group issues into fourteen broad types does not seem to carry obvious moral connotations. Their discounting of links between types, again, is hardly contentious from a normative point of view, although it does help defend the average elector against charges of stupidity (figuring within the theory as a quite sophisticated calculation-minimising device). The association of socialists with a desire for change is surely no more than they (and their opponents) claim for themselves.

Note our assumption is not that electors are against proposals for change, but only against those not carrying immediate benefits. Redistribution, equalisation, comprehensive schooling are all proposals which the majority (who would benefit) support. Since these are the areas where socialist and reformist programmes leave most mark, the assumption about change can hardly be described as reactionary in its implications. Indeed, equality and social justice might be described as what socialism is all about – the core elements in its programme to which state intervention and planning, legal reform, anti-discrimination laws, and so on, are only means. Any assumption that a majority supports redistribution while opposing other types of change is just as 'progressive as it is 'conservative'.

This balance in partisan and philosophical terms does not imply, however, that it is morally vacuous. For it does provide evidence that certain cherished tenets of party dogma are repugnant to a majority of electors in democracies. If, as is generally held, democratic governments should ultimately follow the will of the majority, where it can be ascertained, these tenets should at least be modified in light of electoral disapproval. This would apply to bourgeois parties in so far as they believe in inherent inequalities, though a modified equality of opportunity might be a different matter. It also applies to socialist planning and intervention generally.

No one could, of course, argue that electorally unpopular actions should never be taken. Were the economy to collapse in five years' time for lack of vigorous action at present, electors would blame the government retrospectively. Because unpopular means may be required to secure generally popular ends, governments have to use them and cannot be deterred by their current unpopularity. This is true for both socialist and bourgeois governments.

Nevertheless, if our theory is accepted as a valid description of electoral reality, and if an obligation is recognised to defer to majority wishes, these unpopular tactics – intervention, planning, change – should only be undertaken cautiously, and as a way of securing concrete benefits for the majority rather than as ends in themselves. Here we encounter what may be termed the paradox of responsible government, in that electors who will the ends (stability, prosperity) do not will the means (change, intervention, planning). As we have pointed out, this cannot be called an inconsistency in electors' reasoning since so often such means are not the obvious, only way to achieve the goals. Presumably the very reason why democratic governments are accorded autonomy, and independent decision-making powers, is on occasion to pursue desirable medium-term options at the expense of immediate sacrifices and of concurrent electoral unpopularity. If they turn out to be wrong, they will presumably lose the next election: but if they are right they should gain considerably. Thus the paradox in no way hinders or threatens democratic functioning, compared to that of other systems, provided politicians prove sufficiently intelligent and courageous to use the powers of leadership which democracy places in their hands.

A second more subtle aspect of the typology of issues and of the judgements of direction and magnitude based on opposition to change should also be noted. The consequence of having a whole range of issue types which parties may choose to emphasise in their campaign is to imply that the use of any favourable issue appeal is justified.

We do in fact take the view that matters of general concern should be raised and debated by the major parties, within the constraints of mass communication: no doubt this is a feature, or at least an implicit suggestion, in the theory we have constructed. The alternative is not necessarily that problems will go away if left unraised, but possibly that extremist minor parties will exploit them, or perhaps that they will be voiced and debated by other agencies. In either case, the perceived irrelevance of the major parties to matters of electoral concern constitutes a weakening of their representative function, a dilution of competition between them and hence an undermining of democracy.

The traditional difficulty with the view that any topic is a legitimate subject of public debate and government action (and especially in connection with censorship) comes with the question of response to a majority demand for abrogation of democracy itself. Should the major parties really divide on this rather than uniting to defend the system?

The answer given by our descriptive assumptions is, however, reassuring: this would never be a majority demand since it involves such massive change as to be repugnant to most electors. Nor would widespread censorship of traditional practices be acceptable, since this would simply be change in the guise of stability – and would be rejected by the majority where they had a voice.

Ultimately, therefore, the moral implications of our descriptive theory are reassuring for democracy, if not wholly agreeable either to bourgeois or socialist partisans. Because the majority dislike unpredictable change they will strongly support existing systems. Scope for change exists, however, where immediate benefits outweigh the costs, so electors by no means adhere to a completely static or a hierarchic society. They simply require convincing that proposed courses of action will bring personal benefits. Here lies the challenge and opportunity for socialists and reformers.

References

Alt, J. (1980), *The Politics of Economic Decline* (Cambridge: Cambridge University Press).

Arcelus, F., and Meltzer, A. H. (1975), 'The effect of aggregate economic variables on congressional elections', *American Political Science Review*, vol. 69, pp. 1232–9.

Blalock, H. (1960), *Social Statistics* (New York: McGraw-Hill).

Blondel, J. F. P. (1964), *Voters, Parties and Leaders: The Social Fabric of British Politics* (Harmondsworth, Penguin).

Bloom, P. H. S., and Price, H. D. (1975), 'Voter response to short-run economic conditions: the asymmetric effect of prosperity and recession', *American Political Science Review*, vol. 69, pp. 1240–54.

Børre, O. (1980), 'Recent changes in Danish elections and parties', paper presented to the Conference on Recent Changes in European Party Systems, Minneapolis, 5–9 May.

Boyd, R. W. (1972), 'Popular control of public policy: a normal vote analysis of the 1968 election', *American Political Science Review*, vol. 66, pp. 429–79.

Bryce, J. (1921), *Modern Democracies* (London: Macmillan).

Budge, I. (1973), 'The scientific status of political science: a comment on self-fulfilling and self-defeating predictions', *British Journal of Political Science*, vol. 3, p. 249.

Budge, I., Crewe, I., and Farlie, D. J. (eds) (1976), *Party Identification and Beyond: Representations of Voting and Party Competition* (London and New York: Wiley).

Budge, I., and Farlie, D. J. (1977), *Voting and Party Competition: A Theoretical Critique and Synthesis Applied to Surveys from Ten Democracies* (London and New York: Wiley).

Budge, I., and Farlie, D. J. (1978), 'The potentiality of dimensional analyses for explaining voting and party competition', *European Journal of Political Research*, vol. 6, pp. 203–31.

Budge, I., Farlie, D. J., and Laver, M. (1981), 'What is a rational choice? Shifts of meaning within explanations of voting and party competition', Department of Government, University of Essex, ms.

Budge, I., and Herman, V. H. (1978), 'Coalition and government formation: an empirically relevant theory', *British Journal of Political Science*, vol. 8, pp. 459–78.

Budge, I., and Robertson, D. (eds) (forthcoming), *Comparative Party Strategies: An Analysis of Party Manifestos and Their Equivalents in Seventeen Democracies* (London: Sage).

Butler, D. E., and Stokes, D. E. (1971), *Political Change in Britain* (Harmondsworth: Penguin).

Campbell, A., Converse, P., Miller, W. E., and Stokes, D. E. (1960), *The American Voter* (New York: Wiley).

Castles, F. (ed.) (1982), *Political Parties and Public Policy* (London: Sage).

Converse, P. (1966), 'The concept of a normal vote', in *Elections and the Political*

Order, ed. A. Campbell, P. Converse, W. Miller and D. E. Stokes (New York: Wiley), pp. 9–39.

Crewe, I., and Särlvik, B. (1980), 'Party strategies and issue attitudes', in Z. Layton-Henry (ed.), *Conservative Party Politics*, (London: Macmillan), pp. 244–75.

Crewe, I., Särlvik, B., and Alt, J. (1977), 'Partisan dealignment in Britain 1964–74', *British Journal of Political Science*, vol. 7 (1977), pp. 129–90.

Farlie, D. J., and Budge, I. (1977), 'Newtonian mechanics and predictive election theory', *British Journal of Political Science*, vol. 7, pp. 413–22.

Flanigan, W. H., and Zingale, N. H. (1974), 'The measurement of electoral change', *Political Methodology*, vol. 1, pp. 49–82.

Goodhart, C., and Bhansali, R. (1970), 'Political economy', *Political Studies*, vol. 18, pp. 43–106.

Goodman, S., and Kramer, G. H. (1975), 'Comment on Arcelus and Meltzer: the effect of aggregate economic conditions on congressional elections', *American Political Science Review*, 69, pp. 1255–65.

Hibbs, D. (1978), unpublished ms., Department of Government, Harvard University, ms.

Jackson, J. (1975), 'Issues, party choices and presidential votes', *American Political Science Review*, vol. 69, pp. 193–204.

Kavanagh, D. (1981), 'The politics of manifestos', *Parliamentary Affairs*, vol. 34, pp. 7–27.

Kelley, S., and Mirer, T. (1974), 'The simple act of voting', *American Political Science Review*, vol. 68, pp. 572–91.

Kemp, D. (1978), *Society and Electoral Behaviour in Australia* (St. Lucia, Qd.: University of Queensland Press).

Key, V. O. (1963), *Public Opinion and American Democracy* (New York: Knopf).

Klingemann, H. D., and Taylor, C. (1977), 'Partnership, candidates and issues: attitudinal components of the vote in West German elections', European Consortium for Political Research, Berlin, ms.

Kramer, G. (1971), 'Short-term fluctuations in US voting behaviour 1896–1964', *American Political Science Review*, vol. 65, pp. 131–43.

Le Duc, L. (1975), 'The majority government issue and electoral behaviour in Canada', paper presented to International Political Science Association Committee on Political Sociology Conference on Elections in Complex Societies at Queen's University, Kingston, Ontario.

Le Duc, L. (1977), 'Political behaviour and the issue of majority-government in two federal elections', *Canadian Journal of Political Science*, vol. 10, pp. 311–39.

Lipset, S. M. (1976), 'Radicalism in North America: a comparative view of the party systems in Canada and the United States', *Transactions of the Royal Society of Canada*, ser. IV, vol. XIV, pp. 19–55.

Lipset, S. M., and Rokkan, S. (1967), *Party Systems and Voter Alignments* (New York: The Free Press).

Madsen, H. J. (1980), 'Electoral outcomes and macro-economic policies: the Scandinavian cases', in *Models of Political Economy*, ed. P. Whiteley (London: Sage).

Margolis, M. (1977), 'From confusion to confusion: issues and the American voter', *American Political Science Review*, vol. 71, pp. 31–43.

Miller, W. L. (1978), 'What was the profit in following the crowd? Aspects of

Labour and Conservative strategy since 1970', paper presented to Political Studies Association, Warwick.

Miller, W. L., and Mackie, M. (1973), 'The electoral cycle and the asymmetry of government and opposition popularity', *Political Studies*, vol. 21, pp. 263–79.

Page, B., and Jones, C. C. (1978), 'Reciprocal effects of policy preferences, party loyalties and the vote', paper presented to the American Political Science Convention, New York.

Paldam, M. (1981), 'A preliminary survey of the theories and findings on vote and popularity functions', *European Journal of Political Research*, vol. 9, pp. 181–99.

Pedersen, M. (1980), 'On measuring party system change', *Comparative Political Studies*, vol. 12, pp. 387–403.

Pool, I., Popkins, S., and Abelson, B. (1965), *Candidates, Issues and Strategies* (Boston, Mass.: MIT Press).

Riker, W., and Ordeshook, P. C. (1973), *Positive Political Theory* (Englewood Cliffs, NJ: Prentice-Hall).

Robertson, D. (1976), *A Theory of Party Competition* (London and New York: Wiley).

Stigler, G. J. (1973), 'General economic conditions and national elections', *American Economic Review Papers*, no. 63, pp. 160–80.

Stokes, D. E. (1966), 'Some dynamic elements of contests for the presidency', *American Political Science Review*, vol. 60, pp. 19–38.

Studlar, D. T. (1978), 'Policy voting in Britain', *American Political Science Review*, vol. 72, pp. 46–64.

Tufte, E. R. (1975), 'Determinants of the outcomes of midterm congressional elections', *American Political Science Review*, vol. 69, pp. 812–26.

Tufte, E. R. (1978), *Political Control of the Economy* (Princeton, NJ: Princeton University Press).

Postwar Votes in Twenty-Three Democracies

The major source of information on voting percentages is the *International Almanac of Electoral History*, supplemented by reports in *Keesing's Contemporary Archives, European Journal for Political Research*, and the occasional newspaper report. The sources used are indicated by the letter I, K, E, and N respectively.

Because the political systems in several countries are fragmented, the returns have been simplified by grouping parties into *tendances* of left or right. The groupings are detailed in Table 2.1 (p. 28 above). Where electoral systems have more than one stage in the electoral process, whether by transferable votes or two actual elections, the initial votes are the ones included in the analyses.

Australia 1951–80

Year	Bourgeois Parties		Socialist–Reformist Parties		Source of % Votes
	Issue Score	% Vote	Issue Score	% Vote	
1951	3	50·2	3	47·7	I
1954	7	47·0	3	50·1	I
1955	6	47·6	0	45·2	I
1958	9	46·4	–3	42·9	I
1961	2	42·0	3	48·0	I
1963	6	46·0	2	45·5	I
1966	6	50·0	3	40·0	I
1969	–1	43·3	4	47·0	I
1972	1	41·5	6	49·6	I
1974	0	44·9	1	49·3	E
1975	4	53·0	–2	42·8	E
1977	4	48·1	–6	39·6	E
1980	2	46·2	0	45·4	K

Austria 1953–79

Year	Bourgeois Parties		Socialist–Reformist Parties		Source of % Votes
	Issue Score	% Vote	Issue Score	% Vote	
1953	1	41·3	3	42·1	I
1956	7	46·0	3	43·0	I
1959	4	44·2	3	44·8	I
1962	3	45·4	2	44·0	I

Austria 1953–79 (*continued*)

Year	Bourgeois Parties		Socialist–Reformist Parties		Source of
	Issue Score	*% Vote*	*Issue Score*	*% Vote*	*% Votes*
1966	5	48·3	0	42·6	I
1970	0	44·7	5	48·4	I
1971	0	43·1	6	50·0	I
1975	0	42·9	5	50·4	E
1979	1	41·9	5	51·0	E

Belgium 1951–78

Year	Bourgeois Parties		Socialist–Reformist Parties		Source of
	Issue Score	*% Vote*	*Issue Score*	*% Vote*	*% Votes*
1951	3	47·7	0	34·5	I
1954	1	41·1	3	37·3	I
1958	3	46·5	−1	35·8	I
1961	−1	41·5	4	36·7	I
1965	−2	34·4	−7	28·3	I
1968	−3	31·8	−6	28·0	I
1971	0	30·1	−8	27·2	I
1974	−1	32·3	−9	26·7	E
1977	2	36·0	−6	26·4	E
1978	−1	36·3	−8	25·4	E

Canada 1945–80

Year	Bourgeois Parties		Socialist–Reformist Parties		Source of
	Issue Score	*% Vote*	*Issue Score*	*% Vote*	*% Votes*
1945	0	27·4	0	40·9	I
1949	0	29·7	8	49·5	I
1953	1	31·0	7	48·8	I
1957	6	38·9	−1	40·9	I
1958	9	53·6	−4	33·6	I
1962	3	37·3	2	37·2	I
1963	−3	32·8	3	41·7	I
1965	−1	32·4	7	40·2	I
1968	−3	31·4	9	45·5	I
1972	3	35·0	1	38·5	I
1974	4	35·5	5	43·2	E
1979	5	35·9	0	40·1	E
1980	−1	33·0	5	43·9	K

Denmark 1950–79

Year	Bourgeois Parties		Socialist–Reformist Parties		Source of % Votes
	Issue Score	% Vote	Issue Score	% Vote	
1950	1	47·3	0	39·6	I
1953	1	48·0	3	40·4	I
1953	1	47·7	3	41·3	I
1957	0	49·5	3	39·4	I
1960	4	44·8	3	42·1	I
1964	0	46·2	1	41·9	I
1966	1	45·3	–3	38·3	I
1968	1	53·9	–4	34·1	I
1971	–6	46·7	1	37·3	I
1973	1	32·6	–7	25·7	E
1975	2	35·9	1	29·9	E
1977	1	24·1	1	37·0	E
1979	–3	30·4	1	38·3	E

Finland 1945–79

Year	Bourgeois Parties		Socialist–Reformist Parties		Source of % Votes
	Issue Score	% Vote	Issue Score	% Vote	
1945	–1	41·6	3	48·6	I
1948	4	45·2	0	46·3	I
1951	2	43·5	3	48·1	I
1954	3	44·8	3	47·9	I
1958	4	44·2	2	46·4	I
1962	4	44·4	–3	41·5	I
1966	3	41·5	6	48·4	I
1970	–1	41·1	–3	40·0	I
1972	–2	39·1	–1	42·8	I
1975	–2	40·3	0	43·8	E
1979	0	42·7	–3	41·8	E

France (First Ballot) 1958–81

Year	Bourgeois Parties		Socialist–Reformist Parties		Source of % Votes
	Issue Score	% Vote	Issue Score	% Vote	
1958	5	49·1	–4	45·9	K
1962	3	54·3	–3	41·9	K
1967	3	50·5	5	41·3	K
1968	5	58·1	0	36·5	K
1973	3	49·5	2	44·1	K
1978	1	44·1	4	45·3	K
1981	4	43·3	9	54·3	K

Iceland 1946–79

Year	Bourgeois Parties		Socialist–Reformist Parties		Source of % Votes
	Issue Score	% Vote	Issue Score	% Vote	
1946	1	39·5	0	19·5	I
1949	1	39·5	0	19·5	I
1953	−1	37·1	−1	16·0	I
1956	2	42·4	0	19·2	I
1959	2	42·5	−1	15·2	I
1959	1	39·7	−1	16·0	I
1963	2	41·4	−1	16·0	I
1967	−1	37·5	−3	13·9	I
1971	−4	36·2	−1	17·1	I
1974	4	42·7	0	18·3	E
1978	−5	32·7	3	22·9	E
1979	−3	35·4	−3	19·7	E

India 1951–79

Year	Congress Party		Source of % Votes
	Issues Score	% Vote	
1951	9	44·5	K
1957	10	47·2	K
1962	8	45·1	K
1967	−3	37·9	K
1971	9	43·7	K
1977	−11	34·5	K
1979	3	42·0	K

Ireland 1948–81

Year	Bourgeois Parties		Socialist–Reformist Parties		Source of % Votes
	Issue Score	% Vote	Issue Score	% Vote	
1948	1	19·8	2	41·9	I
1951	5	25·8	6	46·3	I
1954	7	32·0	3	43·4	I
1957	0	26·6	6	48·3	I
1961	2	32·0	0	43·8	I
1965	3	34·1	5	47·7	I
1969	3	34·1	6	45·6	I
1973	3	35·1	4	46·3	E
1977	−5	30·5	9	50·5	E
1981	6	36·6	2	45·4	K

Israel 1949–81

Year	Bourgeois Parties		Socialist–Reformist Parties		Source of
	Issue Score	% Vote	Issue Score	% Vote	% Votes
1949	−1	20·7	6	50·3	I
1951	4	26·1	4	50·0	I
1955	5	27·2	−1	47·7	I
1959	2	24·3	6	51·4	I
1961	4	27·4	0	48·8	I
1965	−2	21·3	7	51·3	I
1969	−4	22·9	−3	46·2	I
1973	4	30·2	−4	39·6	E
1977	7	33·4	−8	24·6	E
1981	10	40·0	−6	39·2	N

Italy 1948–79

Year	Bourgeois Parties		Socialist–Reformist Parties		Source of
	Issue Score	% Vote	Issue Score	% Vote	% Votes
1948	6	48·5	0	18·9	I
1953	2	40·1	0	22·6	I
1958	4	42·4	0	22·7	I
1963	1	38·2	3	25·3	I
1968	3	39·1	3	26·9	I
1972	1	38·8	4	27·2	I
1976	4	38·7	4	34·4	E
1979	4	38·3	4	30·4	E

Japan 1958–80

Year	Bourgeois Parties		Socialist–Reformist Parties		Source of
	Issue Score	% Vote	Issue Score	% Vote	% Votes
1958	7	57·8	3	32·9	I
1960	5	57·6	−1	27·6	I
1963	1	53·9	0	29·0	I
1967	−3	48·8	−1	27·9	I
1969	−2	47·6	−3	21·4	I
1972	5	46·9	3	21·9	I
1976	−3	41·8	0	20·7	E
1979	−5	44·6	−6	19·7	E
1980	−2	47·9	−5	19·3	K

Luxembourg 1954–79

Year	Bourgeois Parties		Socialist–Reformist Parties		Source of
	Issue Score	% Vote	Issue Score	% Vote	% Votes
1954	2	42·4	1	35·1	I
1959	1	36·9	−1	34·9	I

Luxembourg 1954–79 (*continued*)

Year	Bourgeois Parties Issue Score	% Vote	Socialist–Reformist Parties Issue Score	% Vote	Source of % Votes
1964	1	33·3	3	37·7	I
1968	3	35·3	−1	32·3	I
1974	−2	27·9	−4	29·1	E
1979	0	34·5	−6	24·3	E

Netherlands 1946–81

Year	Bourgeois Parties Issue Score	% Vote	Socialist–Reformist Parties Issue Score	% Vote	Source of % Votes
1946	0	51·5	−3	28·3	I
1948	2	53·4	−4	25·6	I
1952	−1	48·9	0	29·0	I
1956	4	50·0	2	32·7	I
1959	0	49·1	1	30·4	I
1963	2	49·2	0	28·0	I
1967	−3	44·6	−3	23·6	I
1971	−3	36·8	0	24·6	I
1972	−3	31·3	3	27·3	I
1977	7	31·9	5	33·8	E
1981	−1	30·8	3	28·3	N

New Zealand 1951–78

Year	Bourgeois Parties Issue Score	% Vote	Socialist–Reformist Parties Issue Score	% Vote	Source of % Votes
1951	3	54·0	1	45·8	I
1954	2	44·3	2	44·1	I
1957	−3	44·2	3	48·3	I
1960	0	47·6	−4	43·4	I
1963	4	47·1	0	43·7	I
1966	2	43·6	0	41·4	I
1969	4	45·2	3	44·2	I
1972	−2	41·5	6	48·4	I
1975	7	47·4	−2	39·7	E
1978	−4	39·7	−3	40·3	E

Norway 1949–77

Year	Bourgeois Parties Issue Score	% Vote	Socialist–Reformist Parties Issue Score	% Vote	Source of % Votes
1949	0	41·6	4	45·7	I
1953	0	47·7	5	46·7	I
1957	1	45·3	6	48·3	I

Norway 1949–77 (*continued*)

Year	Bourgeois Parties Issue Score	% Vote	Socialist–Reformist Parties Issue Score	% Vote	Source of % Votes
1961	1	42·6	1	46·8	I
1965	1	47·6	−4	43·1	I
1969	0	45·0	3	46·5	I
1973	0	44·2	−8	35·3	E
1977	−1	48·6	−1	42·3	E

Sri Lanka 1960–77

Year	Bourgeois Parties Issue Score	% Vote	Socialist–Reformist Parties Issue Score	% Vote	Source of % Votes
1960	5	29·3	0	22·0	K
1960	6	37·6	3	33·6	K
1965	8	39·2	−1	30·0	K
1970	3	37·9	7	36·8	K
1977	8	49·1	−4	31·8	K

Sweden 1948–79

Year	Bourgeois Parties Issue Score	% Vote	Socialist–Reformist Parties Issue Score	% Vote	Source of % Votes
1948	0	47·5	2	46·1	I
1952	1	49·5	2	46·0	I
1956	0	50·4	1	44·6	I
1958	0	50·4	3	46·2	I
1960	1	47·7	3	47·8	I
1964	3	43·9	2	47·3	I
1968	2	42·8	4	50·1	I
1970	3	47·7	2	45·3	I
1973	3	48·8	0	43·6	E
1976	3	50·7	−5	42·7	E
1979	1	49·0	0	43·2	E

Switzerland 1951–79

Year	Bourgeois Parties Issue Score	% Vote	Socialist–Reformist Parties Issue Score	% Vote	Source of % Votes
1951	0	58·7	0	25·8	I
1955	0	58·2	0	26·8	I
1959	0	58·1	0	26·2	I
1963	0	58·3	0	26·4	I
1967	−3	55·8	−3	23·3	I
1971	−4	52·8	−7	22·7	I
1975	3	53·2	3	24·9	E
1979	0	57·2	0	24·4	E

United Kingdom 1950–79

Year	Bourgeois Parties Issue Score	% Vote	Socialist–Reformist Parties Issue Score	% Vote	Source of % Votes
1950	4	43·4	3	46·1	I
1951	4	48·0	3	48·8	I
1955	5	49·7	1	46·4	I
1959	7	49·4	2	43·8	I
1964	2	43·4	3	44·1	I
1966	0	41·9	8	48·0	I
1970	4	46·4	2	43·1	I
1974	−4	37·9	−4	37·2	E
1974	−4	35·8	2	39·3	E
1979	7	43·9	0	37·0	E

United States 1948–80

Year	Bourgeois Parties Issue Score	% Vote	Socialist–Reformist Parties Issue Score	% Vote	Source of % Votes
1948	−1	45·1	1	49·6	I
1952	6	55·1	−4	44·4	I
1956	9	57·4	0	42·0	I
1960	0	49·5	0	49·7	I
1964	−6	38·5	6	61·1	I
1968	1	43·4	−1	42·7	I
1972	6	60·7	−3	37·5	I
1976	0	48·0	0	50·1	E
1980	1	51·0	−1	41·0	K

West Germany 1957–80

Year	Bourgeois Parties Issue Score	% Vote	Socialist–Reformist Parties Issue Score	% Vote	Source of % Votes
1957	8	50·2	0	31·8	I
1961	4	45·3	0	36·2	I
1965	6	47·6	5	39·3	I
1969	6	46·1	7	42·7	I
1972	3	44·9	2	45·8	I
1976	1	48·6	0	42·6	E
1980	−3	44·5	0	42·9	K

Appendix B

Issues and Scorings for Individual Postwar Elections in Twenty-Three Democracies

General

The bulk of this Appendix is devoted to a summary description of issues in each election, and their classification and scoring as specified by Tables 2.1. and 2.6.–2.9. (pp. 28 and 50–6 above), and the coding procedures outlined in Appendix C. First, however, we have to review such points as our choice of countries, time periods, and parties, and to create the sources from which the characterisation of issues was derived.

Countries were chosen on the grounds that they had had reasonably free elections over the postwar periods, and that there was no reason to think this situation would change in the immediate future. The maintenance of free elections meets the most widely accepted 'procedural' definition of democracy, as a competitive struggle for the popular vote under standard liberties of speech and assembly, and so on.

These criteria directed choice of the classical mass democracies of Western Europe, North America and Australasia. India and Sri Lanka were incuded because free elections had taken place from Independence, shortly after the war. Other ex-colonial countries were not studied even though they had free elections from Independence, since the period which had elapsed to the present was rather short. This had two effects: one was to reduce confidence in whether free elections could be maintained over the long run, the other was to render it doubtful whether the party system had stabilised sufficiently for general estimates to be based upon it.

This indeed constituted a problem even in the case of some of the countries we had chosen. The most obvious case is Sri Lanka (Ceylon) where after a near-monopoly of votes and seats by the United National Party in 1948 and 1952 the balance swung wildly in the other direction in 1956. Only in the elections of the 1960s could a more regular pattern of competition be discerned, which enabled general estimates to be made with more confidence. Accordingly the postwar elections examined for Sri Lanka are for 1960 onwards.

This is an extreme case, not paralleled in the case of India where the 'normal' pattern of Congress dominance began early. Even in the case of old established democracies the impact of war and reconstruction – and often the emergence of differently constituted parties – means that we begin with the second or third postwar election, in order to give the new system a chance to settle down. In France we concentrate on the Fifth Republic only, as politics differ so much between the Fourth and Fifth Republics. In countries less affected by the war we tend to start earlier. For defeated countries (Austria, Italy, West Germany and Japan) we begin with the emergence of the normal party structure, after re-establishment of effective independence – earlier for the first two named, later for West Germany and Japan.

These are only the general considerations we have had in mind in choosing elections for study. Choices are also shaped by circumstances peculiar to each country, such as stabilisation of party alliances or the fact that the previous party system emerged relatively unchanged from the war.

The accounts of election prospects and campaigns upon which we based the characterisation of issues are overwhelmingly the distillations of newspaper accounts produced by *Keesing's Contemporary Archives* (London, 1933–81) under the index heading for each country and the subheading 'General Election'. These were supplemented by reports in *The Economist* (London) under the same index headings. These are by far the most accessible accounts of elections and their use also means that we base our characterisation of issues for different countries on reasonably uniform criteria of relevance and a fairly standard format.

In the case of a few important countries these advantages were outweighed by the existence of a uniquely authoritative series of specialised accounts. The prime example is the Nuffield General Election Series for Britain, edited since 1951 by D. E. Butler with various associates (London, Macmillan, various dates). For the United States there is the analogous *Making of the President* series, by T. White (New York: Atheneum Press, various dates). This extends from 1960 to 1976. Earlier descriptions of issues are provided by the voting studies: B. Berelson, P. F. Lazarsfeld and W. McPhee, *Voting* (Chicago: Chicago University Press, 1956): A. Campbell *et al.*, *The Voter Decides* (Evanston, Ill.: R. W. Peterson, 1954) and *The American Voter* (New York: Wiley, 1960). For the Canadian elections of 1972 and 1974 our source has been *Canada at the Polls*, edited by H. Penniman (Washington: American Enterprise Institute, 1975). All other accounts used were in *Keesing's Archives* and *The Economist*.

The parties or *tendances* to which issues were credited in each country are those specified in Table 2.5 (p. 50 above) and in Appendix A. In the summaries below they are generally designated as B (for bourgeois) and S (for socialist–reformist). The specific party or combination of parties so designated for each country can be found by turning to Table 2.5. In general our summaries of issues and types are brief, in view of the large number of elections covered and the need to conserve space. We have made them so far as possible self-explanatory, but wider references and implications cannot be covered. Interested readers can, of course, follow them up independently by turning to the corresponding accounts in *Keesing's* and *The Economist*.

Below we generally give a summary description of the specific issue, a condensed label referring it to a type (for example, (1) refers to the first category in Table 2.1, 'Civil order'); a magnitude and direction indicated by symbols such as +3B, –1S, +2S, and O which imply a large impact favouring the bourgeois parties, a small impact against the socialist–reformist parties, a medium impact favouring the socialist–reformist parties; and in an issue such as government record, zero means the issue was raised but the pros and cons effectively balanced out. A net score is given for all the issue impacts for and against each party.

The individual contribution of each issue to the score has been determined by substituting 3 for large, 2 for medium and 1 for small. The overall score is the one used in our standard calculations – the algebraic sum of individual issue magnitudes for each party. The alternative scores discussed in Appendix D can easily be calculated from the information provided.

Of course all judgements rest on the application of certain procedures to the basic accounts specified above, in the way illustrated in Chapter 3, Section 3.1 (p. 57

above). These procedures are codified in Appendix C, where we also report levels of agreement between independent codings of the same accounts.

ISSUES AND SCORES FOR INDIVIDUAL ELECTIONS

Australian Elections	*Issues and Scores*	*Overall Net Scores*	
		B	*S*
1951	Communist-inspired industrial unrest (1); Menzies' leadership (5); price rises (6); increased pensions and family allowances (11): +3B, +3B, –3B, +3S	+3	+3
1954	Menzies' personality (5); economic growth (6); increased pensions (11); level of taxation (14): +3B, +3B, +3S, +1B	+7	+3
1955	Labour ties with Communists (1); Menzies' leadership (5); Evatt's sympathy with radicals (5); increases in social services (11): +3B, +3B, –3S, +3S	+6	0
1958	Communist domination of trade unions (1); Menzies' leadership (5); Evatt's alleged Communist sympathies (5); general prosperity after difficulties (6): +3B, +3B, –3S, +3B	+9	–3
1961	Prosperity balanced by credit squeeze (6); social service payments, National Health Service (11): +2B, +3S	+2	+3
1963	Australian garrison in Malaysia, American base in N. W. Cape (4); prosperity after credit squeeze (6); Federal–RC Church negotiations on aid to private schools (7); increased social service spending, housing aid (11): –1S, +3B, +3B, +3S	+6	+2
1966	Vietnam involvement, conscription (4); Holt leadership compared to inexperienced labour (5); economic boom (6); finance for Ord River scheme (W. Australia) (9); more for pensioners and education (11): +1B, +1B, +1B, +3B, +3S	+6	+3
1969	Vietnam war involvement (3); recriminations surrounding Gorton (5); attractiveness of Whitlam (5); economic growth (6); proposals for National Health Service (11): –1B, –1B, +1S, +1B, +3S	–1	+4
1972	Forward policy *v.* disengagement in S. E. Asia (3);		

Australian Elections	Issues and Scores	Overall Net Scores	
		B	S
	Whitlam openness and attractiveness (5); recriminations surrounding McMahon (5); inflation balanced by economic growth (6); Chinese resume wheat purchases, revaluation of dollar increases farm sales (10); plans for Health Service (11): +1S, +2S, −1B, +1B, +1B, +3S	+1	+6
1974	Foreign ownership of resources (3); Whitlam personality (5); inflation of 14 per cent (6): +1S, +2S, −2S	0	+1
1975	Governor-General's dismissal of Prime Minister (Whitlam) (2); Fraser image as a 'strong man' (5); economic depression, government corruption balanced by earlier prosperity (6); free market, removal of controls (14): +2B, +1B, −2S, +1B	+4	−2
1977*	Prime Minister Fraser's style (5); Whitlam's unreliability (5); unemployment, sluggish economy balanced by reduction in inflation (6); lack of credibility of alternative government (6); uranium mining (12); industrial disruption, laws to curb trade union activities (13): +3B, −3S, −1B, −3S, +1B, +1B	+4	−6
1980	Prime Minister's style (5); sluggish economy balanced by reduction in inflation (6): +1B, +1B	+2	0

*Effect of personalities underestimated in the original prediction and net scores used were −1 for both parties.

Austrian Elections	Issues and Scores	Overall Net Scores B	S
1953	Greater public expenditure to meet unemployment (11); deflation to balance budget (14): +3S, +1B	+1	+3
1956	Formation of neo-Nazi party (1); end of Allied Occupation (6); public ownership in oil industry (12): +3B, +3 Both, +1B	+7	+3
1959	Minor scandals in People's Party (6); Church–state relations (7); agricultural price policy (10); housing reform (11); tax reforms to benefit small business (14): −1B, +3B, +1B, +3S, +1B	+4	+3
1962	Socialist ministers in coalition mishandled police strike (6); general economic prosperity (6): −1S, +3 Both	+3	+2
1966	Danger of covert Communist entry to power through Socialists(1); People's Party defence of press liberty (2); Socialist leadership splits (5); increases in rail tariffs and milk prices (11): +3B, +2B, −3S, +3S	+5	0
1970	Reduction of army service (4); Kreisky's personality (5); faltering economic progress (6); welfare and housing policies (11): +1B, +2S, −1B, +3S	0	+5
1971	Electoral reforms (2); Kreisky's personality (5); better economic performance balanced by inflation (6); increase in social welfare (11): −2S, +3S, +2S, +3S	0	+6
1975	Kreisky's personality (5); relative economic prosperity (6) balanced by payments difficulties (6); opposition to unemployment (11): +2S, 0, +3S	0	+5
1979	Austrian neutrality (3); Kreisky's personality (5); relative economic prosperity (6); nuclear energy development (12); support for free enterprise (14): +1S, +3S, +2S, −1S, +1B	+1	+5

Belgian Elections	*Issues and Scores*	Overall Net Scores B S
1950	Position of monarchy (2); tax on company profits (14): +2B, +1B	+3 0
1954	Joining European Defence Community (4); unemployment, social reforms (11): +1B, +3S	+1 +3
1958	Reduce conscription, oppose nuclear arms (4); equality for church schools (7): −1S, +3B	+3 −1
1961	Strikes, riots, industrial unrest against Loi Unique (1); loss of Congo (3); Spaak's personality (5); Austerity Programme (6); reduction in unemployment benefit (11): +3B, −1B, +1S, −3B, +3S	−1 +4
1965	Proposals for federalism (2); economic growth balanced by current policies towards Flemish and Walloons (6); language tensions (8): −2S, −2 Both, −3S	−2 −7
1968	Non-response to Flemish/Walloon demands (6); splitting University of Louvain (8); continuing regional disputes over boundaries (9): −3B, −3S, −3S	−3 −6
1971	Constitutional concessions to Flemish (2); language disputes (8); allocation of villages between Liège and Limburg, status of Brussels (9): −2S, −3S, −3S	0 −8
1974	Linguistic constitutional amendments (2); aborted Iran refinery, confused economic situation, government uncertainty over language (6); continuing language tension (8); regionalisation (9): +2B, −3 Both, −3S, −3S	−1 −9
1977	Constitutional changes (2); Tindemans's personality (5); stabilisation programme balanced by poor economic growth (6); creation of cultural councils (8); regional autonomy (9); unemployment (11); cuts in public spending (14): −2S, +1B, +1B, −3S, −3S, +3S, −1S	+2 −6
1978	French language rights (2); Tindemans's popularity (5);	

Belgian Elections	*Issues and Scores*	*Overall Net Scores*	
		B	S

economic recession (6);
socialist split on ethnic issues (8):
–2S, +2B, –3 Both, –3S   –1   –8

Canadian Elections	Issues and Scores	Overall Net Scores	
		B	S
1945	Conduct of war (3); total *v.* partial conscription (4); Mackenzie King's personality (5); rationing, war restrictions balanced by need for strong majority government (6): +3S, +3S, −3S, −3S	0	0
1949	St Laurent's personality (5); Postwar prosperity (6); National Unity (9A): +3S, +2S, +3S	0	+8
1953	Support for NATO (3); St Laurent's personality (5); prosperity, industrial expansion (6); redundancies, government waste (14): +1S, +3S, +3S, +1B	+1	+7
1954	Fear of US domination (3); Diefenbaker's personality (5); bad wheat sales, economic decline balanced by feeling that only Liberals can govern effectively (6): +3B, +3B, −1S	+6	−1
1958	Fear of US domination (3); Diefenbaker's personality (5); Pearson's ineptness (5); good performance of Conservatives in government, credibility as majority government (6); Liberal responsibility for unemployment (6): +3B, +3B, −3S, +3B, −1S	+9	−4
1962	Kennedy's anti-Diefenbaker remarks and support for Liberals (3); Diefenbaker's personality (5); attempted dismissal of Governor, Bank of Canada (Coyne), devaluation, unemployment, balanced by good wheat sales to China (6): +2S, +3B, 0	+3	+2
1963	Nuclear weapons storage BOMARC MISSILES (4); government quarrels, unemployment (6): +3S, −3B	−3	+3
1965	Dispute over Canadian flag (2); unification armed forces (4); Liberals only credible majority government (6); relations with Quebec, preservation of unity (9A); Canadian pension plan (11): +2B, +3S, −3 Both, +1S, +3S, +3S	−1	+7
1968	Trudeau's personality (5); economic prosperity (6); Conservative leadership divisions (6);		

Canadian Elections	Issues and Scores	Overall Net Scores	
		B	*S*
	prospect Quebec independence (9A): +3S, +3S, −3B, +3S	−3	+9
1972	FLQ terrorism law and order (1); suspension civil rights in Quebec (2); Stanfield's personality (5); disappointing Liberal government performance, balanced by Liberals credibility as only effective government (6); bicultural policy to meet Quebec (9A); Western resentment of Quebec biculturalism (9): +3B, −2S, −3B, 0, +3S, +3B	+3	+1
1974	Personality of Trudeau compared with that of Stanfield (5); inflation balanced by credibility of Liberals as majority government (6); resentment of west at Quebec's share of resources and oil price fixing (9); price and wage legislation (12): +3S, +2S, +3B, +1B	+4	+5
1979	Constitutional changes (2); unemployment, inflation (6); threat of Quebec secession (9A); western resentment of concessions to Quebec (9): +2B, −3S, +3S, +3B	+5	0
1980	Trudeau's leadership (5); inflation, unemployment, broken pledges (6); prospect of majority government with Liberals (6); oil pricing (12); interest rates and taxation (14): +2S, −3B, +3S, +1B, +1B	−1	+5

Danish Elections	Issues and Scores	Overall Net Scores	
		B	S
1950	Austerity, economic difficulties (6); maintain employment (11); higher taxes (14): −3S, +3S, +1B	+1	0
1953 April	Slight economic upturn (6); maintain employment (11); +1B, +3S	+1	+3
1953 September	Slight economic upturn (6); maintain employment (11): +1B, +3S	+1	+3
1957	Rise in prosperity (6): +3S	0	+3
1960	Lower voting age, lower representation threshold (2); equipping forces with nuclear weapons (4); economic prosperity, strong government (6); improve position of agriculture (10): +2B, +1B, +3S, +1B	+4	+3
1964	Coalition prospects − SD guarantee no alliance with Left Socialists (6); government housing control (11); tax at source of income (14): −1S, +3S, −1S	0	+1
1966	Membership NATO, defence expenditure (4); economic difficulties (6); new tax system (14): −1S, −2S, +1B	+1	−3
1968	Inflation, wage freeze (6); willingness of three main bourgeois parties to co-operate (6); taxation levy on salaries (14): −3S, +1B, −1S	+1	−4
1971	Entry to EEC (3); inflation, economic difficulties (6); housing (11): +1S, −3B, −3B	−6	+1
1973	Entry to EEC (3); personality of Jorgenson in comparison with that of Glistrop (5); inflation, bad economic situation (6); high taxation (14): +1B, −3S, −3S, −1S	+1	−7
1975	Personality of Jorgenson compared with that of Glistrop (5); economic stabilisation, some tax cuts (6); demand for measures against unemployment (11); high level of taxes (14):		

Danish Elections	*Issues and Scores*	*Overall Net Scores*	
		B	S
	−2S, +1B, +3S, +1B	+2	+1
1977	Defence expenditure agreement (4); economic stabilisation (6):		
	+1B, +1S	+1	+1
1979	Who rules Denmark? – government – TUS (2); Inflation/prices and incomes policy (6); co-ownership in industry (11):		
	−2S, −3B, +3S	−3	+1

Finnish *Elections*	*Issues and Scores*	*Overall* *Net Scores* B S

1945   Purge administration, war trials (2);
relations with Soviet Union (3);
loss of war, cession territory (6);
land redistribution (11);
nationalisation of heavy industry (12):
+2B, +1S, −3B, +3S, −1S   −1   +3

1948   Attempted Communist general strike (1);
half Russian reparations cancelled (3);
hardship over three postwar years balanced by success
of reconstruction (6);
reduction in price of farm products (10);
freedom from controls (12):
+3B, +1S, 0, +1B, −1S   +4   0

1951   Maintenance of relations with Soviet Union (3);
rise in cost of living balanced by almost full reconstruction (6);
measures on behalf of small farmers (10);
increase in rents, housing measures (11);
strikes in metal and timber industries (13):
+1B, −1B, +1B, +3S, +1B   +2   +3

1954   Successful relations with Soviet Union (3);
safe image of President Kekkonen (5);
inflation, rising cost of living balanced by increasing
prosperity (6);
proposed wage cuts of 10 per cent, housing (11):
+1B, +3B, −1B, +3S   +3   +3

1958   Successful balance between Soviet and West (3);
President Kekkonen (5);
inflation, unemployment under bourgeois government
balanced by its credibility as only cohesive government
(6);
price changes for farm produce (10);
demand for cheaper food prices (11);
entry of new trade unions to Trade Union Federation
(13):
+1B, +3B, −1B, +1B, +3S, −1S   +4   +2

1962   Demand for military talks by Soviet Union (3);
Kekkonen's success with Khrushchev (5);
split in Social Democrats (6):
+1B, +3B, −3S   +4   −3

1966   Greater representation of peaceful reformers among
Popular Democrats (6);
development areas for less prosperous regions, regional
education institutes, agricultural subsidies (9);
Socialist demand for major expansion of housing
assistance (11):

Finnish Elections	*Issues and Scores*	*Overall Net Scores*	
		B	*S*
	+3S, +3B, +3S	+3	+6
1970	Relations with Scandinavian Economic Union, EEC (3);		
	divisions among Popular Democrats on Czechoslovakia, painful economic stabilisation after recent boom (6):		
	−1B, −3S	−1	−3
1972	Recognition of East Germany (3);		
	incomes policy, increased taxes (6);		
	size of agricultural subsidies (10);		
	relations between Social Democrats and trade unions (13):		
	−1B, −2B, +1B, −1S	−2	−1
1975	Worsening trade deficit, inflation, increased unemployment, government cuts in welfare and education (6):		
	−2B	−2	0
1979	Inflation and unemployment (6):		
	−3S	0	−3

French Elections	*Issues and Scores*	*Overall Net Scores*	
		B	S
1958	Restoration of state authority in face of disorders (1); new constitution (2); Algerian war (3); failure of Socialist Party government (6): +3B, +2B, −1S, −3S	+5	−4
1962	Direct election of President (2); Algerian settlement (3); no credibility in left government (6): +2B, +1B, −3S	+3	−3
1967	Stability of Fifth Republic (2); relations with NATO and EEC (3); Mitterand's popular appeal (5); unity of non-Communist left (6); social reforms needed (11): +2B, +1B, +1S, +1S, +3S	+3	+5
1968	Events of May (1); Pompidou as symbol of order (5): +3B, +2B	+5	0
1973	Danger to Fifth Republic from election of left (1); Mitterand's personality (5); economic prosperity balanced by relative inertia of government (6): +3B, +2S, 0	+3	+2
1978	Chirac (5); Mitterand as moderate reformer (5); unemployment and austerity balanced by signs of reduction in inflation (6); Socialist coolness to Communists (6); Nuclear energy development (12); Barre Plan (14): +1B, +3S, −2B, +1S, +1B, +1B	+1	+4
1981	Proposals for greater legislative autonomy (2); Mitterand's personality and prestige (5); credibility of left-wing government without Communist domination (6); job creation, increase in basic wages, health centres (11); nationalisation of industry and financial institutions (12); higher taxes (14): +2B, +3S, +3S, +3S, +1B, +1B	+4	+9

Icelandic Elections	Issues and Scores	Overall Net Scores	
		B	S
1946	Agreement with United States for use of Keflavik base (3):		
	+1B	+1	0
1949	Inflation balanced by economic development under Marshall Aid (6):		
	+1B	+1	0
1953	Membership of NATO, US troops in Iceland (3); financial difficulties (6):		
	−1S, −1B	−1	−1
1956	Presence of US troops at Keflavik (3); settlement of fisheries dispute with UK over conservation (12):		
	+1B, +1B	+2	0
1959 June	Reform of constituency system (2); reaction to Hungarian rising, internal disputes in Communist Party (6):		
	+2B, −1S	+2	−1
1959 October	New electoral law (2); inflation and devaluation under minority government left in by Independence Party (6); fishing 'war' with Britain over conservation, proposed controls over business (12):		
	+2B, −1B, −1S	+1	−1
1963	Four-year development plan to diversify economy (6); internal Communist dispute (6):		
	+2B, −1S	+2	−1
1967	Split among Communists (6); economic recession balanced by previous prosperity (6):		
	−3S, −1B	−1	−3
1971	Proposed withdrawal of US troops from Keflavik (3); mediocrity of government leadership (5); devaluation, bad economic situation (6); Communist divisions (6); extension of territorial waters to conserve fish (12):		
	−1B, −2B, −2B, −1S, +1B	−4	−1
1974	Continuance of NATO base at Keflavik (3); severe inflation, wage and price freeze increases credibility of Independence Party government (6); dispute over extent of fishing limits (12):		
	+1B, +2B, +1B	+4	0
1978	Withdrawal from NATO, closing base at Keflavik (3); uninspiring leadership of Independence Party (5); inflation and devaluation (6); unemployment and price increases (11):		
	+1B, −3B, −3B, +3S	−5	+3
1979	Uninspiring leadership of Independence Party (5);		

Icelandic Elections	*Issues and Scores*	*Overall Net Scores*	
		B	*S*
	inflation, inadequate measures (6): −3B, −3S	−3	−3

Indian Elections	*Issues and Scores*	*Overall Net Scores S*
1951	Lack of alternatives to Nehru (5); successful consolidation of Independence (6); limited land reform, advancement of minorities and women (11): +3S, +3S, +3S	+9
1957	Union with Goa (3); 'obviousness' of Nehru as Prime Minister (5); relatively successful conduct of government by Congress Party (6); promise of guaranteed minimum wage, social reform (11): +1S, +3S, +3S, +3S	+10
1962	Reconstitution of states on linguistic basis (2); campaign over Goa (3); Nehru's personality and position (5); development, somewhat improved economic conditions (6); promise of greater educational opportunity, social reforms (11): −2S, +1S, +3S, +3S, +3S	+8
1967	Defeat and insecurity with regard to China (4); appeal of Mrs Gandhi (5); economic development balanced by increasing corruption, divisions in Congress Party, rising prices (6); demands for local linguistic rights (8); government control of commanding heights of the economy (12): −1S, +1S, +1S, −3S, −1S	−3
1971	Relative foreign security through alliances, peaceful co-existence with China (3); decisiveness of Mrs Gandhi (5); strong government provided since explusion of 'Syndicate' (6); promises of social reform, measures to reduce princes' income and powers (11); nationalisation of banks (12): +1S, +3S, +3S, +3S, −1S	+9
1977	Sporadic disorder and terrorism (1); emergency regulations, censorship, sterilisation campaign (2); promotion of Sanjay Gandhi (5); government corruption and arbitrariness, high food prices (6); railway strikes (13): −3S, −2S, −2S, −3S, −1S	−11
1979	Strikes in army and police, disorder in rural areas (1); Mrs Gandhi's leadership (5);	

Indian Elections	*Issues and Scores*	*Overall Net Scores* S
	Congress only effective governing party (6): −3S, +3S, +3S	+3

Irish Elections	*Issues and Scores*	*Overall Net Scores*	
		B	*S*
1948	de Valera's personality (5); cost of living (6); taxation (14): +3S, –1S, +1B	+1	+2
1951	de Valera's personality (5); Costello's personality (5); internal dissensions balanced by government reforms (6); mother and child health scheme (11): +3S, +3B, +2B, +3S	+5	+6
1954	de Valera's personality (5); Costello's personality (5); prices, cost of living, credibility of coalition as alternative to Fianna Fáil (6); reduction of taxes (14): +3S, +3B, +3B, +1B	+7	+3
1957	de Valera's personality (5); Costello's personality (5); unemployment, emigration (6); reunification and opposition to partition (9A): +3S, +3B, –3B, +3S	0	+6
1961	Joining EEC (3): +2B	+2	0
1965	Lemass's personality (5); Dillon's personality (5); industrial development, economic prosperity (6): +3S, +3B, +2S	+3	+5
1969	EEC negotiations (3); Lynch's personality (5); Cosgrove's personality (5); economic development and moderate prosperity (6): +2S, +3S, +3B, +1S	+3	+6
1973	Protection of civil liberties in IRA emergency (2); relationships with Britain in Northern Ireland (3); Lynch's personality (5); Cosgrove's personality (5); arms-smuggling conspiracy, economic difficulties (6); housing, price control, social reform (11): +3S, –2S, +3S, +3B, –3S, +3S	+3	+4
1977	Lynch's popularity (5); Cosgrove's unpopularity (5); unemployment, recession, new compact with Labour (6); end of partition by agreement (9A); more effective price control (11); lower taxation (14): +3S, –3B, –3B, +3S, +3S, +1B	–5	+9
1981	Crime and vandalism (1);		

Irish Elections	*Issues and Scores*	*Overall Net Scores*	
		B	S
	Fitzgerald's popularity (5); bad economic record balanced by pre-election concessions (6); hunger strikers in Northern Ireland (9A): +3B, +3B, −1S, +3S	+6	+2

Israeli Elections	*Issues and Scores*	*Overall Net Scores* B	S
1949	Demand for expansion in Transjordan (3); Ben-Gurion's personality (5); achievement of Independence (6): −1B, +3S, +3S	−1	+6
1951	Ben-Gurion's personality (5); consolidation of the state (6); which authority to supervise religious education of child immigrants in work camps? (7); planned economy controls (12): +3S, +1S, +3B, +1B	+4	+4
1955	Arab Commando activity (1); proposal to change electoral system (2); government handling of Kastner case (6): +3B, +2B, −1S	+5	−1
1959	Election reform (2); personalities of Ben-Gurion and Dayan (5); divisions among (right-wing) general Zionist leadership (6); discontent among Oriental Jews (8); social reforms to help disadvantaged groups (11): +2B, +3S, −3B, +3B, +3S	+2	+6
1961	Reform of electoral system (2); role of Zionist organisation (3); civil control over army activities (4); personalities of Ben-Gurion, Dayan, etc. (5); divisions in government over Lavon affair (6): +2B, +1B, +1B, +3S, −3S	+4	0
1965	Israeli and Western containment of Nasser (3); personalities of Ben-Gurion and Dayan (5); inflation, balanced by success of voluntary pay restraints, breakaway of Rafi and split in Liberals over alliance with Herut (6); alliance with Ahduth Havoda and more reformist policies (11); abolition of controls (12): +1S, +3S, −3B, +3S, +1B	−2	+7
1969	External security after 1967 War (3); distrust of Begin (now nearer to power) (5); economic overheating, inflation, divisions in coalition leadership (6); strikes (13): +1 Both, −2B, −3 Both, −1S	−4	−3
1973	Opposition to concessions made to get peace settlement (3); future defence preparations, stalemate in war (4); Sharon's popularity (5);		

Israeli Elections	*Issues and Scores*	*Overall Net Scores*	
		B	S

government preparedness for attacks (6):
+1B, –1S, +3B, –3S .... +4 ... –4

1977   Change in electoral system (2);
stalemate over peace settlement (3);
waste in defence budget (4);
financial charges against Rabin and Housing Minister (5);
inflation, unemployment (6);
discontent of Oriental Jews (8);
denationalisation (12);
compulsory arbitration in labour disputes (13):
+2B, –1S, –1S, –3S, –3S, +3B, +1B, +1B .... +7 ... –8

1981   Election campaign violence (1);
West Bank, Iraqi raid (4);
Begin's personality (5);
Perez's personality (5);
inflation balanced by pre-election boom (6);
factionalism amongst Alignment (6);
discontent of Oriental Jews (8);
tax cuts (14):
+3B, +1B, +3B, –3S, –1B, –3S, +3B, +1B .... +10 ... –6

Italian Elections	*Issues and Scores*	*Overall Net Scores*	
		B	S
1948	Adherence to Western Alliance (3); reconstruction and distribution of aid (6); clergy direction to vote DC (7): +1B, +2B, +3B	+6	0
1953	Election Reform Bill (2): +2B	+2	0
1958	Economic prosperity (6); Communist opposition to 'religious totalitarianism' (7): +1B, +3B	+4	0
1963	Economic prosperity: tempered by 'opening to the left' (6); urgency of social and economic reforms (11): +1B, +3S	+1	+3
1968	Economic affluence balanced by internal disunity of left–centre coalition and absence of large initiatives (6); introduction of regional governments (9); need for social economic reform (11): 0, +3B, +3S	+3	+3
1972	Activity of neo-Fascists (1); reduction of East–West tension (3); Andreotti's personality (5); weakness of the lira, economic difficulties (6); referendum on divorce (7); need for socioeconomic reform (11): +3B, +1S, –2B, –3B, +3B, +3S	+1	+4
1976	Riots, assassinations (1); retention of NATO membership, remaining in Western Alliance (3); Berlinguer's personality (5); economic difficulties, weakness of the lira, government corruption as opposed to Communist constructive opposition (6); Support of church for PDC (7); need for social reforms (11): +3B, +1B, +1S, –3B, +3B, +3S	+4	+4
1979	Terrorism (1); effect on NATO of Communists in government (3); Berlinguer's personality (5); need for social reforms (11): +3B, +1B, +1S, +3S	+4	+4

Japanese Elections	Issues and Scores	Overall Net Scores B S

1958   Revision of constitution (2);
relations with China and United States, claims to islands (3);
size and function of defence force (4);
Kishi's popularity (5);
union of the socialist parties (6):
+2B, +1B, +1B, +3B, +3S   +7   +3

1960   Anti-Eisenhower riots (1);
constitutional changes (2);
security treaty with United States (3);
economic growth balanced by internal factionalism, replacement of Kishi by Ikeda (6);
splits in Socialist Party (6):
+3B, +2B, +1B, −1B, −1S   +5   −1

1963   Trading relations with China (3);
economic growth and prosperity balanced by LDP faction fights (6):
+1B, 0   +1   0

1967   Security treaty with United States cultural revolution in China (3);
'black mist' of government scandals, increase in consumer-goods prices (6):
−1S, −3B   −3   −1

1969   Students riots (1);
Return of Okinawa (3);
government corruption and divisions (6):
−3S, +1B, −3B   −2   −3

1972   *Rapprochement* with China, attacks on US Security Treaty (3);
increased defence expenditure (4);
inflation, rise in cost of living, balanced by Liberal–Democratic position as only credible governing party (6);
'Remodelling Japanese Archipelago' Plan (9);
greater welfare provisions (11):
+1B, +1B, 0, +3B, +3S   +5   +3

1976   Lockheed bribes scandal (6):
−3B   −3   0

1979   Ohira unable to unite factions (5);
uninspiring leadership of JSP (5);
government corruption and divisions (6);
disunity within JSP (6):
−3B, −3S, −2B, −3S   −5   −6

1980   Japanese Socialist Party support of military non-alignment (4);
sympathy vote for Ohira who died during campaign (5);

Japanese Elections	*Issues and Scores*	*Overall Net Scores*	
		B	S
	corruption, factionalism within government (6); internal disunity and weakness of JSP (6); nuclear power (12):		
	−1S, +1B, −3B, −3S, −1S	−2	−5

Luxembourg		*Overall*	
Elections	*Issues and Scores*	*Net Scores*	
		B	*S*
1954	European Defence Community (4); recovery in economic prosperity after stagnation, unemployment in coal and steel 1952–3 (6): +1B, +1 Both	+2	+1
1959	Bodson (Socialist minister) suppressed action in bribery case (6); higher protection for agriculture (10): −1S, +1B	+1	−1
1964	Economic prosperity upturn in steel, 6 per cent inflation (6); need for social reforms (11): +1B, +3S	+1	+3
1968	Right- and left-wing conflict in Socialist Party (6); state schools question (7); social welfare, workers participation (11); higher taxes to finance Socialist proposals (14): −3S, +3B, +3S, −1S	+3	−1
1974	Leftism causes secession in Socialist Party (2); Werner too long in office as Prime Minister (5); higher inflation (6); proposed abortion laws (7); agricultural problems (10); strikes (general strike, October 1973) (13): −2S, −2B, −3B, +3B, −1S, −1S	−2	−4
1979	Unemployment and inflation (6); abortion reform (7): −3S, −3S	0	−6

Netherlands *Elections*	*Overall* *Issues and Scores*	*Net Scores*	
		B	*S*
1946	Indonesian Independence (3); low wages, economic dislocation (6); social reform (11); nationalisation (12); seamens', dockers' strikes (13): –1S, –3S, +3S, –1S, –1S	0	–3
1948	Communist, left strength in light of Czech coup (1); Indonesia War, Benelux Union (3); reconstruction achievements (6); irritation at rationing controls (12); deregulation of prices (14): –3S, –1 Both, +1 Both, –1S, +1B	+1	–4
1952	Internal divisions in Catholic Party (6); low unemployment, prosperity balanced by housing shortage (6); freedom for business *v.* trade unions (13); lower taxes (14): –3B, +2 Both, –1S, –1S	–1	0
1956	Drees's personality (Prime Minister) (5); economic prosperity, full employment balanced by housing shortage (6); bishops' appeal to vote for Catholic Party (7): +1S, +1 Both, +3B	+4	+2
1959	West New Guinea crisis (3); economic prosperity, full employment balanced by housing shortage (6); rent control proposal (11); divisions in government over subsidies and controls (12); defeat of Socialist tax proposals (14): –1 Both, +1 Both, +3S, –1S, –1S	0	+1
1962	Economic prosperity balanced by housing shortage (6); reduction in taxes (14): +1B, +1B	+2	0
1967	Recession, credit squeeze (6): –3 Both	–3	–3
1971	Economic recession, inflation, expenditure cuts (6): –3B	–3	0
1972	Economic recession, inflation, government disunity (6); measures against unemployment (11): –3B, +3S	–3	+3
1977	South Moluccan terrorism (1); Personality of den Uyl (Prime Minister) (5); recession, high unemployment balanced by active government expenditure, good payments balance (6); abortion law (7); profit-sharing, worker participation (11);		

Netherlands Elections	Issues and Scores	Overall Net Scores B	S
	land planning, conservation (12); strikes (13):		
	+3B, +3S, −1 Both, +3B, +3S, +1B, +1B	+7	+5
1981	Cruise missiles (4); unemployment and poor economic conditions (6); level of social benefits (11); nuclear energy (12):		
	+1B, −3B, +3S, +1B	−1	+3

New Zealand Elections	Issues and Scores	Overall Net Scores	
		B	*S*
1951	Industrial unrest connected with Communists (1); cost of living (6): +3B, +1S	+3	+1
1954	Inflation (6); state control of economy (12); level of taxation (14): +2S, +1B, +1B	+2	+2
1957	Inflation, falling export prices (6); improvements in welfare provision (11): −3B, +3S	−3	+3
1960	Economic difficulties (6); level of taxation (14): −3S, −1S	0	−4
1963	Holyoake's personality (5); high prices for exports (6): +1B, +3B	+4	0
1966	Vietnam War, negotiations with UK and EEC (3); Holyoake's personality (5): +1B, +1B	+2	0
1969	Industrial unrest linked to Communists (1); Vietnam War (3); Holyoake's personality (5); Kirk's personality (5): +3B, −1B, +2B, +3S	+4	+3
1972	British entry to EEC – trade negotiations (3); Marshall's personality (5); Kirk's personality (5); bad economic performance (6); increased social spending (11): −1B, +2B, +3S, −3B, +3S	−2	+6
1975	EEC and access to UK market (3); Muldoon's personality (5); Kirk's personality (5); inflation and public spending (6); Polynesian and other immigration (8): +1B, +3B, +1S, −3S, +3B	+7	−2
1978*	Muldoon's personality (5); unemployment and inflation balanced by firm government and world conditions (6); weak Labour opposition (6); strikes and Industrial Relations Reform Bill (13); reduction in taxation (14): −3B, −2B, −2S, −1S, +1B	−4	−3

* Effect of personality underestimated in predicting election.

Norwegian Elections	Issues and Scores	Overall Net Scores	
		B	S
1949	Speed of reconstruction (6); regulation of house rents (11); government regulations (12): +2S, +3S, −1S	0	+4
1953	Good economic performance (6); price regulation (11); direction of economy (12): +3S, +3S, −1S	0	+5
1957	Hungarian crisis, negotiations over Nordic Common Market (3); personality of (Labour) Prime Minister (5); good economic performance (6): +1B, +3S, +3S	+1	+6
1961	Membership NATO, EEC (3); economic growth (6); farming, fishing policy (10); tax levels (14): +1B, +3S, −1S, −1S	+1	+1
1965	Membership of NATO (3); economic situation, mining disaster, bourgeois parties greater credibility (6); taxation and bureaucracy (14): +1B, −3S, −1S	+1	−4
1969	Vietnam War (3); desire for strong united government (6): +1S, +2S	0	+3
1973	Negotiations over EEC (3); economic difficulties, viability of bourgeois parties (6); fears of outlying regions over future development (9); fears of farmers over future under government policy (10): −1S, −3S, −3S, −1S	0	−8
1977	Concession on fishing limits (3); government maintained prosperity (6); lack of unity in bourgeois opposition (6); expansion of oil drilling (12): −1S, −1B, +1S, −1S	−1	−1

Sri Lankan Elections	*Issues and Scores*	*Overall Net Scores*	
		B	S
1960 (1)	State of emergency, press censorship (2); Prestige of D. Senanayake (5); Mrs Bandaranaike's campaign on behalf of SLFP (5); complicity of government ministers in Bandaranaike assassination (6): +2B, +3B, +3S, –3S	+5	0
1960 (2)	Prestige of D. Senanayake (Prime Minister) (5); Mrs Bandaranaike now leader SLFP (5); accusation of pact SLFP–TAMIL (8): +3B, +3S, +3B	+6	+3
1965	Legislation to change control of press (2); Prestige of D. Senanayake (5); Mrs Bandaranaike (Prime Minister) (5); unemployment, high cost of living (6); Buddhism as official religion, teetotalism (7): +2B, +3B, +2S, –3S, +3B	+8	–1
1970	Independence from Western powers (3); prestige of D. Senanayake (Prime Minister) (5); popularity of Mrs Bandaranaike (5); recovery of economy balanced by decreased rice ration (6); promised rice ration, social reforms (11): +1S, +3B, +3S, 0, +3S	+3	+7
1977	State of emergency, danger of disorder among youth like 1971 (1); Jayawardene's personality (5); nepotism, corruption, decline of economy, unemployment (6); government alienation of Buddhist priesthood (7); railway strikes (13); more scope for business (14): +3B, +1B, –3S, +3B, –1S, +1B	+8	–4

Swedish Elections	Issues and Scores	Overall Net Scores	
		B	S
1948	Shortage of housing balanced by abolition of bread rationing (6); holiday provisions, welfare state, low interest rates (11); wartime controls (12): 0, +3S, −1S	0	+2
1952	Friction with Soviet Union (3); economic performance balanced by rising prices (6): +1B, +2S	+1	+2
1956	Economic prosperity modified by rising prices and housing shortage (6); level of taxation (14): +2S, −1S	0	+1
1958	New additional pension scheme (11): +3S	0	+3
1960	Extended holiday provisions, cuts in child allowance and pension scheme proposed by bourgeois parties (11); cuts in taxes proposed by bourgeois parties (14): +3S, +1B	+1	+3
1964	Housing shortage (6); policy in Norrland (9); use of pension funds (11): −1S, +3B, +3S	+3	+2
1968	Palme's personality (5); economic prosperity (6); public-sector spending, government investment in banking (12); cuts in taxes (14): +1S, +3S, +1B, +1B	+2	+4
1970	Palme's personality (5); economic growth, balanced by unemployment, rising prices (6); Norrland development (9): +1S, +1S, +3B	+3	+2
1973	Falldin's personality (5); rising prices, unemployment, credible alternative combination of bourgeois parties (6); pension scheme and use of funds (11); less government control of life (12): +2B, −3S, +3S, +1B	+3	0
1976	Falldin's personality (5); rising prices, unemployment and credibility of bourgeois combination (6); nuclear development (12); trade union power (13); level of taxation, bureaucracy (14): +2B, −3S, +1B, −1S, −1S	+3	−5

Swedish Elections	*Issues and Scores*	*Overall Net Scores*	
		B	*S*
1979	Tax cuts and reduction in public spending (14): +1B	+1	0

Swiss Elections	Issues and Scores	Overall Net Scores	
		B	S
1951	No national issues	0	0
1955	No national issues	0	0
1959	No national issues	0	0
1963	No national issues	0	0
1967	Cost of living (6):		
	–3 Both	–3	–3
1971	Schwartzenbach's personality (5); high cost of living (6); reduction in foreign workers (8):		
	–3 Both, –1 Both, –3S	–4	–7
1975	Economic stability in world depression, fewer foreign workers (6);		
	+3 Both	+3	+3
1979	No national issues	0	0

United Kingdom Elections	*Issues and Scores*	*Overall Net Scores*	
		B	*S*
1950	Threat from Russia (4); Attlee's personality (5); Churchill's personality (5); cost of living, unemployment (6); Welfare State (11); nationalisation (12): +1B, +2S, +2B, −2S, +3S, +1B	+4	+3
1951	Peace (3); Attlee's personality (5); Churchill's personality (5); cost of living, unemployment (6); housing problem (11); nationalisation (12): +1S, +2S, +3B, −3S, +3S, +1B	+4	+3
1955	Eden's personality (5); Attlee's personality (5); economic prosperity (6): +2B, +1S, +3B	+5	+1
1959	Post-imperial defence, unilateralism (4); Macmillan's personality (5); economic growth and prosperity (6); pensions (11); nationalisation (12); level of taxation (14): +1B, +2B, +3B, +3S, −1S, +1B	+7	+2
1964	Defence East of Suez (4); Wilson's personality (5); balance of payments (6); Immigration Bill (8); housing, pensions, health, education (11); nationalisation (12); trade unions (13): +1B, +2S, −2B, +3B, +3S, −1S, −1S	+2	+3
1966	Entry to the Common Market (3); Wilson as sound Prime Minister (5); aversion of immediate balance of payment crisis (6); social services improvements (11); trade union powers (13): +1S, +2S, +3S, +3S, −1S	0	+8
1970	Opposition to the Common Market (3); Wilson as best Prime Minister available (5); Price rises, wage freeze (6); control of immigration (8); housing shortages, shortfalls in social services (11); high level of taxation (14):		

United Kingdom Elections	Issues and Scores	Overall Net Scores	
		B	*S*
	+1S, +1S, −3S, +3B, +3S, +1B	+4	+2
1974 February	'Who Governs Britain?' (2); entry to the Common Market (3); Heath as confrontationist maladroit Prime Minister (5); industrial relations, rising prices, wage freeze (6); disunity of Labour Party (6); nationalisation (12); miners' strike (13):		
	+2B, −1 Both, −2B, −3B, −1S, −1S, −1S	−4	−4
1974 October	Entry to the Common Market (3); Heath as unsuccessful Prime Minister (5); settlement of industrial troubles, prices, higher wages (6); housing shortages and promised remedies, social legislation (11); nationalisation (12):		
	−1 Both, −3B, +1S, +3S, −1S	−4	+2
1979	Law on picketing (1); fair deal from EEC (3); moderation of Callaghan (5); firmness of Thatcher (5); economic crises, unemployment, inflation (6); quangos (12); trade union reform (13); high level taxation (14):		
	+3B, +1S, +1S, +1B, −2S, +1B, +1B, +1B	+7	0

United States Elections	Issues and Scores	Overall Net Scores B	S
1948	Cold War, Berlin crisis, national collapse in China (3); impact of Truman as sitting President (5); post war prosperity tempered by rising prices (6); states rights (9); price control opposed by (Rep) Congress (11); Taft–Hartley Act (13): +3B, +3S, +1S, –3S, –3B, –1B	–1	+1
1952	Internal communism, subversion (1); war in Korea (3); prestige of Eisenhower (5); government corruption, scandals (6): –3S, +3B, +3B, –1S	+6	–4
1956	Korean peace, world détente (3); Eisenhower as reassuring President (5); economic prosperity, rise in living standards (6): +3B, +3B, +3B	+9	0
1960	Democratic criticism of foreign policy (3); economic recession, quiescent domestic policy (6); Kennedy's Catholicism (7); social reforms (11): –3S, +3S, –3S, +3S	0	0
1964	Johnson as sitting and reassuring President (5); economic prosperity, firmness of Democratic administration compared to lack of credibility of Republican (6); threat to position of underprivileged groups (8); threat to social services and welfare (11): +3S, +3S, –3B, –3B	–6	+6
1968	Law and order (1); war in Vietnam (3); domestic reforms of Democratic administration (6); social reforms – medicine, welfare and education (11); bussing, federal powers (14): –3S, –3S, +2S, +3S, +1B	+1	–1
1972	Peace negotiations in Vietnam (3); McGovern's projected cuts in defence expenditure (4); prestige of Nixon as sitting President (5); lack of credibility of Democrat administration – untrustworthiness in Eagleton affair (6); proposal for payments to poor by Federal Government (11); McGovern's general advocacy of 'big government' (14): +3B, –2S, +3B, –3S, +3S, –1S	+6	–3
1976	Prestige of Ford as sitting President (5); Watergate, domestic inflation, and unemployment (6):		

United States Elections	Issues and Scores	Overall Net Scores B S

	+3B, −3B	0 0
1980	Lack of success of government foreign policy (3); prestige of Carter as sitting President (5); economic recession balanced by relative prosperity (6); Republican tax cuts (14):	
	−3S, +3S, −1S, +1B	+1 −1

West German Elections	*Issues and Scores*	*Overall Net Scores*	
		B	S
1954	Proposal to withdraw from NATO (3); defence policy (4); Adenauer's personality (5); economic prosperity (6):		
	+1B, +1B, +3B, +3B	+8	0
1961	Berlin crisis (3); economic miracle (6):		
	+1B, +3B	+4	0
1965	Nazi threat (NPD) (1); Brandt's personality (5); economic prosperity (6); housing, urban transport (11):		
	+3B, +2S, +3B, +3S	+6	+5
1969	Revaluation, Nazi threat (NPD) (1); electoral reform (2); Ostpolitik (3); Brandt's personality (5); grand coalition achievements with SD participation (6); educational measures (11); worker control (12):		
	+3B, +2B, +1B, +3S, +2S, +3S, −1S	+6	+7
1972	Baader–Meinhof affair (1); Ostpolitik (3); Brandt's personality (5); economy slowing down (6):		
	+3B, +1S, +3S, −2S	+3	+2
1976	Delicate relations with East Germany (3); Schmidt *v.* Strauss as assurance of stability (5); poor economic performance, though relatively good in world depression (6):		
	+1B, +2S, −2S	+1	0
1980	Distrust of Strauss (5):		
	−3B	−3	0

The Coding of Issues: Procedures and their Validity

The major guide to coding issues and their effects are the groupings made in Table 2.1 (p. 28 above) and the characterisations of direction and magnitude for each grouping made in Table 2.6 (p. 50 above) (and in Tables 2.7–2.9 pp. 52–6, for US, Canadian and Irish parties respectively). Our coders also based decisions on the supplementary instructions given here. We give the text of these below. They were subjected to the usual check of having different coders independently categorise the same material (postwar election issues for five countries) using the tables and supplementary instructions. The degree of correspondence between the independent coding decisions was then estimated. The quite satisfactory results of this check are reported at the end of the appendix.

Supplementary Coding Instructions

Sources

(1)   In all cases but the UK, United States and Canada 1972 and 1974, use *Keesing's Contemporary Archives* for initial search, focusing on entries under '(Country Name) – General Election', from before election (preferably one to two months before). Having identified issues from *Keesing's* compare with reports in *The Economist*. Use only these two sources. If no identifiable issues are mentioned in either, conclude that there are no issues and score parties zero.

(2)   For the UK use Nuffield Election Series as only source. Concentrate on specific assessments and discussions of what were the salient issues.

(3)   For the United States use specified voting studies and *Making of the President* as only sources. Concentrate on specific assessments and discussions of what were the salient issues.

(4)   For Canada 1972 and 1974 use *Canada at the Polls*. Concentrate on specific assessments and discussions of what were the salient issues.

(NB Predictions of future elections will use available newspaper and *The Economist* reports.)

Categorising Specific Issues

(5)   Always code a specific issue into only one category.

(6)   In cases of doubt, preference should be giving to coding specific issues into issue types with fixed magnitude and direction.

(7)   Issues which are salient but do not favour either major party/*tendance* under consideration should be noted as balancing out.

(8)   If more than one specific issue falls into the same type, type is not counted twice, with the undernoted exceptions.

(a) However, to aid calculation of the overall balance of effects, positive aspects of government record (if any) can be noted and notionally scored, and the same done for negative aspects. To get overall effects under '6 Government record and prospects' add the two, then record them as one component to the final calculation. A similar procedure can be followed with '5 Candidate reactions'.

(b) Two separate records of '5 Candidate reactions' and '6 Government record and prospects' can be made if they refer to different actions/attributes of different parties. For example, government can get reward or penalty for performance, *at same time as* opposition can get reward or penalty for its promises.

Fixed Issues

(9) Codes are to be strictly applied where there is fixed direction and magnitude of effect, for example, even if in the case of a particular election '1 Civil order' seems to favour the left rather than right, it must still be counted for the party fixed in the code. If this is not done all issue types become erratic and we shall be unable to generalise about their effects. Obviously in most cases the evidence will point to them acting in the way anticipated – otherwise we would change the coding scheme.

(10) Initial presumption is that issues will be associated positively with parties which their general type is 'fixed' to favour (but note exceptional case of '12 Government control and planning' – 12 below). Only if there are strong indications from the context that the issue negatively affects other party/*tendance* should it be assigned as a negative score to that party.

(11) However, in certain countries (India, Scandinavia excluding Finland) one party is so generally dominant that most issues relate to it (either positively or negatively). Only if issue is very strongly associated with another party should it be attributed elsewhere.

(12) In spite of general provision (10 above) about 'positive attributions' of issue types, note that government control, planning and particularly nationalisation (all in '12 Government control and planning') are usually to be attributed negatively to left party. Where there are pledges to free business and individuals from bureaucratic control, give a positive attribution to the bourgeois party under '14 Initiative and freedom'. Note that conservation of environment and natural resources fall under '12 Government control and planning'.

(13) Trade union power, strike action, trade union support of a particular party all fall into '13 Government regulation in favour of individual'. This is often negative for left rather than positive for bourgeois (but note that in United States, Canada and Ireland this type favours the *reformist* party).

Erratic Issues

(14) '3 Foreign relationships' is usually positive or negative for the party(ies) forming the government, since the Opposition is less able to make its mark here than elsewhere.

(15) (a) Note that '5 Candidate reactions' refers to personal qualities of candidates –personal attractiveness, ability, past success. It does not relate to issues with which candidate happens to be associated, which should be coded into other categories.

(b) Generally the presumption is against candidates having any appeal, especially in countries with an institutionalised socialist/bourgeois confrontation. In these cases, where a candidate is prominent there is also a presumption in favour of small as against medium or large effects.

(c) There is usually more emphasis on candidates in the United States, Canada and Ireland, recognised in the overall codes by these countries having invariant large effects associated with the saliency of a candidate.

(d) In the United States when a sitting President is running for office, he must be coded as salient with a large positive effect for his party.

(e) Note also provision under 8(b).

(16)   Note that '6 Government record and prospects' covers both past record and future promise (especially for Opposition parties).

(a) The actual record and performance of government can only reward or penalise government parties, not divert bonus to Opposition.

(b) Similarly, Opposition promises or prospects can only reward or penalise Opposition.

(c) Note also provisions under 8(a).

Agreement between Independent Codings

Five countries were coded independently by each of the three coders who between them prepared all the material in Appendix B (Barlow, Budge and Foster). These provided checks of consistency between Barlow–Foster (UK), Barlow–Budge (Australia, New Zealand, West Germany) and Budge–Foster (Italy). Aggregate levels of agreement between all the separate coding attempts were reported below: agreement was also high, however, between each pair of coders and for each of the countries involved.

Comparison of Original and Check Coding

Check Codes	Original Codes						
	−4 to −3	−2 to −1	0 to 1	2 to 3	4 to 5	6 to 7	8 to 9
−4 to −3	0	4	0	0	0	0	0
−2 to −1	3	1	1	0	0	0	0
0 to 1	0	2	10	6	1	0	0
2 to 3	0	1	3	15	2	0	0
4 to 5	0	0	2	4	8	4	0
6 to 7	0	0	0	2	1	8	2
8 to 9	0	0	0	0	0	1	1

Overall Differences in Codings (Check-Original)

Difference	−4	−3	−2	−1	0	1	2	3	4
Frequency	1	2	9	12	34	12	5	5	2

Average difference $=\dfrac{5}{82}=+0\cdot06$ Average|Difference|$= 1\cdot04$

Individual Differences in Codings

IB – RB (rest)	0	2	6	9	19	8	4	2	2
PF – RB (UK)	0	0	2	2	10	2	0	2	0
PF – IB (Italy)	1	0	1	1	5	2	1	1	0
Difference	−4	−3	−2	−1	0	1	2	3	4

Note: IB = Ian Budge; PF = Peter Foster; RB = Roger Barlow.

Appendix D

Scoring Election Issues: Assumptions and Performances of Alternative Schemes

It is clear that in order to get any quantified estimate of issue effects at all, we must score issues so as to relate the various fluctuations in issue advantages as exactly as possible to fluctuations in vote. Ignoring magnitude altogether and assuming that each issue type has equal impact (so that its presence could be designated by 1 and its absence by 0) we could simply add ones for or against each party over all issues salient in the election. In this way each party would have an overall issue score to relate to vote, stemming immediately from the assignments of direction.

Since some types of issue (such as a threatened breakdown of order) seem to have more impact than others (such as 'creeping bureaucracy') we felt it essential to give them different weights. At the same time we did not feel qualified to distinguish very finely between them, and so confined ourselves to a very broad assessment of 'large' and 'small' impact, with an allowance also made, in one or two cases, for 'medium' effects. The simplest scoring scheme and the one we have used encapsulates these judgements in numbers, making large = 3, medium = 2, small = 1, and failure of an issue to achieve prominence at all equal to 0.

Of course, any form of scoring rests on certain assumptions, and ours is no exception. The most important assumptions are: (a) Our procedure implies that the difference between 'large' and 'medium' impacts, equals that separating 'medium' from 'small' impacts. This is, of course, the simplest numerical equivalence to make. Evidence that it does not produce systematic bias in residuals is presented in Chapter 5, Section 5.2 p. 119 above). We can also see whether it relates to votes better than its competitors by making straight comparisons, as we do at the conclusion of this appendix. We assess its performance mainly in relation to the uniform scoring system (every salient issue counts 1).

Another possible way of scoring is with unequal intervals (for example, large = 5, medium = 2, small = 1). A difficulty is, of course, that there are so many unequal intervals that might be employed, whereas all systems with equal intervals are essentially equivalent (being readily transformed from one to another through multiplication or division by a constant number).

Because of the infrequent occurrence of 'medium' impacts (of issues with fixed effects only the constitutional type of issue (2) in Table 2.6 (p. 50 above) is assigned a 'medium' effect) our own scoring system in its practical applications tends to approximate to one type of unequal scoring in any case, running in general from 0 for non-occurrence of an issue, 1 for small-impact issues and 3 for large-impact issues. Given the variety of unequal scores that might be applied, this operational equivalence does not guarantee that other forms of unequal scoring might not produce different and possibly better results. Given the very good results we have had, the scope for improvement is limited, however, while the permutations of unequal scoring are almost endless. Since we cannot within our constraints of time and resources make a final evaluation against all types of unequal scores, and since our procedure at any rate relates closely to one of the more obvious alternatives, we do not make direct comparisons but concentrate instead on the other possibilities discussed below.

(b)   A second assumption involved in the transition from ranking issues in terms of magnitude to actually assigning them numbers, is that these can be assigned and added independently for each party, without affecting the support obtained by the other. This opens up a complicated series of possibilities about the vote transfers going on in the real world, under the impact of issues.

We have already noted that issue effects of interest for an analysis of election outcomes are those relating to net rather than gross change. We know that many more voters alter their party choices than appears from voting returns, simply because most individual moves cancel each other out. It is the non-reciprocal, unbalanced changes – the net excess of moves to a party over moves from it – which affect outcomes and which, consequently, are of interest to us.

The voting process which allowed us to add party scores separately and independently, would be a real-life situation where the major parties made no net gains or losses from each other but gained and lost only in regard to third parties and non-voters. That is to say that direct switching between the major parties would be limited, because of their adherents' firmer and more fully-worked-out allegiances which discourage change to the rival party. When direct movement did occur it would be for reasons which produced balanced and reciprocal flows between the parties. The main impact of negative issues would be on the enthusiasm of major party supporters, pushing them into non-voting or into a protest vote for a third party. Conversely, a positive issue impact would pull non-voters and third-party supporters into the major party in such numbers as to produce a surplus of entrants over leavers.

Given such a situation, where the only flows between major parties were mutually balancing, and net gains or losses came from an external pool, we should be justified in assuming that a major party could increase its issue score without necessarily diminishing the score of its rival (or lose on issues without directly benefiting the other). For evidence on whether such balanced flows actually occur, we can turn to a direct analysis of the voting flows attributable to a specific issue. This is an examination by L. Le Duc of 'The majority government issue and electoral behaviour in Canada' (Le Duc, 1975; slightly revised in Le Duc, 1977). Towards the end of this paper a set of electors was isolated who switched, or who entered the electorate for the first time between the elections of 1972 and 1974, and who reported that they were influenced 'a great deal' in their decision by the majority government issue (so that we are sure as we can be with survey responses that we are dealing with electors who changed purely under the impact of that issue).

These electors were divided according to the type of change which brought them from their previous position in the 1972 election into the two major parties (Liberals and Progressive Conservatives) in 1974. Analysis was restricted to these particular 'paths' of change, on the reasoning that concern about majority government could only have the effect of inducing electors to vote for one of the two parties which had any hope of a majority. Among this group, changers from Conservatives to Liberal accounted for 0·4 per cent of the electorate, changers from minor parties and non-voters to Liberals for 1·1 per cent, and changers from Liberals to Conservatives for 0·2 per cent.

Flows between Liberals and Conservatives thus roughly balance out. The great bulk of the Liberals' overall gain comes from the minor parties and previous non-voters (including new voters). Since we have never claimed that our scoring was more than a rough approximation, the broad balancing of flows supports our general assumption that net party gains and losses on each issue are broadly independent of each other, coming from the 'reservoir' of third-party voters and non-voters, or returning to it, so that issue scores can be aggregated separately for the major parties and blocs. (But see Miller, 1978, table 1 for indirect evidence that this might not always be the case.) Of course, this is not to say that between elections only balanced flows occur. We know quite well that the advantaged party(ies) attract more voters from their rival(s) than they lose. But this occurs under the impact of a succession of issues so it is quite compatible with our assumptions.

As a direct check we investigate below the performance of various 'reciprocal' scoring systems (taking something away from one party to give to the other) compared with the 'independent' scores we have discussed so far (where the level of each party's score does not affect the other).

The same point can be made of reciprocal scoring as of unequal intervals – which level of reciprocity should we allow for? There are many trade offs which could take place between the major parties – for each increment to one the other could lose a corresponding quarter, half, three-quarters, and so on. (Not the total amount, however – some gains will still be made elsewhere.) There is an additional question of whether some issue types require reciprocal scoring, while others require independent scoring. A natural division here would be between the relatively transient issues (1–6) where major party supporters, faced with a novel problem, were more likely to transfer; and 'cleavage' issues (7–14) where their opinions were relatively fixed and imbalanced flows occurred only to and from the 'pool' of non-voters and third-party supporters.

The advantage of applying independent scores with equal intervals to all issue types is that it forms a single unique alternative – not a set of different alternatives out of which we have to choose arbitrarily – and that it is simple to apply. It has also worked well for our actual comparative analysis and so has considerable empirical weight behind it.

(c)   The third assumption involved in all the scoring procedures considered above is that issue types always exert the same electoral effects whether they appear alone or in combination. There are, for example, no interactive processes whereby the effect of 'socio-economic redistribution' by itself or in combination with 'civil order', differs significantly from its effects in combination with 'government record and prospects', 'candidate reactions', or with any other type, or types, of issue. Again this is a possibility it is difficult to check directly. Our real safeguard lies in the grounds on which we distinguish between different types of issue in the first place – the electors view them separately and discretely, and react differently to them. If we have succeeded in building these qualities into the classification, then we certainly will not encounter interactive effects. These would follow only if electors carried over reactions to a class issue into an ethnic or regional one, and vice versa. If this is the case, then our typology is faulty, and the damage extends far beyond interactive effects to the whole basis of our analysis. If, on the other hand, the typology corresponds more or less to our specification, then interactive effects are necessarily eliminated.

The general considerations just discussed are supported by the success with which our typology and scoring system have related to voting. Further support is provided by comparison of this performance with that of other possible scoring systems when they, too, are related to vote across the democracies through precisely the same procedures followed in Chapters 3 and 5. That is to say, for each party in each country we have scored issues by one of six different scoring systems and related them to voting percentages, as we did for the original scores in the United Kingdom in Figure 3.1 (p. 61 above.). From the (45 × 6) resulting graphs for all parties, we can derive average lines and estimates of slope, which are estimates of issue effects for the different parties, analogous to those already reported. We can then see whether the new estimates work as well as the originals in producing equally plausible relationships with vote.

The scoring systems we compare are not exhaustive (given the almost unlimited range of possibilities they could not be). They do, however, cover the leading alternatives discussed above:

(a)   Our original, equal interval scoring system where large = 3, medium = 2, small = 1 and scores are summed algebraically for each of the parties or party-groups in a country, separately and independently.

(b)   A 'reciprocal' scoring system where large = 3, medium = 2, and small = 1 and one party's gain on an issue type is subtracted from the other party for 'transient' issues (1–6) but independent scoring is applied on enduring 'cleavage' issues (7–14).

(c)   The same as (b), except that on 'transient' issues only half one party's gain is taken from the other party.

(d)   The same as (c), except that half one party's gain is taken from the other party on *all* issue types.

(e)   The same as (b), except that uniform scoring of 1 for all salient issues is employed.

(f)   The same as (c), except again that uniform scoring is employed.

Obviously, all these systems are related because they derive from the typology of Table 2.1 (p. 28 above) and the assignments of magnitude and direction in Table 2.6 (p. 50 above). The purely technical aspects of scoring do, however, vary sufficiently between the seven procedures, to make comparisons of their success a real test of different measurement assumptions.

The results of the comparisons can be briefly summarised: (1) On the whole, over all graphs relating vote to issue scores for the forty-five parties involved, the best-fitting lines are those produced by our original scoring system. That is to say that the scatter of points about the average line is least when issues are scored according to our original system, and greatest when issues are secured uniformly. Scoring in various 'reciprocal' modes with equal intervals, produces more of a scatter than our original scores but less than uniform scores.

(2)   Putting all the party estimates of issue impact together, and examining the extent to which they vary cross-nationally for each scoring system, it is clear that the estimates which diverge least, and converge most strongly on a common median value, are those produced by our original scores. The median values for the various reciprocal scoring systems with equal intervals are all very similar but many more of the individual estimates diverge from the median. The variability of estimates overall is greatest for the uniform scoring systems.

(3)   Taking estimates for bourgeois and socialist–reformist parties separately, it is clear that the cross-national variability of the bourgeois slope (i.e., issue) estimates is greater than that for socialist–reformist parties for each of the scoring systems. This is an interesting (substantive rather than technical) finding, although the relationship which holds between all the scoring systems means that its replication has less significance than if they were totally independent. It does confirm the impression that bourgeois parties are less well fitted by the common coding and estimates than are socialist–reformist parties. We are, in other words, on firmer ground when we generalise about the left than the right. To a certain extent the finding supports our earlier theoretical assertion that bourgeois parties have a much wider choice of issues and strategies than do socialists. There is only one possible winning combination for the latter but many for the bourgeois. One might therefore expect greater variability of effects from their constantly changing appeals than from the relatively fixed attractions of the other side.

From the point of view of evaluating scores the first two findings are more important than the third. It is clear from these that the system of independently counting large as 3, medium as 2, small as 1, and non-saliency as 0, produces the most consistent and best-fitting set of results in the case of most individual party relationships and in general. Since it has also worked well in the major comparative analyses producing an acceptable general estimate for issue effects, there seems every reason to base our conclusions on it.

Index